Christian Hammer

Information Flow Control for Java
A Comprehensive Approach Based on Path Conditions in Dependence Graphs

Information Flow Control for Java

A Comprehensive Approach Based on Path Conditions
in Dependence Graphs

by
Christian Hammer

universitätsverlag karlsruhe

Dissertation, Universität Karlsruhe (TH)
Fakultät für Informatik, Tag der mündlichen Prüfung: 01.07.2009

Impressum

Universitätsverlag Karlsruhe
c/o Universitätsbibliothek
Straße am Forum 2
D-76131 Karlsruhe
www.uvka.de

Universitätsverlag Karlsruhe 2009
Print on Demand

ISBN: 978-3-86644-398-3

Information Flow Control for Java

A Comprehensive Approach Based on Path Conditions in Dependence Graphs

zur Erlangung des akademischen Grades eines

Doktors der Ingenieurwissenschaften

von der Fakultät für Informatik
der Universität Fridericiana zu Karlsruhe (TH)

genehmigte

Dissertation

von

Christian Hammer

aus Eichstätt

Tag der mündlichen Prüfung: 1. Juli 2009

Erster Gutachter: Prof. Dr.-Ing. Gregor Snelting

Zweiter Gutachter: Prof. Dr. Sabine Glesner

Acknowledgments

I am thankful to my adviser Prof. Gregor Snelting for providing the academic and personal support, advice, and freedom for my research. His constant trust in my abilities were the foundations of this thesis. I thank Prof. Sabine Glesner for contributing the second review of this thesis.

I would also like to thank Dr. Frank Tip (IBM Research) and his research group, for giving me the opportunity to participate in this team as a visiting researcher for half a year and for funding during that time. The results are not described in this thesis, but inspired my scientific work nonetheless.

Many discussions with my colleagues in Passau and Karlsruhe clearly influenced my research. First of all, I'd like to thank Jens Krinke, our discussions culminated in several papers. Dennis Giffhorn was the other leading member in the Joana group and provided a large number of algorithms and deep insight of Eclipse programming. His contributions will be described in detail in a forthcoming thesis. But I would also like to mention the fruitful discussions with my other colleagues and their helpful comments on preliminary parts of this thesis. In particular I thank Torsten Robschink, Maximilan Störzer, Mirko Streckenbach, Daniel Wasserrab, Jürgen Graf, Matthias Braun, Denis Lohner, and Andreas Lochbihler.

I had immense help from many master students in Passau to realize this thesis. Especially the graphical user interfaces would never have reached this degree of maturity without the projects of Bernd Nürnberger, Rüdiger Schaade, Siegfried Weber, Martin Grimme, Kai Brückner, Frank Nodes, Alexander Stockinger, Marieke Westerheide, Thomas Unfried, Tobias Eichinger, Andreas Busler, and Josef Heiduczek.

Special thanks go to Tanja Amtmann for her confidence in me and my work. Being with her inspired my imagination. She also reminded me that "mens sana in corpore sano". Finally, I would like to thank my parents and my family for providing the first and fundamental education and support that enabled my career.

The Valsoft/Joana project was funded in part by Deutsche Forschungsgemeinschaft (DFG grant Sn11/9-1 and Sn11/9-2).

Zusammenfassung

Trotz der derzeitigen Diskussion über Sicherheit in der Informatik können aktuelle Sicherheitstechniken nur die Herkunft und Identität eines Software-Artefakts überprüfen. Die Semantik eines Artefakts wird nicht berücksichtigt, wodurch Trojanische Pferde, Würmer und andere Formen von bösartiger Software begünstigt werden. Durch die allgegenwärtigen Netzwerke unserer Zeit werden diese Probleme umso gravierender.

Informationsflusskontrolle ist eine Technik, die die Sicherheit eines gegebenen Programms hinsichtlich einer Sicherheitspolitik überprüft. Im Gegensatz zur traditionellen Sicherheitstechnik berücksichtigt sie auch die Programmsemantik. Das wohl bekannteste Beispiel einer Sicherheitspolitik, Nichtinterferenz, verlangt zum Beispiel, dass geheime Eingaben eines Programms nicht zu öffentlichen Ausgaben fließen dürfen. In der Tat dürfen öffentliche Ausgaben noch nicht einmal von geheimen Eingaben beeinflusst werden. Obwohl Informationsfluss in der letzten Dekade Ziel intensiver Forschung war, verwenden die eingesetzten Techniken nur einen sehr begrenzten Teil der Programmanalyse, nämlich hauptsächlich Typsysteme. Typsysteme öffneten erfolgreich die Tür für Programmanalyse als eine Form der Informationsflusskontrolle, aber andere Techniken bieten höhere Präzision oder benötigen geringeren Annotationsaufwand, um die Sicherheitspolitik zu spezifizieren.

Das sog. Program Slicing hängt erwiesenermaßen stark mit Informationsflusskontrolle zusammen und bietet mehrere Dimensionen, um die Analysegenauigkeit zu erhöhen. Diese Arbeit präsentiert ein präzises Modell von objektorientierten Programmen in einer klassischen Datenstruktur für Program Slicing, dem Systemabhängigkeitsgraphen. Die Slicingalgorithmen wurden dahingehend erweitert, dass sie präzise Informationsflusskontrolle und, falls nötig, eine Möglichkeit zur Herabstufung geheimer Information bietet. Pfadbedingungen geben tiefere Einsicht, wie eine Anweisung eine andere beeinflussen kann. Sie ergeben somit Bedingungen für unlauteren Informationsfluss oder zeigen auf, dass ein vermuteter Fluss in Wirklichkeit unmöglich ist.

Obwohl die präsentierte Analyse im Allgemeinen teurer ist als ein Typsystem, zeigt eine Evaluation, dass unsere Technik für die Sicherheitskerne skaliert, deren Analyse wir beabsichtigen. Gleichzeitig reduziert sich der Aufwand deutlich, die Sicherheitspolitik zu spezifizieren. Das wichtigste Ergebnis dieser Arbeit ist allerdings, das wir die erste Analyse bieten, die eine realistische Programmiersprache zertifizieren kann: Unser System analysiert Java Bytecode in vollem Umfang.

Abstract

Despite the current discussion on security in computer science, current security mechanisms can only validate origin and identity of a software artifact. The semantics of an artifact are not taken into account, giving rise to all forms of trojan horses, worms and other malware. With the ubiquity of networks in modern life, these problems become all the more serious.

Information flow control is a technique to assert the security of a given program with respect to a given security policy. In contrast to traditional security, it also takes the program semantics into account. The most prominent example of a security policy, noninterference, requires that secret input of a program may not flow to public output; in effect, public output may not even be influenced from secret input. While information flow has been intensively researched in the last decade, the techniques for checking security policies only leverage a very restricted part of program analysis technology, mostly type systems. While type systems were a successful door opener for program analysis as a means of information flow control, other techniques offer higher precision or lower annotation burden for specifying the security policy.

A technique called program slicing has been shown closely connected to information flow control and offers many dimensions for improving analysis precision. This thesis presents a precise model for object-oriented programs in a classic data structure for slicing, the system dependence graph. It extends the algorithms for program slicing to allow for precise information flow control and provide a means to downgrade secret information, if necessary. Path conditions provide further insight into how one statement influences another. They may thus lead to conditions for illicit information flow, or they may provide evidence that an assumed flow is impossible.

While the presented analysis is clearly more expensive than type systems, an evaluation shows that our techniques scale well to the security kernels which we have in mind. At the same time, the burden for specifying the security policy is reduced significantly. But most importantly, we offer the first security analysis that can certify programs written in a realistic programing language: Our system can analyze full Java bytecode.

Contents

List of Algorithms

List of Figures

List of Tables

Chapter 1

Introduction

There are no great discoveries or great progress
so long as there is an unhappy child on the earth.
(Albert Einstein)

This thesis presents several precise techniques that analyze object-oriented
languages for security violations, together with evaluations on Java benchmarks.
The key question that will be targeted throughout this work is "Can a given
statement directly or indirectly influence another statement, and if this is possible, how can this influence happen during program execution?" Several branches
of computer science ask slight variations of this question, but the basic idea remains the same for all their targeted problems. A seminal technique to answer
the first part of the question has been presented by Weiser [Wei84] which has
been coined *program slicing*. Program slicing as presented by Weiser and many
other authors, determines the set of statements that potentially affect the execution of a given statement.

Program slicing has been extended to procedural languages like C and implemented in frameworks like CodeSurfer [AT01] or ValSoft [SRK06]. But for the
predominant programming paradigm of our time, object-oriented programming
(OOP), no clear and sound model was available when this thesis started. Apart
from that, whereas support for multi-threading is integrated into contemporary
languages like Java, and several algorithms for slicing multi-threaded applications had been proposed, no precise data flow analysis had been defined, which
seems to be imperative for precise slicing algorithms. As a remedy, this thesis
presents novel methods for modeling key features of languages like Java – objects, dynamic binding, exception handling and concurrency – for the purpose of
program slicing. A precise analysis for computation of inter-thread dependences
is defined that prunes most of the false positives that crude implementations do
include.

Further, the second part of the key question presented in the first paragraph, *how* one statement can influence another statement, cannot be answered
with program slicing alone. A technique called *Path Conditions* (*PC*) had been
proposed by Snelting [Sne96] and was refined and implemented by Robschink
and Krinke [Rob05, SRK06], however only for procedural languages. The resulting conditions sometimes become rather long and unintuitive, so that other

techniques like automated constraint solving need to be leveraged. The constraint solver checks the satisfiability of the condition and, if possible, generates program input that trigger the influence in question, thus acting as a digital "witness". However, we found that naively extending path conditions to object-oriented constructs results in conditions that such solvers cannot reduce to input. So generating witnesses would be impossible. As part of this work, path conditions are extended to object-oriented language features. Furthermore, we present how to refine the terms generated by naive extension, such that a constraint solver can handle these terms and generate witnesses. Complementary, this thesis proposes an approach to increases precision of path conditions by dynamic profiling data.

All these analyses form the foundation for our main application, information flow control (IFC). Information flow control basically aims at proving that (almost) no sensitive data can leak to untrusted users or other uncontrolled channels like the Internet. While it was folklore that IFC could be done with program slicing [ABHR99], only one mechanism and implementation of this technique for imperative languages was known, and none for object-oriented languages; research was almost exclusively concerned with type systems that guarantee correct information flow [SM03]. Unfortunately type systems are a rather coarse means of program analysis and usually allow no flow-, context-, field-, or object-sensitive[1] analysis. Further, type systems must restrict the programming language and require abundant annotations, both of which may be prohibitive for real applications. Thus type systems are too restrictive for practical use in realistic security-sensitive applications. As an alternative approach, this thesis develops an information flow control mechanism based on dependence graphs and program slicing. It allows a more precise analysis in all dimensions presented in the sequel. As many intuitively secure programs contain a negligible information flow from secret input data to public output, which is prohibited by standard noninterference, we added an extension for declassification, and present a technique to determine context-sensitive results in spite of declassification's intransitive nature.

All the approaches presented in this thesis have been implemented. This implementation will be described, together with a presentation of the Eclipse integration. Finally, the scalability and precision of the presented approaches will be evaluated.

1.1 Principles of Program Analysis

Program analyses infer a given property from the analyzed program. However, for any non-trivial property, it is in general undecidable whether the program satisfies the property [Ric53]. As a consequence every program analysis is subject to several conflicting requirements:

Correctness is mandatory for many program analyses. Correctness stipulates that the analysis will find all instances of the property in the given pro-

---

[1]These terms are explained in the next section.

gram. This holds even more for security analysis, where one wants to ensure that any security violation in the program is actually found.

Precision requires that only those cases that satisfy the given property are reported. For security analyses, it means that there are no false alarms: any program condemned by the analysis must indeed contain a security leak.

Scalability demands that the analysis can handle realistic programs (e.g. 100 kLOC), written in realistic languages (e.g. full Java bytecode).

Practicability demands that an analysis is easy to use. This property subsumes precision, as users are averse to excessive false positives; but it also entails little user interaction (i.e. a low number of program annotations), and understandable descriptions of the analysis results.

Unfortunately, in consequence to the aforementioned undecidability result, any program analysis can only guarantee either correctness *or* precision. Hence, correct algorithms are *conservative approximations*: The analysis is guaranteed to determine all cases that satisfy the given property, but the result will contain some spurious cases in general. These spurious cases do not satisfy that property and are thus often referred to as *false positives*. For purposes like testing or bug finding, one often trades some correctness for precision or scalability. In these applications it is more important to find the majority of the problems fast and to keep the false positive rate very low, as manual inspection is tedious. In contrast, this thesis generally opts for correct analyses, which is paramount for security purposes. Although correctness prevails for our purposes, we must nonetheless optimize precision. The most prominent dimensions of precision in contemporary program analysis are presented in the next section. But note that precision also influences scalability: usually better precision means worse scalability; fast algorithms are not precise. Yet, this is only a rule of thumb: Sometimes increased precision removes excess analysis overhead resulting from imprecision, which compensates for the increased complexity.

1.2 Dimensions of Program Analysis

Due to the conflicting requirements presented before, designing a program analysis always constitutes a trade-off between analysis speed and precision. This section will therefore discuss the major dimensions of precision of contemporary program analysis research. In the field of program analysis a large collection of techniques has been developed such that the engineer can choose from a spectrum between cheap/imprecise and precise/expensive analysis algorithms; depending on the purpose of the analysis. In particular, the engineer can choose whether an analysis should respect:

Flow-sensitivity An analysis is called flow-sensitive if it accounts for the control flow inside a method. Usually a separate solution is computed for each program point. Flow-insensitive analyses ignore the intra-procedural statement order and compute only one solution for each method. Dataflow analysis (see section 2.1) is inherently flow-sensitive, but for other forms of program analysis like pointer analysis flow-sensitivity was widely considered too expensive to scale to realistic applications. Still, current research presents promising exceptions (e.g. [LL03, NR03]. As a remedy, flow-sensitivity is often approximated by static single assignment form (see section 2.1.3).

Context-sensitivity A context-sensitive analysis distinguishes different calling contexts when analyzing the target of a function call. Separate information is computed for different calls of the same method. A context-insensitive analysis merges information from all invocation contexts of a method at the expense of possibly losing precision. The mechanisms to achieve context-sensitivity will be presented with the particular analyses.

Field-sensitivity Field-sensitive analyses distinguish the flow of values stored in different fields of an object. Field-insensitive analyses merge all fields of a given object.

Object-sensitivity Object-sensitive analyses[2] take different 'host' objects for the same field (attribute) into account, while object-insensitive analyses merge the information for a given field over all objects of the same class (and its subclasses).

Virtual method resolution Most inter-procedural analyses are based on a pre-computed call graph[3] to approximate virtual method resolution. Typical analysis techniques for determining such a graph are class hierarchy analysis (CHA) [DGC95], rapid type analysis RTA [BS96] and its extension XTA [TP00]. Points-to analysis[4] allows its computation *on-the-fly*, meaning that the call graph is computed in the course of points-to analysis. Since points-to analysis is more precise than the other techniques, the on-the-fly call graph is most precise, often reducing the number of possibly called methods of a virtual method call to just one.

Several empirical studies have shown that these dimensions dramatically improve precision, in particular for large or automatically generated programs. Even so, due to the increase in analysis time, a trade-off between all kinds of sensitivity and scalability must be found.

1.3 Contributions

This thesis aims to be self-contained and presents previous work for that purpose. The key accomplishments of this work are:

---

[2]In points-to analysis, object-sensitive analysis is a variant of context-sensitive analysis [MRR02], where each method is analyzed separately for each target object on which the method may be invoked.

[3]For a definition confer section 2.5

[4]See section 2.3

- Modeling of side-effects soundly in system dependence graphs. In particular, object parameters are represented as trees according to the instance field nesting structure. Based on pointer analysis results, our analysis handles recursive data structures in a precise but conservative fashion. This modeling is congruous with previous definitions of system dependence graphs, thus the standard linear time context-sensitive slicing algorithm can be leveraged.

- When a language offers dynamic thread creation as in Java, there is another source of undecidability of precise slicing even in the intraprocedural case.

- A new approach to compute interference dependence for Java's memory model. It prunes most of the spurious cases that previous slicers included. In contrast to existing definitions, our algorithm considers the precise aliasing situation and not just type or thread escape information.

- Extending path conditions to object oriented languages which offer language constructs such as dynamic dispatch, instanceof operators and exceptions. This leads to precise static path conditions operating only on the program's variables. The gain in precision allows leverage of automatic constraint solving techniques.

- Dynamic path conditions that enrich static path conditions with dynamic trace data. As a consequence, the conditions are no longer correct for all program runs but only for the current execution. But after an unexpected program behavior has been perceived, the enriched conditions allows a flight recorder principle. This yields precise conditions for the program failure which help to prevent such problems in the future.

- Information flow control is defined in terms of an analysis on the system dependence graph. The basic notion guarantees classical noninterference as presented by Goguen and Meseguer [GM84].

- For the cases where noninterference is too restrictive, a means for declassification is defined. Special declassification summary edges and nodes in the system dependence graph allow for context-sensitive IFC in the presence of declassification.

- All algorithms are implemented. The evaluation illustrates the scalability and practicability of our algorithms and compares with previous work.

Chapter 2

Dependence Graphs and Slicing for Object-Oriented Languages

This chapter gives an overview of dataflow analysis, dependence graphs and program slicing, as a prerequisite for the development of the author's contributions. It does, however, not try to give a complete survey of program slicing literature, as the number of publications in this area has exploded in the last decade. A little outdated but still valuable is Tip's survey on program slicing [Tip95]; other surveys on slicing techniques, applications and variations can be found in [BG96, dL01, HH01, BH04]. Krinke [Kri03a, Kri05] gives another incomplete, but more recent picture of the slicing literature. The most recent overview probably can be found in [MM07]. We will first consider procedure-less programs (the intra-procedural case) and then move on to procedural programs (the inter-procedural case). Section 2.1 will therefore present intraprocedural dataflow analysis starting from the control flow graph and reaching definitions analysis that allow to transform a program into static single assignment form. From that intermediate representation, section 2.2 describes program slicing as a program transformation technique and how to compute slices on a data structure called the program dependence graph. In the second part, techniques to extend dependence graphs to programs that consist of multiple procedures are discussed and how this impacts program slicing. The next section defines points-to analysis and aliasing, prerequisites for precise analysis of all object-oriented languages. This analysis is heavily leveraged in section 2.4, which extends dependence graphs to language features like dynamic dispatch, exception handling, and most prominently, objects and instance fields. A precise analysis of inter-procedural side-effects is presented in section 2.5, together with a correctness proof. This analysis allows computation of precise data dependences between instance fields in the presence of method calls.

A preliminary exposition about the analysis presented in this chapter was published under the title "An improved Slicer for Java" – Christian Hammer and Gregor Snelting [HS04] at the 5th ACM SIGPLAN-SIGSOFT workshop on Program Analysis for Software Tools and Engineering 2004.

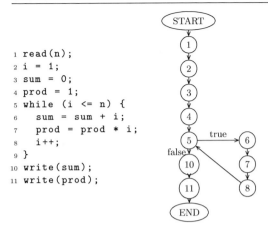

```
1  read(n);
2  i = 1;
3  sum = 0;
4  prod = 1;
5  while (i <= n) {
6      sum = sum + i;
7      prod = prod * i;
8      i++;
9  }
10 write(sum);
11 write(prod);
```

Figure 2.1: Example program and its CFG

2.1 Intraprocedural Dataflow Analysis

Dataflow Analysis (DFA) is a major branch of program analysis. It answers questions of the form "Can a value computed at a certain statement flow to another given statement?" For DFA it is customary to represent a program as a directed graph, where the nodes are the statements or predicates of the program and the edges describe the *control flow*, i.e. possible execution sequences of the statements. The graph-based representation allows analysis of programs with structured and unstructured control flow, like goto's or exception handling.

Definition 2.1 (Control Flow Graph). *A* Control Flow Graph *(CFG) is a directed attributed graph* $G = (N, E, n_s, n_e, \nu)$. *$N$ is the set of nodes representing statements and predicates which contains two distinguished nodes n_s (START) and n_e (END) representing the beginning and termination of the program respectively. E is the set of* control flow edges $(n, m) \in E$, *also written $n \xrightarrow{cf} m$. E contains a control flow edge $n \xrightarrow{cf} m$ iff the statement represented by m may execute immediately after the execution of the statement represented by n. Therefore, START has no predecessors and END no successors. The total attribute function $\nu : E \to \{true, false, \epsilon\} \cup \mathbb{Z}$ maps the edges to an attribute: Nodes representing a predicate have two successors where the edge to one node is attributed with $true$, the other with $false$ in accordance with the predicate's outcome.* switch *statements may have a variable number of successors where each edge is attributed with the integer value that the predicate variable must equal for control flowing to the edge's target. All other edges are attributed with ϵ, the empty attribute. The functions* pred *and* succ *return for each node in the CFG its predecessors and successors, respectively.*

Example 2.1. *Figure 2.1 shows an example program along with its control flow graph. The nodes are represented with the line number of the corresponding statement.*

Since the nodes and their corresponding statements are bijectively mapped, we will use both meanings interchangeably in the sequel.

Reachability in the CFG One of the most fundamental properties of a program is the question if an execution of the program exists, where a given node is traversed and later in this execution another given node is reached, i.e. whether a given statement is reachable in a program execution from another given statement. A path $p = (n_1, ..., n_k)$ is called *realizable* if an execution exists, where the nodes are executed in the order induced by the path. This question, however, is undecidable in general and so one conservatively assumes that all paths in the CFG correspond to a valid execution. This corresponds to treating conditionals like non-deterministic choice operators.

2.1.1 Monotone Dataflow Analysis Framework

Monotone dataflow analysis frameworks (*MDFAF*) are the most important class of dataflow analysis. Under a certain condition, they always compute the most precise solution in a finite number of steps, even if loops in the CFG may allow infinitely long paths. The basic data structure of a MDFAF is a lattice of values:

Definition 2.2 (Semi Lattice). *A (join) semi lattice* $\mathcal{L} = (L, \leq, \bot, \sqcup)$ *consists of a set of values L with a partial order[1] $\leq$, and a binary operator supremum (join) $\sqcup$ where the least element $\bot := \sqcup \varnothing$ in L is called bottom and the following properties hold:*

1. $a \leq b := a \sqcup b = b$

2. $(a \sqcup b) \sqcup c = (a \sqcup b) \sqcup c$ *(associativity)*

3. $a \sqcup b = b \sqcup a$ *(commutativity)*

4. $a \sqcup a = a$ *(idempotence)*

A (meet) semi lattice $\mathcal{L} = (L, \leq, \top, \sqcap)$ *consists of a set of values L with a partial order $\leq$, and a binary operator infimum (meet) $\sqcap$ where the greatest element $\top := \sqcap \varnothing$ in L is called top and the following properties hold:*

1. $a \leq b := a \sqcap b = a$

2. $(a \sqcap b) \sqcap c = (a \sqcap b) \sqcap c$ *(associativity)*

3. $a \sqcap b = b \sqcap a$ *(commutativity)*

4. $a \sqcap a = a$ *(idempotence)*

Definition 2.3 (Complete Lattice). *A complete lattice* $\mathcal{L} = (L, \leq, \bot, \top, \sqcup, \sqcap)$ *consists of a set of values L with a partial order $\leq$ such that $\mathcal{L} = (L, \leq, \bot, \sqcup)$ is a join semi lattice and $\mathcal{L} = (L, \leq, \top, \sqcap)$ is a meet semi lattice. The least element in L is $\bot$ (bottom), the greatest is $\top$ (top). The binary operators infimum (meet) $\sqcap$ and supremum (join) $\sqcup$ have the additional properties:*

---

[1] A partial order is a reflexive, antisymmetric and transitive relation

1. $a \sqcap (a \sqcup b) = a$

2. $a \sqcup (a \sqcap b) = a$ *(absorption)*

3. any *subset* $X \subseteq L$ *has a supremum* $\sqcup X$ *in* L.

It is straightforward to show that finite lattices are always complete, which suffices our needs in this thesis.

Definition 2.4 (Monotone Function Space). *A set of functions* $\mathcal{F}$ *defined on a join semi-lattice* $\mathcal{L} = (L, \leq, \top, \sqcap)$ *is a monotone function space, if*

1. $\exists id_L \in \mathcal{F} : \forall x \in L : id_L(x) = x$ *(identity function)*

2. $\forall F \in \mathcal{F} : \forall x, y \in L : x \leq y \implies F(x) \leq F(y)$ *(monotonicity)*

3. $\forall F, G \in \mathcal{F} : F \circ G \in \mathcal{F}$ *(closed under composition)*

4. $\forall F, G \in \mathcal{F} : F \sqcap G \in \mathcal{F}$ *(pointwise infimum)*

Definition 2.5 (Monotone Dataflow Analysis Framework). *A monotone data-flow analysis framework* (MDFAF) $\mathcal{A} = (\mathcal{L}, \mathcal{F})$ *consists of a*

1. *a complete semi-lattice* $\mathcal{L} = (L, \leq, \top, \sqcap)$ *with a supremum operator for the abstract values of the dataflow analysis, and*

2. *a monotone function space* $\mathcal{F}$ *defined on* $\mathcal{L}$.

If all functions in $\mathcal{F}$ are distributive over $\sqcap$, i.e. ($\forall F \in \mathcal{F} : \forall x, y \in L : F(x \sqcap y) = F(x) \sqcap F(y)$), it is called a distributive MDFAF. The desired solution of a monotone dataflow analysis framework is the *meet-over-all-paths* (*MOP*) solution, which is defined in terms of paths in the control flow graph. The transfer function for a path $P = (n_1, .., n_k)$ can be constructed with the recursive definition:

$$F_{(n_1, ..., n_k)} : L \to L : F_{(n_1, ..., n_k)}(x) = F_{n_k}(F_{(n_1, ..., n_{k-1})}(x))$$

Since there are usually infinitely many paths in a control flow graph, there is in general no algorithm to compute the MOP, which is $\displaystyle\bigsqcap_{\text{Path } P_i} F_{P_i}$ directly. However, an efficient solution can be found using a different definition, which is equivalent or conservative to the MOP for monotone transfer functions.

Definition 2.6 (Fixed point). *A fixed point of an operator* f *on a semi-lattice* L *is an element* $x \in L$ *such that* $f(x) = x$. *A fixed point* x *for* f *is called minimal* (*MFP*) *if* $\forall y \in L : f(y) = y \implies x \leq y$.

The efficient algorithm for computing the MFP solution of a MDFAF, which has been invented by Kildall [Kil73], can be seen as pseudocode in Algorithm 1. Kam and Ullman [KU77] have shown that the monotonicity of the function space guarantees termination and that a MFP exists. The MFP solution is always a conservative solution but if the MDFAF is not distributive it is not necessarily the most precise solution.

Algorithm 1 Kildall's algorithm to compute the MFP

---

1 **Input:** CFG a control flow graph
2 F_q transfer functions of a monotone dataflow analysis framework
3 **Output:** A an array of lattice elements containing the MFP of the MDFAF
4 **foreach** $n \in CFG$ **do**
5 $A[n] = \bot$
6 **od**
7 **do**
8 $change = false$
9 **foreach** $n \in CFG$ **do**
10 $temp = \displaystyle\bigsqcap_{q \in pred(n)} F_q(A[q])$
11 **if** $temp \neq A[n]$
12 $change = true$
13 $A[n] = temp$
14 **fi**
15 **od**
16 **until** !$change$

Theorem 2.1 (Coincidence Theorem [KU77]). *Let* $P_1, P_2, \ldots$ *be all (maybe infinitely many) paths from* $START$ *to the program point* s; *let the transfer functions* F_B *be distributive; let* $A[s] = fix(s) \in L$ *be the value computed by the fixed point iteration. Then follows:*

$$fix(s) = \bigsqcap_{Path\ P_i\ ending\ in\ s} F_{P_i}(\bot)$$

In the general case of non-distributive transfer funtions, the MFP is only less or equal to the MOP.

2.1.2 Reaching Definitions

Reaching definitions is a traditional dataflow problem of optimizing compilers but is also a prerequisite for computing the program dependence graph. It answers the question, if a definition of a variable at one given statement can reach the use of that variable at another statement without being redefined on the way. A definition is a statement that assigns some value to a variable, while a use is a statement that takes a variable as parameter. A definition can reach another statement, if there is a path from the definition to that statement in the CFG without any other definition of the same variable on that path:

Definition 2.7 (Reaching Definitions). *Let* Def(n) *be the set of variables defined at a node* n *in the CFG* G, *then a definition* d *of a variable* $var(d) := v$, *where* $v \in$ Def(n), *reaches a (not necessarily different) node* n', *if there is a path* $P = (n = n_0, \ldots, n_k = n')$ *in* G *with* $k > 0$ *such that* $\forall i \in 1, \ldots, k - 1 : v \notin$ Def(n_i).

Reaching definitions can be expressed as a distributive monotone data flow framework with the powerset of D, the set of all definitions, as the lattice elements L in $\mathcal{L} = (L, \leq, \varnothing, D, \cup, \cap)$. The transfer functions are derived from the abstract semantics of variable assignment:

$$F_n(X) = X \setminus kill(n) \cup gen(n)$$

A statement n defines the variables in $\text{Def}(n)$, so all definitions in D that define the same variables can no longer be visible after n has executed, i.e. they are overwritten or "killed" by this definition. All elements of $\text{Def}(n)$ are "generated" by that statement and thus visible after its execution. This can be formalized as follows:

$$gen(n) := \text{Def}(n)$$

$$kill(n) := \bigcup_{v \in \text{Def}(n)} D_v, \text{ where } D_v := \{d \in D \mid v = var(d)\}$$

As reaching definitions is a distributive monotone dataflow analysis framework, its MFP computed by Kildall's algorithm with which the MOP solution coincides.

2.1.3 Static Single Assignment Form

A very popular program representation is called *static single-assignment (SSA)* form [CFR+91]. It effectively separates a program's values from the program's variables and thus enables several more effective optimizations. A program is in static single-assignment form if every variable is assigned at most once in the source code. It is called *static* because the variable may very well be assigned to multiple times during program execution, e.g. in a loop. For program analysis, the outstanding property of SSA form is that it makes def-use chains, as computed by reaching definitions in the last section, explicit and allows flow-sensitive analysis for the program's variables, as each variable is assigned to exactly once. Because of that, SSA form has become a standard intermediate representation in program analysis.

To compute the static single-assignment form [CFR+91], one usually introduces a subscript for each variable that is incremented at each assignment statement. At join points in the control flow graph, new assignments with a so-called Φ-operator need to be inserted that represent the choice of the appropriate variable according to the program's flow. Note that programs in SSA form are equivalent to the original program. As an example, consider Figure 2.2, where a program is depicted alongside its SSA form. In line 5 of the SSA form, sum_2 is defined as either sum_1, if the while loop has not yet been entered, or else as sum_3, the last value defined in the loop body.

2.2 Program Slicing

A program slice contains only those statements of a program that potentially influence the execution of a given statement of interest. The idea of (static) program slicing was first presented by Weiser [Wei79, Wei81, Wei84] in 1979. Weiser formulated the seminal idea that, while debugging, programmers build

```
1  read(n);
2  i = 1;
3  sum = 0;
4  prod = 1;
5  while (i <= n) {
6    sum = sum + i;
7    prod = prod * i;
8    i++;
9  }
10 write(sum);
11 write(prod);
```

```
1  read(n);
2  i₁ = 1;
3  sum₁ = 0;
4  prod₁ = 1;
5  while [i₂ = Φ(i₁, i₃)
         sum₂ = Φ(sum₁, sum₃)
         prod₂ = Φ(prod₁, prod₃)]
         (i₂ <= n) {
6    sum₃ = sum₂ + i₂;
7    prod₃ = prod₂ * i₂;
8    i₃ = i₂ + 1;
9  }
10 write(sum₂);
11 write(prod₂);
```

Figure 2.2: Example program and SSA form

a program abstraction in their minds [Wei82] for which he coined the name *program slice*. In his definition, a slice is an executable program, with some statements of the original program P removed. For a given so-called *slicing criterion* $C = (n, V)$, a tuple consisting of a statement and a subset of the program's variables, such a reduced program S is called a program slice if it fulfills the following properties:

1. S must be a valid program, and

2. whenever P halts for a given input, S also halts for that input, computing the same values for the variables in V whenever the statement n is executed.

A formal definition of this idea was presented in [Wei84]. Trivially, every program is a slice of itself. A slice is called *statement-minimal* for a given criterion, if no other slice for that criterion contains fewer statements. Unfortunately, statement-minimal slices are not unique in general, and their computation is undecidable. Weiser also formulated the first algorithm for slicing [Wei84], an iterative dataflow analysis on the source code level.

Semantics of Slicing   Slicing does not preserve traditional program semantics in which the program and its slices are defined [CF89, GM03]. The problem with the standard semantics lies in that slicing may remove non-terminating portions of a program, i.e. transform a non-terminating program into a terminating one. In this case, the slice clearly has different semantics than the original program. However, recently, a non-standard semantics has been found that is preserved under program slicing. Danicic et al. [DHHO07] present a non-strict semantics for a simple while language that is consistent with program slicing.

2.2.1 Slicing in the PDG

Later, Ottenstein and Ottenstein [OO84] presented an alternative way of slicing:
They reformulate slicing as a reachability analysis in a program representation
called *Program Dependence Graph (PDG)* as defined by Ferrante et al. [FOW87].
In the PDG, slicing can be done in time linear to the number of statements, with
a single backward-traversal of dependences between these statements (defined
later). In contrast to the executable slices of Weiser's algorithm, slices in the
PDG do not necessarily represent executable slices, i.e. the first property of a
slice may be violated. The notion of a static slice with a PDG is rather the set
of statements that may directly or indirectly affect the slicing criterion. Thus
the slice may not represent a syntactically correct program, or some structural
statements like `gotos` can be missing, which changes the program's semantics.
To circumvent these restrictions, several extensions of slicing in PDGs were
presented that also compute executable slices [BH93, CF94, Agr94, HD98, HLB06]

The PDG is defined in terms of the control flow graph: it contains all the
nodes of the CFG, but not its edges. Instead, nodes are connected by data and
control dependence edges.

Control Dependence

Control dependence exists between two statements, if a statement directly controls the execution of the other statement. In structured programs, control
dependence is equivalent to the nesting level of source code: Each statement
that is indented by exactly one additional level is control dependent on the
directly enclosing branch or loop predicate. In the presence of arbitrary control flow, control dependence is defined in terms of post-dominance [FOW87]. A
node x in the CFG is *post-dominated* by node y if all paths from x to END pass
through y. Some definitions exclude the case that a node does postdominate
itself.

Definition 2.8 (Control Dependence). *A node y is control dependent on node*
x $(x \rightarrow_{cd} y)$ *if*

- *there exists a path p from x to y in the CFG, such that y post-dominates
  every node in p (except for x),[2] and*

- *x is not post-dominated by y*

There is always an *immediate post-dominator* for each statement that has a
post-dominator, i.e. a post-dominator that does not post-dominate another post-
dominator of the same statement. Therefore, post-dominance can be depicted as
a tree, where only the immediate post-dominator relation is depicted, transitive
post-domination can be found by paths in the tree. As an example, consider
Figure 2.3, which shows the post-dominator tree (left) and the corresponding
control dependence (sub)graph for the example program in Figure 2.2. For
example, node 11 is immediately post-dominated by END. There is a control
dependence $5 \rightarrow_{cd} 7$, as 7 can be avoided on the path from 5 to END, and 7
post-dominates all nodes on the path $\langle 5, 6, 7 \rangle$ except 5.

---

[2]If post-dominance is not reflexive, then also except for y

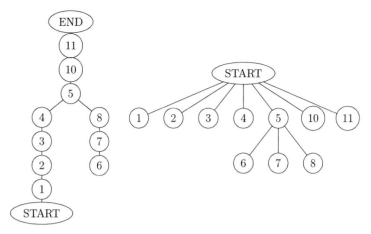

Figure 2.3: Post-dominator tree and control dependence subgraph for the example program in Figure 2.2. Edges are implicitly directed downwards

Definition 2.8 is equivalent to the intuition outlined above for structured programs. Ferrante et al. [FOW87] presented an approach to compute control dependence: They first compute the post-dominator tree with the fast Lengauer-Tarjan algorithm [LT79]. Then, for every edge $x \xrightarrow{\text{cf}} y$ where y is not postdominated by x, one moves upwards from y in the post-dominator tree. Every node z visited before x's parent is control dependent on x. The control dependence edge $x \rightarrow_{cd} z$ is labeled with $\nu(x, y)$, the label of the control flow edge. To obtain a connected control dependence graph, usually a synthetic control flow edge (with label false, the original edge from $START$ to the first statement is labeled true) is inserted between $START$ and END. Therefore, the $START$ node will be the root in the control dependence subgraph. This synthetic edge is only inserted while computing control dependence and ignored for other analyses.

Data Dependence

Originally [FOW87], *data dependence* comprised several types of dependences like *flow dependence*, *output dependence* and *anti-dependence*, but for the purpose of slicing, usually only flow dependence is relevant. For that reason, the term data dependence is generally used interchangeably with flow dependence in that context. The intuition behind a flow dependence $x \rightarrow_{dd} y$ is that a node x computes a value that may be used at node y in some feasible execution. In some cases, a distinction between loop-carried and loop-independent data dependences is made, representing if the dependence may or may not arise as a result of loop iterations. In the sequel, data dependence will stand for loop-carried or -independent flow dependence. In the CFG, this can be formalized as follows:

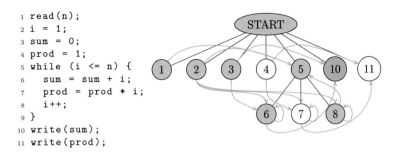

```
1  read(n);
2  i = 1;
3  sum = 0;
4  prod = 1;
5  while (i <= n) {
6    sum = sum + i;
7    prod = prod * i;
8    i++;
9  }
10 write(sum);
11 write(prod);
```

Figure 2.4: Program dependence graph of the example

Definition 2.9 (Data Dependence). *Let* $\mathrm{Ref}(x)$ *denote the set of variables referenced at node* x. *Then a node* y *is data dependent on node* x ($x \rightarrow_{dd} y$) *if*

- *there exists a variable* v *with* $v \in \mathrm{Def}(x)$ *and* $v \in \mathrm{Ref}(y)$, *and*

- *there exists a path* P *in the CFG from* x *to* y *where the definition of* v *in* x *is not definitively killed (i.e.* x *is a reaching definition of* y.)

As mentioned earlier, the program dependence graph consists of the nodes of the CFG (sometimes the END node is omitted as it has no in- or outgoing dependence edges) with control and data dependence edges replacing the control flow edges. Consider the program dependence graph of our example program in Figure 2.4. The data dependences are depicted in green, control dependences in blue. Since statement 1 defines the variable n that is referenced at line 5 and not overwritten in-between, there is a data dependence from 1 to 5. The condition in line 5 determines if and how often the loop is executed, so all the statements in the loop body are connected by control dependence to node 5. Note that dependence graphs may contain loops (see the data dependence at node 6) and multiple edges between two nodes, i.e. they are multigraphs in general.

Data dependence can be computed with reaching definitions analysis directly. But it is already explicit for programs in SSA form, as each variable name is only defined once. So computing DD from SSA form is finding the definition of the referenced variable and – if this definition is in a Φ-function – building the transitive hull of variables in referenced Φ-functions.

As an example, consider Figure 2.2 again. The definition of sum_3 depends on the variable sum_2, which is defined in a Φ-function. This function in turn references sum_1 and sum_3, none of which is defined in a Φ-function. So sum_3 is data dependent on itself and on the initialization. This can be seen in Figure 2.4 as data dependences from node 3 to node 6 and from 6 to 6.

Slicing

The *slicing criterion* for dependence graph based slicing is usually defined different from Weiser's original: Instead of a tuple (n, V), a statement and a set of variables, it is only a node v in the dependence graph. This yields a more coarse-grained kind of slicing criterion, as it is equivalent to the slicing criterion, where n is the statement corresponding to the criterion node v, and $V = \mathrm{Ref}(v) \cup \mathrm{Def}(v)$. To compute a slice for a variable not in V one needs to alter the program and insert a synthetic reference of that variable, but this difference should be negligible in practice.

Definition 2.10 (*Intraprocedural Backward Slice*). *The (backward) slice $BS(v)$ of v is defined as the reflexive, transitive closure of $\{v\}$ under the predecessor relation in the PDG, denoted as $\to^*$, where the predecessor relation subsumes both kinds of dependence edges:*

$$BS(v) = \{x \in PDG | x \to^* v\} \tag{2.1}$$

So slicing in the PDG becomes a simple graph reachability problem, which stems from the transitivity of data and control dependence.

In our example program in Figure 2.4, nodes in the backward slice of node 10 are shaded. Lines 4, 7, and 11 could therefore be deleted from the program if one were only interested in the sum, but not in the product.

A common variation of slicing is the forward slice, that computes which statements may be influenced by the slicing criterion, as opposed to backward slicing, which determines those statements that can influence the criterion:

Definition 2.11 (*Intraprocedural Forward Slice*). *The forward slice $FS(v)$ of v is defined as the reflexive, transitive closure of $\{v\}$ under the successor relation in the PDG, again subsuming both kinds of dependence edges:*

$$FS(v) = \{x \in PDG | v \to^* x\} \tag{2.2}$$

2.2.2 Interprocedural Analysis

When analyzing procedural languages, the calling structure of the program must be taken into account. A standard data structure for that purpose is the *call graph* [Ryd79, CCHK90, GDDC97], which can be derived from the interprocedural control flow graph.

Definition 2.12 (interprocedural control flow graph). *An interprocedural control flow graph (ICFG) $G = ((G_p)_{p \in P}, \mathsf{main}, \mathsf{Call}, \mathsf{Ret})$ for a program P consists of a family $(G_p)_{p \in P}$ of CFGs $G_p = (N_p, E_p, \mathsf{Entry}_p, \mathsf{Exit}_p)$ for procedures $p \in P$, an entry procedure main, and sets of call and return edges Call and Ret such that*

1. *Both $(N_p)_{p \in P}$ and $(E_p)_{p \in P}$ are each pairwise disjoint.*

2. *If $(u, v) \in \mathsf{Call}$, then $u \in N_p \backslash \{\mathsf{Entry}_p\}$ and $v = \mathsf{Entry}_{p'}$ for some $p, p' \in P$, and there is a matching return edge $(\mathsf{Exit}_{p'}, u') \in \mathsf{Ret}$ such that $u' \in N_p$ is the only successor to u in G_p. p is the caller and p' the callee for that call edge. We say that u and u' match each other and call (u, u') a call-return edge.*

3. *Conversely, every return edge in* Ret *has a matching call edge in* Call.

Nodes with outgoing call edges (incoming return edges) are called call nodes *(return nodes)*

In an ICFG, label each call edge $(u, \text{Entry}_{p'})$ with $\big(\!\!\big|_{p'}^{u}$ and each return edge $(\text{Exit}_{p'}, u')$ with $_{p'}^{u}\big|\!\!\big)$ where u is the matching call node for u' and label all call-return edges with $\perp$. All other edges are labeled according to Definition 2.1

Definition 2.13 (*interprocedural realizable path* [RHSR94, Kri03a]). *For a path π in ICFG G, let* $\mathsf{EL}(\pi)$ *denote the concatenation of labels of the edges in π. π is balanced iff* $\mathsf{EL}(\pi)$ *is in the language of balanced parentheses generated from the nonterminal M by the context-free grammar with this set of productions* $\{M ::= M \ \big(\!\!\big|_{p}^{u} \ M \ _{p}^{u}\big|\!\!\big) \mid true \mid false \mid \epsilon \mid i \mid MM\}$ *where* $(u, \text{Entry}_{p'}) \in$ Call $\wedge i \in \mathbb{Z}$. *π is left balanced iff there are paths π_1, π_2 in G such that $\pi = \pi_1 \pi_2$ is the concatenation of π_1 and π_2, π_2 is balanced and* $\mathsf{EL}(\pi_1)$ *contains no labels of the form $_{p}^{u}\big|\!\!\big)$ and $\perp$. π is right balanced iff there are paths π_1, π_2 in IG with $\pi = \pi_1 \cdot \pi_2$ such that π_1 is balanced and* $\mathsf{EL}(\pi_2)$ *contains no labels of the form $\big(\!\!\big|_{p}^{u}$ and $\perp$. π is realizable iff π is left balanced or right balanced.*

Note that realizable paths in the ICFG are not closed under concatenation. A common abstraction of the ICFG is the call graph, which models the invocation structure of a program:

Definition 2.14 (Call Graph). *A call graph in our setting is a directed bipartite graph $G_c = (N_p^* + N_c, E)$ consisting of the procedure entry nodes of the program $(N_p^* := \{v \in N_p \mid v = \text{Entry}_p$ for some $p \in P\})$ and the call sites of the program $(N_c := \{u \in N_p \mid (u, v) \in$ Call$\})$, where the edges E represent*

  1. *containment: An edge $e = \text{Entry}_p \rightarrow c$ is included in E for each call site $c \in N_c$ that appears in procedure $p \in N_p^*$.*

  2. *invocation: An edge $e = c \rightarrow \text{Entry}_p$ is contained in E iff call site $c \in N_c$ may invoke procedure $p \in N_p^*$.*

This graph effectively represents the interprocedural control-flow of the program. Containment is a static property, that can easily be determined using the ICFG. With static binding, each call site has out degree of 1, namely the called procedure. But function pointers or dynamic dispatch make ICFG and call graph construction more difficult. We will see later how pointer analysis can be leveraged for constructing precise call graphs in the presence of dynamic dispatch.

Slicing Procedural Programs

To slice programs that consist of a set of procedures Horwitz et al. [HRB90] extended the PDG: The *System Dependence Graph* (SDG) models multi-procedure programs using a call-by-value-result parameter passing semantics. Each procedure is represented by a dependence graph similar to a PDG, the *Procedure Dependence Graph*, which is also abbreviated to PDG. It is always clear from

```
1  main() {
2    a=3;
3    b=4;
4    v=add(a,b);
5    w=add(v,b);
6  }
7  add(x,y) {
8    return x+y;
9  }
```

————→ data dependence
————— control dependence
- - -→ summary edge
- - - -→ parameter edges
- - - - - call dependence

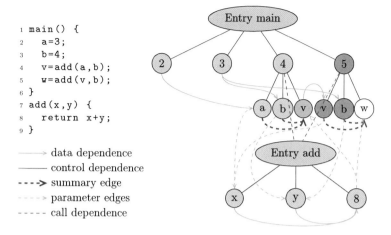

Figure 2.5: Interprocedural example with system dependence graph

the context, if PDG represents only a procedure or a whole program. At each call site, the PDG contains an *actual-in node* per parameter of the invoked procedure, modeling the assignments of the parameters to temporary variables (this assignment is supposed to take place before the actual call). The called procedure's PDG holds, in analogy, one *formal-in node* for each formal parameter, representing the assignment of the corresponding temporary variable to the formal parameter. At the end of the procedure the opposite schema is applied: the return parameters are copied to temporary variables in *formal-out nodes* and, after returning to the caller, those temporaries are copied back to the variables receiving the return values in *actual-out nodes*. Globally visible variables (e.g. static variables in Java) receive special treatment: They are handled like additional read-write-parameters of that procedure [HRB90] and are thus ignored in the subsequent discussions.

The SDG consists of all the PDGs involved in the program connected by interprocedural edges, which are inserted in accordance to the invocation edges of the call graph: An actual-in parameter node is connected to its corresponding formal-in node with an *parameter-in edge* (pi), formal-out nodes to their corresponding actual-out nodes with an *parameter-out edge* (po). Finally, the node representing a call-site is connected to the entry node of the callee with a *call edge* (cl).

As an example, consider Figure 2.5, which shows an example program and the corresponding SDG. The straight edges in blue represent control dependence, the curved edges in green data dependence. Interprocedural edges are shown as dashed edges: The call edges from nodes 4 and 5 to the entry of procedure add, parameter-in edges from variables a and v to x, parameter-out edges from the return statement in node 8 to the variables v and w.

While this representation does allow program slicing, the slice according to equation 2.1 is correct but not context-sensitive due to the calling-context

37

problem: A slice may enter a callee by a parameter-out edge but leave it towards a different procedure using a parameter-in edge towards a different call-site, so this kind of slicing is called *context-insensitive*.

When slicing the example program in Figure 2.5, the context-insensitive backward slice of node v from call site 4 is shown in Figure 2.5 as shaded nodes. However, a dataflow from in-parameters of statement 5 to the slicing criterion is infeasible in any program execution, because statement 5 executes only after statement 4.

As the SDG makes all side-effects visible, the actual-out parameters of any call-site can only be (transitively) dependent on actual-in parameters of the same call-site. This inspired the inclusion of so-called *summary edges* [HRB90] to enrich the SDG. Summary edges are inserted between actual-in and actual-out nodes of the same call-site, if there exists a realizable path in the callee between the corresponding formal parameters. These edges represent interprocedural summary information of dependences between procedure parameters and thus allow preservation of the calling context.

In our example in Figure 2.5, there are four summary edges depicted in red and dashed: from a and b of call site 4 to v, and from v and b of call site 5 to w. These correspond to the transitive dependences between the formal parameters x and y and the return statement in node 8.

With summary edges, context-sensitive slicing becomes a two-phase algorithm which is still in $O(|SDG|)$. The first phase traverses all edges (including summary edges) except for parameter-out edges. Thus all dependences of the slicing criterion's procedure and its transitive callers are included. The second phase starts at all omitted formal-out nodes and traverses all edges but call and parameter-in edges, thus omitting all callers (whose effects have already been included because of the summary edges). The context-sensitive slice is the union of the nodes encountered in both phases.

The result of the context-sensitive two-phase algorithm for the program in Figure 2.5 is shown in Figure 2.6. It traverses the summary edges to a and b and from there the nodes 2, 3, 4 and the entry of main (gray nodes). The second phase starts with node 8 which has been omitted due to the formal-out edge to v and includes the nodes x and y and the entry of add (depicted in light gray). Note that the nodes at call site 5 are correctly not included in the context-sensitive slice, but in the context-insensitive slice (Figure 2.5).

Computing Summary Information

Summary edges have been proposed by Horwitz et al. [HRB90] as a means to allow context-sensitive slicing in time linear in the size of the dependence graph. Their algorithm to compute these edges based on attribute grammars, however, is asymptotically slower than an alternative algorithm presented by Reps et al. [RHSR94]. An optimization of this latter algorithm, which trades space for time in the map fragmentPath, is presented in Algorithm 2. Its worst case complexity is in $O(n^3)$ where n is the size of the dependence graph. After summary edges have been computed, each slice can be determined in linear time.

Algorithm 2 Pseudocode for computing summary edges

---

1 **function** ComputeSummaryEdges
2 **Input**: G an SDG
3 **Output**: $SummaryEdge$ set of summary edges
4 **declare** $PathEdge, SummaryEdge, WorkList$: set of edges
5 **declare** $fragmentPath$: map **from** vertex **to** set of edges
6 **begin**
7   PathEdge := $\varnothing$; SummaryEdge := $\varnothing$; WorkList := $\varnothing$
8   **foreach** $w \in FormalOutNodes(G)$ **do**
9   insert $(w \to w)$ into PathEdge
10   insert $(w \to w)$ into WorkList
11   **od**
12   **while** WorkList $\neq \varnothing$ **do**
13   **select** and **remove** an edge $v \to w$ **from** WorkList
14   **switch** v
15   **case** $v \in ActualOutNodes(G)$:
16   **foreach** x such that $x \to v \in SummaryEdge \lor x \to_{cd} v \in G$ **do**
17   Propagate$(x \to w)$
18   **od**
19   **esac**
20   **case** $v \in FormalInNodes(G)$:
21   **foreach** $c \in \{G_c \mid (c \to Entry(w)) \in E\}$ **do**
22   **let** $x = $ CorrespondingActualIn(c, v)
23                     $y = $ CorrespondingActualOut(c, w) **in**
24   insert $x \to y$ into SummaryEdge
25   **for** each a such that $y \to a \in$ fragmentPath(y) **do**
26   Propagate$(x \to a)$
27   **od**
28   **end let**
29   **od**
30   **esac**
31   **default** :
32   **foreach** x such that $x \to_{dd} v \in G \lor x \to_{cd} v \in G$ **do**
33   **if** $x \to_{dd} v$ or x and v are not both parameter nodes **then** // *exclude object trees*
34   Propagate$(x \to w)$
35   **fi**
36   **od**
37   **end switch**
38   **od**
39   **return**(SummaryEdge)
40 **end**
41
42 **procedure** Propagate$(e:$ edge $(v \to w))$
43 **begin**
44   **if** $e \notin$ PathEdge **then**
45   insert e into PathEdge
46   insert e into WorkList
47   **if** $v \in ActualOutNodes(G)$
48   insert e into fragmentPath(w)
49   **fi**
50   **fi**
51 **end**

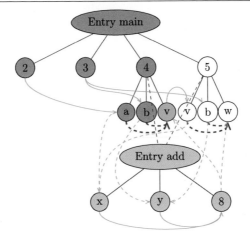

Figure 2.6: Backward slice of node v at call site 4 in the example

Correctness of graph-based Slicing

Horwitz et al. [HPR88] showed that PDGs (for a while language including arrays) are adequate for representing a program's execution behavior: If the PDGs
of two programs are isomorphic, then for a given input either both programs
diverge, or terminate with the same final values for all variables. Backward
intraprocedural slicing based on the PDG for a simple while language has been
proved correct in [RY88]. Their Slicing Theorem shows that for any initial state
on which the program terminates, the program and its slice compute the same
sequence of values for each element of the slice. This result was extended to
the SDG by Binkley et al. [BHR89] and to programs with heap-allocated storage (based on a LISP-style cons operator) and pointers [PS91], in the spirit
of [HPR89]. It is well-known that such an operator is sufficient to model complex heap structures and even Java-like objects. Still, our extension of SDGs in
section 2.5 is presented together with a correctness argument for interprocedural
data dependences to illustrate the soundness of our modeling of method parameter passing. Syntax-preserving slicing in the presence of unstructured control
flow has been solved independently by Ball and Horwitz [BH93] and Choi and
Ferrante [CF94]. Both solutions include a correctness proof. Harman and Danicic [HD98] extend the solution of Agrawal [Agr94] and present a correctness
proof.

2.3 Points-To Analysis

Points-to analysis is a major prerequisite for analyzing heap-manipulating programming languages. For an object-oriented language, it answers the question

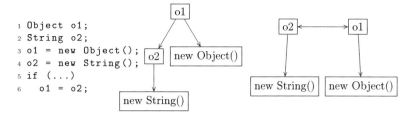

```
1  Object o1;
2  String o2;
3  o1 = new Object();
4  o2 = new String();
5  if (...)
6     o1 = o2;
```

Figure 2.7: Code fragment and possible points-to graphs

which objects a given pointer or reference may point to at runtime. Based on this analysis one can derive related questions, like *may-aliasing*, i.e. whether two variables may refer to the same location in memory – thus to the same object, and under certain conditions also *must-aliasing*, i.e. if two variables always point to the same object.

Since the basic techniques were presented by Andersen [And94] and Steensgaard [Ste96], hundreds of papers have targeted this issue (e.g. [SS00b, RMR01, RLS+01, MRR02, NR03, LH03, LL03, WL04, LH08]) and thereby refined the technique such that today, pointer analyses scale well for realistic programming languages and program sizes. However, even though points-to analysis seemed worn out [Hin01] years ago, there are still papers at major conferences on that topic that improve precision and scalability substantially.

Points-to analysis is usually solved by constraint based program analysis: From the control flow graph a number of constraints is extracted that must hold due to the program semantics. These constraints can be solved and yield a conservative solution for the points-to relation. The constraint system is traditionally represented as a *points-to graph*, where (in the intra-procedural case)

- there is one node for each pointer variable in the program,

- one node for each representative of an object (usually an *object creation site*). Due to undecidability, objects created by the same creation site in different iterations of a loop can in general not be distinguished and are therefore all represented by the same creation site; and

- an edge $p \rightarrow q$, where p and q are nodes in the graph, is inserted if p might point to q during program execution.

A pointer p may point to an object created at a creation site o ($o \in$ points-to(p)) iff there exists a path $p \rightarrow \cdots \rightarrow o$ in G.

As an example, consider Figure 2.7, where a program fragment is depicted together with possible points-to graphs. There are nodes for each variable o1 and o2 and for both creation sites. The assignment in line 3 and 4 yield edges between the variables and the corresponding creation sites. The assignment in line 6 creates another edge between the two variables.

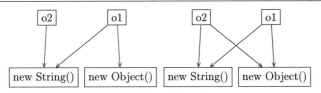

Figure 2.8: Points-to relations for the graphs in Figure 2.7

2.3.1 Inclusion-Based vs. Unification-Based Analysis

Two fundamental approaches in determining points-to relations have been presented:

Steensgaard [Ste96] proposed a unification-based approach, where pointers are either unaliased or point to the same set of objects. Its big advantage is the near-linear complexity of $\mathcal{O}(n \cdot \alpha(n))$ (where α is the inverse Ackermann function), based on the fast Lengauer-Tarjan algorithm [LT79]. In the example of Figure 2.7, the rightmost graph corresponds to Steensgaards algorithm. Since unification means that the points-to set of o1 equals the one of o2, the edge between their corresponding nodes points in both directions. Unfortunately, applying this algorithm to Java yields several undesirable properties. Streckenbach [SS00b] has found that strongly typed languages like Java loose type safety with unification-based approaches, which can be seen in Figure 2.8, where a reference of type `String` is determined to possibly point to a variable of declared type `Object`. This has dramatic implications on the approximation of dynamic binding, where the called method is dependent on the target object: When `String.charAt(int)` is called on o2, the analysis cannot determine such a method in `java.lang.Object`, the type of the first allocation. Since bytecode lacks typing information, it is now unclear, if the bytecode is unsafe, the analysis contains a bug, or this flaw is simply due to over-approximation.This problem led to years of research in scalability for the inclusion-based approach.

Andersen's points-to graph is inclusion-based and inserts only uni-directed edges between pointer nodes of an assignment. This approach will only generate constraints that obey type-safety[3], which corresponds more thoroughly to an assignment's semantics, as can be seen in Figure 2.7 (middle): Here, only o1 might point to o2 but not vice versa. Thus the points-to relation becomes more precise than with the unification-based approach (see left graph in Figure 2.8). However, the cost of solving the constraint system is in $\mathcal{O}(n^3)$ where n is the number of statements in the program. Despite this relatively high worst case complexity, inclusion-based analyses have become predominant in the last years, due to advances in runtime based on recent research e.g. by using better data structures like BDDs [WL04, LH08].

---

[3]In some representations, explicit downcasts may generate constraints violating type-safety, too: Code of the form `if (x instanceof A) A y = (A) x;` needs to take into account that y's type is guaranteed to be `A`, however, since bytecode is untyped, this requires program analysis.

2.3.2 Inter-procedural Analysis and Dynamic Dispatch

For inter-procedural analysis, the predominant implementation technique is graph cloning, i.e. one adds a points-to graph for each procedure in each context. A context may be the traditional calling context as in [WL04]. Alternatively, for object-oriented languages the target object of virtual bound methods has been found effective as context [MRR02], which has been termed *object-sensitive pointer analysis*. Using calling contexts for contexts is problematic in that it requires conservative approximations in case of recursion and often a precomputed call graph is needed, which hinders on the fly computation. Therefore, using target objects as contexts is – while more conservative for some cases – more practical, as no call graph is needed for context computation and contexts need not be constructed in a complicated manner. Still, it has been found efficient for many typical problems, like factory methods or containers, which context-insensitive analysis treats in a too conservative way.

Object-oriented languages like Java either need a pre-computed call graph for points-to analysis, with the drawbacks that an additional analysis needs to be done in advance and that the generated call graphs are typically relatively imprecise. Alternatively, the call graph may be computed on the fly during points-to analysis. While this makes points-to considerably more complex, additional analysis is omitted and the generated call graph is as accurate as the analysis itself, typically much more precise than simple algorithms like class hierarchy analysis (CHA) [DGC95] or more refined analyses like 0-CFA [GDDC97], VTA [SHR+00], Rapid Type Analysis (RTA) [BS96] and the XTA algorithm [TP00].

The algorithm to conservatively approximate dynamic binding on-the-fly during points-to analysis consists of [HBCC99, SS00b]:

- Construct the initial points-to relations from assignments and statically dispatched method calls.

- Propagate the points-to relations along the graph edges.

- For each virtual call o.f(x1, ..., xn) determine points-to$(o) = \{o_1, \ldots o_k\}$ in the current graph

- Use static lookup to determine the call target f_i of method o_i.f(x1, ..., xn) and insert an edge from the call site to its target f_i in the call graph.

- Connect the parameters and return value of the call to those of f_i in the points-to graph, but only add an edge between the this-pointer of f_i and o_i instead of o. This last restriction guarantees type safety.

- Iterate until a fixed point of the points-to-relation is reached

The high technical complexity of this algorithm – an adaption of Lhoták [LH03] – especially when propagating points-to relations with a worklist algorithm, stems from the fact that the call targets f_i usually have not yet been analyzed and need to be added to the points-to graph first. This is even more true for call targets in f_i, which often need to be analyzed and added as well,

and those methods can in turn contain calls to new methods. But even after
analyzing and adding all new methods, the complexity remains that a worklist
algorithm must know which nodes need propagation. When analyzing new code
it is not sufficient to just add the parameters of the call to f into the worklist,
but the targets of all edges from newly analyzed code to "elder" nodes, that
already have been propagated to, may also require propagation. However, it is
difficult to keep track of which nodes are old and which are not. As a remedy,
on can conservatively propagate all method-spanning assignment edges after
adding new methods.

Algorithm 3 shows the adaption of Lhoták's [LH03] algorithms to on-the-fly
call graph computation. The main algorithm starts in line 1 and iterates until no
more elements are in the worklist. As expected, processing the new virtual call
target is most challenging. This procedure directly reflects all items described
in the list above.

2.3.3 Aliasing

For our application — program slicing — points-to information is mainly required for alias determination. Two references are said to be aliased [HLW+91],
if they point to the same memory cell. We distinguish two flavors of aliasing:

Definition 2.15 (Aliasing). *Two references are* must-aliased, *if they point to
same memory cell in every execution of the program; they are* may-aliased, *if
they point to the same memory cell in some executions of the program.*

May-alias information is needed when computing data dependences, where
a dependence must be inserted if the two statements may accesses the same
memory cell. Must-aliasing information allows strong updates (i.e. insertion
into the kill-set of an update) and thus reduces the number of spurious data
dependences. However, aliasing is known to be statically undecidable [Ram94],
so conservative approximations must be applied. In practice this means that
only a subset of the must-aliases and thus strong updates can be determined,
some spurious dependences remain in the dependence graph. And for may-
aliasing, one must find a superset of all definitive may-aliases, in order to get
all possible data dependences.

May-aliasing based on points-to relations is easily determined, even that
easily, that points-to and aliasing are sometimes used interchangeably:

Definition 2.16 (May-aliasing). *For two references [or pointers] p and q,*

$$\text{may-alias}(p, q) := (\text{points-to}(p) \cap \text{points-to}(q) \neq \varnothing)$$

Little work can be found on must-aliasing, probably because may-aliasing
(and points-to) is already hard enough for realistic languages and often local
reasoning is sufficient. Must-aliasing is hard to determine, as the points-to
relation is already a conservative approximation (here specifically due to flow-
insensitivity). One problem lies in the fact that each allocation site in the points-
to set stands for an equivalence class of dynamic allocations that are possible at
runtime. For example, an allocation in a loop can create an unbounded number

---

Algorithm 3 Points-to analysis with on-the-fly call graph computation.

---

1   process allocations
2   **repeat**
3   **repeat**
4   **remove** first node p **from** worklist
5   process each assignment edge $p \leftarrow q$
6   process each store edge $p \leftarrow q.f$
7   process each store edge $q \leftarrow p.f$
8   process each load edge $p.f \leftarrow q$
9   **until** worklist is empty
10   process every store edge
11   process every load edge
12   process new virtual call targets
13   **until** worklist is empty
14
15 **procedure** process allocations
16   **foreach** allocation edge $new1 \leftarrow p$ **do**
17   points-to(p) $\cup= \{new1\}$
18     $worklist \cup= \{p\}$
19   **od**
20   **foreach** assignment edge spanning method boundaries $p \leftarrow q$ **do**
21     $worklist \cup= \{q\}$
22   **od**
23
24 **procedure** process assignment edge $(p \leftarrow q)$
25   points-to(q) $\cup=$ points-to(p)
26   **if** points-to(q) was changed **then**
27     $worklist \cup= \{q\}$
28   **fi**
29
30 **procedure** process store edge $(p \leftarrow q.f)$
31   **foreach** allocation node $a \in$ points-to(q) **do**
32   points-to$(a.f)$ $\cup=$ points-to(p)
33   **od**
34
35 **procedure** process load edge $(p.f \leftarrow q)$
36   **foreach** allocation node $a \in$ points-to(p) **do**
37   points-to(q) $\cup=$ points-to$(a.f)$
38   **if** points-to(q) was changed **then**
39       $worklist \cup= \{q\}$
40   **fi**
41   **od**
42
43 **procedure** process new virtual call targets
44   **for** each virtual call $o.f(x_1, ... x_n)$ **do**
45   **for** each allocation node $a \in$ points-to(o) **do**
46   determine $a.f(y_1, ... y_n)$ with static lookup
47   add $(a.f(y_1, ..., y_n).this \rightarrow a)$ in the graph
48   connect other parameters and return value in the graph
49   **od**
50   **od**
51   add all targets of created edges **to** worklist
52   **if** new methods have been added **to** the graph or new connections have been created **then**
53   process allocations
54   **fi**

---

of objects at runtime, none of which is must-aliased but to itself. The same goes
for allocations in recursive cycles of the call graph. Still, provided an allocation
a is not in any cycle in the interprocedural control flow graph, two accesses
x, y where points-to$(x) =$ points-to$(y) = \{a\}$ are known to be must-aliases.
This is trivial for the case where both references may never be null, but also
straightforward, if one reference might be null, as then the corresponding use
or definition will not take place but the program will branch to error handling
code. So such a dependence is impossible and redundant, so must-aliasing may
induce killing definitions here.

As references in Java are immutable, must-aliasing becomes a simple form
of *Global Variable Numbering* [RWZ88]. Therefore, another local analysis is
possible with an intermediate representation in SSA-form: If two statements
in the same method access the same SSA-variable, they are must-aliases, no
matter how many elements their points-to set contains. Usually the employed
SSA-form is not minimal, so mere renamings of the form $x_2 = \Phi(x_1, \ldots x_1)$ can
also be detected as must-aliases.

2.4 Slicing Object-oriented Languages

The slicing techniques presented in the previous sections and other research in
program slicing has produced systems such as CodeSurfer [AT01] or VALSOFT
[Kri03a, RS02], which can slice realistic programs written in the full C language
with reasonable precision and performance.

2.4.1 Dynamic Dispatch

Several extensions of the SDG to object-oriented features have been proposed,
and all of them are capable of handling dynamic dispatch and inheritance
[LH96, KMG96, Zha00, LH98, WRW03, MMKM94, TAFM97, HDZ00]. Usually,
dynamic dispatch is treated similar to function pointers in C [GH96]. Today,
approximation of dynamic dispatch in slicers for object-oriented languages is
reasonable precise and efficient, thanks to powerful call-graph and points-to
analysis algorithms supporting the SDG construction. For every method that –
according to the call graph (see Definition 2.14) – might be called at runtime,
one adds a call edge to the entry of this method [TAFM97]: Each $c \to m \in G_c$
induces a call edge $c \to_c$ Entry$_m$ in the SDG. As the number and type of
parameters must be identical for redefined methods, the parameter nodes at
the call site can be taken from any appropriate method definition. However,
global variables and fields of parameters that are used or modified may differ
for redefinitions. This problem will be discussed in section 2.5.

2.4.2 Exception Handling

Java offers exception handling in a try ... catch ... finally construct, which
must be taken into account, when building the control flow graph: Each instruction that may throw a subtype of the type given in a catch block must have
a successor at the associated exception handler code. As Java allows multiple

catch blocks for the same try block, where only the first matching catch block is executed [LY99], only the first matching block should be a successor, to achieve maximum precision. Finally blocks are executed in any case, and thus are incorporated into the control flow after all[4] code in the try and catch blocks has been executed. If no appropriate exception handler is present, it is nevertheless executed before the procedure returns abnormally (throwing the exception to the caller) and must therefore be included just before the method's exit node.

Building PDGs just according to explicit exception handling constructs renders it incomplete for the full Java semantics: In Java, many bytecode instructions may throw an *implicit exception* (subtypes of RuntimeException) in case operands are inconsistent. For example, nearly every bytecode instruction that manipulates objects may throw a NullPointerException, those for arrays may throw ArrayIndexOutOfBoundsExceptions. To get a sound analysis result, control flow due to implicit exceptions must be taken into account. In our model, each bytecode instruction that may throw an implicit exception is preceded by code that checks a bytecode's precondition for normal execution, and if it is not satisfied, control flow branches to exception handling code or else to code for abnormal termination [CPS+99].

An exception without appropriate exception handler is passed to the caller of the causative method. If this caller method has an appropriate handler installed at the invocation bytecode, this handler is branched to in order to handle the exception; if not, then the caller method terminates abruptly as well, "rethrowing" the causing exception. This schema is employed until an appropriate handler is found somewhere above in the call stack, or else this thread of execution terminates and the causing exception is printed to the user. Again, this is incorporated into the control flow graph by introducing an extra predicate node with two successors for each possibly excepting call instruction: one successor models normal termination and one is for abrupt termination of the called method.

As an example, consider Figure 2.9, which shows a code snippet and the corresponding SDG. Line 3 in the code corresponds to several nodes: First the node bar with its children representing the parameter s and the synthetic return-parameter $exc. And second the predicate node exc==null, which models branching according to normal or abrupt termination of bar. If it terminates abruptly (the predicate is true), the statement of line 6 is executed.

In the subgraph for method bar, the precondition for an arraylength bytecode is that the array reference may not be null, which is checked in a synthetic predicate node. If it is true, an exception is thrown, otherwise the statement of line 10 is executed.

In case there are multiple catch blocks for one try block, the control flow graph contains a so-called typeswitch statement, which is similar to a traditional switch statement. For each possible catch block with exception type e there exists an edge labeled e to the corresponding code block.

---

[4]See Allan and Horwitz [AH03] for a discussion of inlining for finally blocks.

```
 1  void foo(Object[] s) {
 2    try {
 3      bar(s);
 4    } catch (
 5        NullPointerException e) {
 6      print("null");
 7    }
 8  }
 9  void bar(Object[] s) {
10    print(s.length);
11  }
```

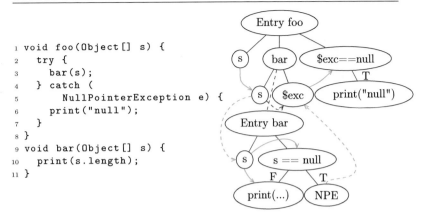

Figure 2.9: Example code for exception handling with SDG

2.4.3   Objects and Fields

Program slicing in the presence of objects and fields is not so different from slicing composite data types in traditional languages. Horwitz et al. [HPR89] already noticed that to extend the concept of data dependence for languages that manipulate heap-allocated storage, it is necessary to phrase its definition in terms of memory locations rather than variables:

Definition 2.17 (Data Dependence for Composite Data Structures). *Program point q has a* data dependence *on program point p if p writes into a memory location loc that q reads, and there is no intervening write into loc along the execution path by which q is reached from p.*

Even though Horwitz et al. did only consider a Lisp-style cons operator, it can model more complex data structures. However, with objects and fields, it is not always decidable, if two program points access the same memory location. Agrawal et al. [ADS93] give a classification of memory accesses into complete, maybe and partial intersection of abstract memory locations: *Complete intersection* arises, if the objects of both accesses are must-aliases and they access the same field. Maybe intersection for field access is possible due to aliasing: if two accesses reference the same field but they are only may-aliases, this is called *maybe intersection.* Another case of maybe intersection arises with arrays, as the field index is generally unknown at compile time. Arrays combine this maybe intersection with *partial intersection,* as only one element of the whole array is accessed. Most work on arrays treats arrays as a single location in memory, thus ignoring the index which is, in general, only known at runtime. We follow this conservative convention by modeling arrays as a field with the reserved name []. Lyle [Lyl84] proposed that array updates should be handled like a reference to and subsequent update of the whole array (killing modifications). This results in data dependences between array updates a[i] $\rightarrow_{dd}$ a[j] when the first statement reaches the second, even if i may not equal j.

```
1 int z;
2 T a, b;  // initialization omitted here
3 a.x = 1;
4 b.x = 2;
5 a.y = 3;
6 b.y = 4;
7 a = b;
8 z = a.y;
9 }
```

Figure 2.10: Example program illustrating field sensitivity

For computing precise results for data dependence it is necessary to base intersection decision on the results of pointer and alias analysis. Tonella et al. [TAFM97] were the first to propose to use points-to analysis [And94, Ste96, SS00b] for SDG generation of OO programs.

Field sensitive analysis

Several approaches for determining the type of intersection have been proposed in literature. Each approach has its own strengths and weaknesses. For example, a straightforward intersection computation based on scalar replacement [Kri03a], where any access to a variable is (recursively) replaced by accesses to the contained fields, does not necessarily give the most precise data dependences. Consider the program in Figure 2.10 where variable z is only dependent on the definition in line 6. The C-Framework of ValSoft [Kri03a] computes a slice containing line 4 due to the inherent loss of precision of its virtual scalar replacement. CodeSurfer [AT01] employs a non-virtual scalar replacement strategy that blows up the code by replacing the assignment a = b with a.x = b.x; a.y = b.y beforehand, which allows the computation of the precise slice. Such a replacement may be appropriate for procedural languages like C, where nesting of structures is not too common, for object-oriented languages like Java with deeply nested objects, this would require a large overhead, which can be omitted in intraprocedural cases using a definition of data dependence without explicit scalar replacement.

The definition of data dependences can be refined for the case of field access to a field f, which is referenced by its fully qualified name (including name and defining class):

Definition 2.18 (Data Dependence for Field Access). *A PDG has a data dependence edge from node n_1 to node n_2 due to field access iff all the following conditions hold:*

- *n_1 is a node that defines the field f of variable x*

- *n_2 is a node that uses the field f of variable y*

- *x and y are potential aliases (may-aliases)*

- *control flow can reach n_2 after n_1 via a path in the CFG along which is
  no intervening definition of f*

With this definition, we get the precise slice in Figure 2.10 without expensive scalar replacement strategies just by inspecting the reaching definitions of the last line, which contains both assignments to the y field. With the flow-sensitivity in pointer analysis gained by SSA form, the criterion will be determined data dependent only on the definition in line 6. So while this last definition of data dependence is always field-sensitive, its precision relies heavily on the precision of the underlying alias analysis.

2.5 Interprocedural Dataflow-Analysis

For interprocedural analysis, a conservative approximation is required of how a program manipulates its data at the call-graph level. For program slicing, this mainly covers knowledge about what side-effects a method[5] call may impose on its parameters[6]. Side-effects of called methods produce new definitions that may reach a use and thus require transitive data dependences. Algorithms to compute such side-effects are known in the literature [Ban79, Muc97], but they are presented for procedural languages only, without covering extensive use of objects and their field structures. Side-effect analysis for multi-level pointers [RLS+01] is, however, too intricate for Java's single-level references. While some authors targeted how to represent objects for slicing [LH96, LH98], their approaches either have flaws or are not explicit on how to handle nested and recursive object structures conservatively. Tonella [TAFM97] already noted that points-to information is a prerequisite for precise side-effect analysis of object-oriented languages. The following section will present a new approach for computing a precise but conservative approximation of the side-effects of methods and their invoked methods that allows context-sensitive slicing of objects. It allows field-sensitive slicing and takes possible aliasing into account.

To allow field-sensitive analysis also in the interprocedural case, we need to explicitly represent all the fields of parameter objects and accessed static variables at the method entry nodes and call sites [PS91]. This corresponds to the non-virtual *scalar replacement* strategy in the intra-procedural case (cf. section 2.4.3).

In analogy to previous work [Ban79, Muc97] we characterize side-effects as two functions from statements to the set of locations they may access. A *memory location* is an abstraction of a cell in the heap and is represented as a sequence of fields[7] rooted at a parameter of the given method, such that dereferencing the fields in the list yields a pointer to the given abstract location. For example, if an object may be accessed with the expression a.f.g from the parameter a, then $a.f.g$ is an abstract location for the memory storing that object. While this representation is not necessarily unique, it is sufficient for our algorithm. We

---

[5]The object-oriented term *method* will be used instead of procedure in the sequel

[6]As static variables are modeled as extra parameters in SDGs the term parameter will cover both normal parameters and synthetic ones for static variables in the sequel

[7]To achieve disambiguity, the fully qualified field name must be used.

will write $a.f.g$ for an abstract location rooted in the parameter a which may be accessible in one execution through dereferencing first f and then g. We say that a location $x = a.f.g$ *extends* location $y = a.f$ when the list of fields of y is a prefix of x's and they share the same root. We will also write $x = y.g$ where y is another location as an abbreviation of the extension of y with g. Finally, we define $root(a.f_1...f_n) := a$. The side-effects for a method m are described by the following functions [Ban79]:

$Ref(m) = $ set of locations that may be referenced by executing m and
$Mod(m) = $ set of locations that may be modified by executing m

These sets are prefixed with letters to represent interprocedural versions (see next paragraph). By definition, $Ref(m) \supset Mod(m)$ and the same relation holds for the prefixed variants.

The first step in computing side-effect is to determine which side-effects a method may produce without considering other methods called in that method. We call these sets $IRef$ and $IMod$ to indicate that they are intra-procedural only.

2.5.1 Intraprocedural IRef and IMod Computation

Before going into the details of the algorithm, the notation used in the sequel is presented: For a method m, the set $\mathrm{Param}(m)$ denotes all formal parameters of m. The notation $\mathrm{loc}\, y.f$ represents an abstract memory location. We will write $\mathrm{Subobject}(x)$ for the set of locations that are transitively reachable by dereferencing fields of x. This set can easily be determined by Class Hierarchy Analysis [DGC95], but the results of pointer analysis generally allow much more refined sets, as only fields of classes in the points-to set of x (and transitively reachable locations) need to be considered. The notation $base(y.f)$ refers to the base object location of a composite location $y.f$ and is defined as $base(y.f) = y$, the field can be obtained by $field(y.f) := f$.

The locations that may be referenced or modified by executing the method alone, i.e. without taking effects of method calls into account, are computed according to the following recursive definitions. Therefore, we are interested in their minimal fixed point:

$$IRef(m) = \{\mathrm{loc}\, y.f \mid y \in \mathrm{Param}(m) \cup IRef(m) : \exists \text{ statement } r \in m$$
$$\exists\, \mathrm{loc}\, x.f \in Mod(r) \cup Ref(r) : \text{may-alias}(x,y)\} \cup IMod(m) \cup \mathrm{Subobject}($$
$$\{\mathrm{loc}\, y.f \in IRef(m) : \exists r \in m\ \exists\, \mathrm{loc}\, x.f \in Def(r) : \text{may-alias}(x,y)\}) \quad (2.3)$$

The memory locations that may be directly referenced in a method consist of the parameters of the analyzed method m as well as memory locations transitively reachable from these ($IRef$) by access through a field f whose base object x is a may alias of a memory location that may be referenced. Apart from that, all memory locations that may be written ($IMod(m)$) must be included into $IRef$ by definition, as not all paths in that method must redefine those fields. In that case, the original value will be synthetically referenced. Finally, the subobjects of all memory locations that may be used when writing another memory location need to be included. The reason is that, when an object is written, its whole

subobject structure changes due to its changed field values, and these changes
come from the field values of the used object.

As an example, in Figure 2.10, line 7 defines a using b, therefore all definitions
concerning the subobject of b need to be included in the backward slice for a.

$$IMod(m) = \{loc\, y.f \mid y \in \mathrm{Param}(m) \cup IRef(m) : \exists\, \text{statement}\, r \in m$$
$$\exists\, loc\, x.f \in \mathrm{Def}(r) : \text{may-alias}(x, y)\} \cup \mathrm{Subobject}(IMod(m) \cup \{\$ret, \$exc\})$$
$$(2.4)$$

The set of memory locations that may be modified in the method m directly
subsumes all locations that are directly or indirectly accessible via parameters
and are used at a statement $r \in dom(Mod)$ with a possible aliasing situation of
their base locations. Apart from that, the whole set together with the synthetic
variables $\$ret, \$exc$ that representing the return value or the thrown exception
of method m, respectively, is transitively closed with respect to the subobject
relation.

Note that in the presence of recursive data structures, $IRef$ and $IMod$ may
contain an infinite number of locations with finite length. For example, a linked
list might contain $\{head, head.next, head.next.next, \dots\}$. We will show later,
that for computation purposes, it is sufficient to determine only a finite number
of representatives for an equivalence relation, so these sets can be considered
finite in the meantime.

Figure 2.11 presents a small Java program which we will use as a running example for illustrating interprocedural dataflow-analysis. Its intermediate SDG
after the traditional SDG generation steps is depicted in Figure 2.12. It only
contains five accesses to abstract locations: $Mod(3) = \{this.x\}$, $Mod(10) =$
$\{this.a\}$, $Ref(12) = \{this.a\}$ and $Ref(13) = \{a.x\}$. In the constructor A.init,
$IRef(A.init) = \{this.x\}$ and thus $IMod(A.init) = \{this.x\}$. $IRef(B.init) =$
$\{this.a\}$ and thus $IMod(B.init) = \{this.a\}$, $IRef(foo) = \{this.a\}$, $IRef(bar) =$
$\{a.x\}$ and all other $IRef$s and $IMod$s are empty. This result can be seen in
Figure 2.13 where $IRef$ and $IMod$ are represented in the tree domain, however, with $IRef(A.init)$ omitted, as the instance members of the this object
are uninitialized at invocation of the constructor.

The Unfolding Criterion

Liang and Harrold [LH98] already pointed out that in the presence of recursive
data structures the object trees cannot be unfolded until all leaves are primitive
types. As mentioned in section 2.5, their solution, namely to limit the depth to a
fixed level, is unsatisfactory. In our approach we unfold the tree until we reach a
fixed point with respect to the aliasing situation of the containing object. Thus
we obtain a safe criterion telling us whether further unfolding can be stopped
without losing dependences. The criterion is based on points-to information and
works as follows. We define a reflexive, symmetric relation $R \subseteq loc \times loc$:

$$l_1 R\, l_2 \Leftrightarrow l_1 = l_2 \vee ((l_1 \text{ extends } l_2 \vee l_2 \text{ extends } l_1) \wedge$$
$$\text{points-to}(base(l_1)) = \text{points-to}(base(l_2)) \wedge field(l_1) = field(l_2)) \quad (2.5)$$

```
1  class A {
2    int x, y;
3    A(int i) { x = i; }
4  }
5
6  class B {
7    A a;
8    B() {
9      A n = new A(2);
10     this.a = n;
11   }
12   int foo() { return bar(a); }
13   static int bar(A a) { return a.x; }
14   public static void main(String[] args) {
15     B b = new B();
16     int z = b.foo();
17   }
18 }
```

Figure 2.11: An example program

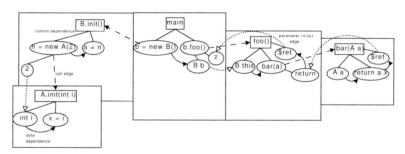

Figure 2.12: Intermediate SDG for class B after traditional SDG generation.

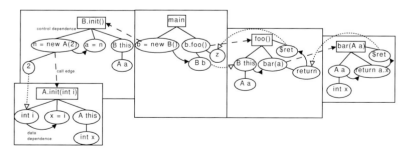

Figure 2.13: Intermediate SDG for class B after intraprocedural IREF/IMOD analysis.

```
 1 class C {
 2   C f;
 3   public static void main(String[] args) {
 4     C c = new C();
 5     C.rec(c);
 6     C x = c.f;
 7     C y = x.f;
 8   }
 9   static void rec(C c) {
10     c.f = new C();
11     C x = c.f;
12     x.f = c;
13   }
14 }
```

Figure 2.14: Example program illustrating recursive data structures.

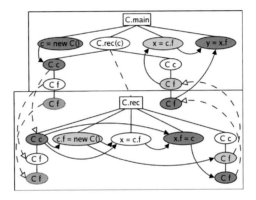

Figure 2.15: SDG (without summary edges) for Figure 2.14 including object trees.

The idea is to stop unfolding, when the same field has been observed earlier in this branch of the object tree and the base pointers of these two locations have the same points-to sets. In this case, both locations are equivalent with respect to all properties used for computing data dependences, so including the second tree would just add the same information again, rendering one of these locations redundant. The transitive closure $\sim$ of R yields an equivalence relation which we leverage to find a unique representative:

When computing the quotient sets $IRef/_\sim$ and $IMod/_\sim$, we choose the shortest entry (i.e. the infimum in terms of the *extends* relation) as representatives. These sets are finite due to the sets in the points-to relation being finite. We will show later that including these quotient sets (i.e. these representatives) into the dependence graph is sufficient to compute correct slices with respect to field access. This is due to Definition 2.18 of data dependence, which is also based on the aliasing situation.

54

As an example, consider Figure 2.15, which shows the SDG for class C in Figure 2.14. Note that no data dependence points to the formal-out parameter node C c, as Java only supports call-by-value, such that this node does not represent a reference of c. Its only purpose is to reflect the tree structure of the formal-in parameters. The points-to set of c contains only the new statement in C.main, while the points-to set of field f in c contains only the new instruction in C.rec. Our algorithm adds the first level for field f due to the write to c.f. The second level is added in our approach as the points-to sets of the root and the first level node are not equal. A third level is not added as the points-to sets of the c and c.f.f nodes are equal. The representative of c.f.f.f's equivalence class is c.f. Adding the field f a third time, would just result in the same dependences as c has because of the aliasing situation. In contrast, k-limiting as proposed by Liang [LH98] would cut off the trees and miss the purple shaded nodes for $k = 1$, hence dependences and slices would be incomplete. Liang is not specific on how to approximate these missing dependences.

2.5.2 Interprocedural Analysis

The previous section only determined side-effects up to method boundaries. The next step must therefore determine these side-effects up to the call graph level. This involves propagating side-effects along call sites and then again from the actual parameters to formal parameters if necessary. A fixed point iteration is required until all side-effects have been propagated to methods that transitively call them. Before going into the technical descriptions, we need to define some auxiliary functions: To this end, we overload the Param function to call sites such that $Param(m, c)$ denotes all locations that are passed to method call c which resides in method m. We assume temporary variables are leveraged when a complex expression is passed to c and in cases of parameter aliasing. For example, the call f(x+y) is replaced by t = x+y; f(t), where t is a fresh variable. When c may call method m' then the function $bind_{m,c,m'} : Param(m') \rightarrow Param(m, c)$ returns the actual parameter of call c that corresponds to the formal parameter of method m'. For convenience, we extend this function to sets, where the set of actual parameters corresponding to a given set of formal parameters is returned.

Since the global side-effects $GRef$ and $GMod$ (defined later) include the local ones $IRef/_\sim$ and $IMod/_\sim$ (as defined in [Ban79, Muc97]), we can determine the side-effects of the directly called method at a call site according to the following definitions:

$$CRef = \{(m, c, t) \mid t \in bind_{m,c,m'}(GRef(m'))\} \qquad (2.6)$$
$$CMod = \{(m, c, t) \mid t \in bind_{m,c,m'}(GMod(m'))\} \qquad (2.7)$$

For convenience, we define the curried versions $CRef(m, c) = \{t \mid (m, c, t) \in CRef\}$ and $CMod(m, c) = \{t \mid (m, c, t) \in CMod\}$. Intuitively, $CRef$ and $CMod$ represent the set of side-effects $IRef$ and $IMod$ of the possibly called methods m' at the call-site c, however with the formal variable names replaced by the actual variables passed to m' at c. As we are using $GRef$ and $GMod$ instead of $IRef$ and $IMod$, a fixed point iteration needs to be done to include the global side-effects, i.e. the side-effects that include those of called methods as well.

Figure 2.16 shows the results of applying these definitions to the local side-effects $IRef/_\sim \subset GRef$ and $IMod/_\sim \subset GMod$ of our running example as determined in section 2.5.1: $CMod \supset \{(B.init, newA(), n), (B.init, newA(), n.x)\}$ and $CRef \supset \{(foo(), bar(), a), (foo(), bar(), a.x)\}$. Note that the implicit variable $this$ of $A.init$ has been renamed to the name of the actual parameter a. Moreover, the corresponding nodes in the graph have already been connected by parameter-in and -out edges, except for the root of $IMod(A.init)$. This exception reflects Java's call-by-value parameter passing scheme, which does not propagate changes to formal parameter variables back to its callees.

The method entry vertex contains parameter trees with one formal-in node for every location in $GRef$, and one formal-out node for every location in $GMod$. For a virtual method call this means that there is not exactly one actual node ($CRef/GRef$) for every formal node: Different (re)definitions of virtual methods may very well access a different set of fields of a parameter. Thus, every actual tree in $CRef/CMod$ is a union of all corresponding formal trees in $GRef/GMod$ of all possibly called methods in the approach presented here.

Now the side-effects of called methods are visible at the call site but they may in turn represent side-effects of the method containing the call. For example, the definition of `a.x` in B's constructor is also a side-effect of this method. Therefore, we need another function $bind_{m,c} : \mathrm{Param}(m, c) \rightarrow \mathrm{Param}(m) \cup IRef(m)$, which returns, for a given parameter of a method call c in method m, the formal parameters or locations in $IRef(m)$ that are aliased:

$$bind_{m,c}(x) := \{y \in Param(m) \cup IRef/_\sim(m) : mayAlias(x, y)\} \qquad (2.8)$$

Again, this definition is extended to sets of parameters. In our example program, $bind_{B.init, newA()}(n) = \{this.a\}$ and $bind_{foo(), bar()}(a) = \{this.a\}$. For two locations y and z, the append function @ returns the location of the concatenation of the access paths of y and z:

Definition 2.19 (Append). *For two locations $y = v.f_1...f_n$ and $z = w.g_1...g_m$ where* may-alias(y, w) *the concatenation* $y@z = v.f_1...f_n.g_1...g_m$.

Now, the global side-effects of method calls [Ban79] can be included into the parameters of a method:

$$GRef = \{(m, t) \mid t \in IRef/_\sim(m) \vee (t = y@z : \exists c \in Calls(m) :$$
$$z \in CRef(m, c) \wedge y \in bind_{m,c}(root(z)))\} \quad (2.9)$$

$$GMod = \{(m, t) \mid t \in IMod/_\sim(m) \vee (t = y@z : \exists c \in Calls(m) :$$
$$z \in CMod(m, c) \wedge y \in bind_{m,c}(root(z)))\} \quad (2.10)$$

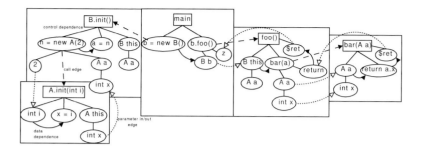

Figure 2.16: Intermediate SDG for class B after first iteration of interprocedural CRef/CMod propagation.

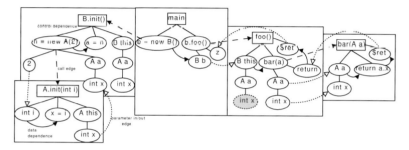

Figure 2.17: Intermediate SDG for class B: First iteration of GRef/GMod.

Again, we define the convenience functions $GRef(m) = \{t \mid (m,t) \in GRef\}$ and $GMod(m) = \{t \mid (m,t) \in GMod\}$. $CRef$ and $GRef$ are mutual recursive, as well as their Mod counterparts, and the minimal fixed point gives the desired solution. It is again sufficient to consider representatives of the $\sim$ relation in the $GRef$ and $GMod$ definitions, so this fixed point is guaranteed to exist.

Considering our running example again, Figure 2.17 shows the first iteration of the $GRef$ and $GMod$ computation: $GMod \supset \{(B.init, this), (B.init, this.a), (B.init, this.a.x)\}$ and $GRef \supset \{(foo(), this), (foo(), this.a), (foo(), this.a.x)\}$.

After the second iteration, $CRef/CMod$ contain the locations depicted in Figure 2.18 where $CMod \supset \{(main, newB(), b.a), (main, newB(), b.a.x)\}$ and $CRef \supset \{(main(), foo(), b), (main(), foo(), b.a), (main(), foo(), b.a.x)\}$. Since $bind_{main,foo}$ is constantly empty (for main only having args as formal parameters), the fixed point iteration ends here.

2.5.3 Data Dependences

When all global side-effects have been computed, data dependence for fields is determined according to Definition 2.18. To this end, elements of $GRef$ are considered as elements of Def of the corresponding method entry node,

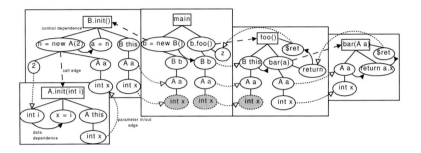

Figure 2.18: Intermediate SDG for class B: Fixed point after second CRef/CMod propagation

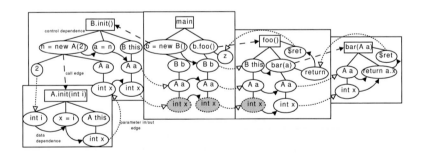

Figure 2.19: SDG for class B including data dependences (but without summary edges). Shaded nodes are cut off by 1-limiting.

elements of $GMod$ as elements of Ref of the corresponding exit node [HRB90]. In contrast, elements of $CRef$ are inserted in Ref of the call node and $CMod$ in Def, respectively [HRB90]. The kill sets of the standard intraprocedural reaching definitions analysis are only populated with definitions where the must-aliasing relation of the base objects holds. Data dependence is subsequently determined using Definition 2.18.

In our running example, Figure 2.19 shows the result of this step: In A.init, the definition x = i reaches the exit node, so we get a data dependence between this definition and the synthetic use of this.x in $GMod$. Similarly, the synthetic definition based on $GRef(bar)$ a.x reaches the return statement and therefore produces a data dependence edge. In main, the synthetic definitions based on $CMod(main, newB())$ reach the synthetic uses of $CRef(main, foo())$, so data dependences are inserted between these locations.

Summary Edges for Object Trees When computing summary edges with object trees, an optimization is crucial to obviate combinatorial explosion: With the original algorithm for summary edges, if a child of an actual-in parameter has a summary edge to node n, then the parent(s) would get such an edge to n as well. But these edges are redundant, as one can always follow the child's summary edge and ascend to the parent, so slicing will yield the same with or without these edges. As a consequence, Algorithm 2 does not follow control dependences from parameters to their parents (line (33)).

2.5.4 Correctness of Object Tree Algorithm

Previous work [RY88, BHR89, PS91] has shown several dimension of slicing correct (in particular interprocedural slicing and heap objects, see page 40). As a combination of interprocedural slicing with heap objects has not been explicitly proven correct, we focus on the soundness of interprocedural data dependences for heap objects. Thus, to show the soundness of our algorithm, we need to prove that all dynamic data dependences are approximated by static data dependences, i.e. when a statement defines a field value in an execution and this value is later used at another statement, then there must be a dependence chain between the corresponding nodes of the SDG. For a method call $call$, we assume that in a dynamic execution, the successor of the last statement of the invoked method is again $call$, to assign the returned value to the result variable.[8] In the sequel, we denote the kind of dependence of an SDG edge e with $label(e)$, e.g. $label(x \rightarrow_{dd} y) = dd$. $correspondingCall(n)$ denotes the call statement that created the stack frame of statement n, where n is typically a return statement.

Theorem 2.2 (Correctness of Object Tree Algorithm). *For all runs of the program p whose SDG G was built according to section 2.5, if the execution E contains a path $P = \langle p_1, \ldots p_n \rangle$ where p_1 defines memory cell mem and p_n reads mem, where either $p_1 = correspondingCall(p_n)$ and both p_1 and p_n are synthetic field assignments due to parameter passing or p_1 is a regular field assign-*

---

[8]This assignment is not assumed to constitute an interprocedural statement.

$ment$,[9] and $\forall p_i \in \{p_2, \ldots, p_n\}$ we have that p_i is not a regular field assignment statement to memory mem, then $\exists$ path $S \in G$ with $S = \langle p_1 = s_1, \ldots, s_m = p_n \rangle$ where $label(s_i, s_{i+1}) \in \{DD, PI, PO\}$.

Proof. The proof is an induction over the number q of interprocedural statements in the execution trace P, where interprocedural statements are either `call`, `return`, or `throw` statements. Without loss of generality, we assume that we have no `throw` statements, as these are functionally equivalent to `return` statements (using the synthetic variable $\$exc$ instead of $\$ret$ (see section 2.5.1)).

Base case: $q = 0$ **(intra-procedural case)** We have that $P = \langle p_1, \ldots, p_n \rangle$ is a subsequence of E where p_1 defines memory cell mem and p_n reads mem, thus $p_1 \in \text{Def}(f)$ and $p_n \in \text{Ref}(f)$ for a field f and may-alias($base(p_1)$, $base(p_n)$). As none of $p_i \in \{p_2, \ldots, p_n\}$ redefines memory mem in this execution, the definition of p_1 reaches p_n in the CFG and points-to(p_1) $\cap$ points-to(p_n) $\neq \varnothing$. Therefore definition 2.18 applies, such that we get a data dependence $p_1 \to^{dd} p_n$

Inductive step: $q \to q + 1$

The last interprocedural statement p_i in P is a call

$$\lceil \!\!\!\! \longrightarrow \cdots p_n$$

$p_1 \longrightarrow \ldots, p_i$: `call`

Three kinds of statements may have access to a memory cell:

a) A regular field access statement in Java can only access a memory cell via a parameter[10], so we know that there exists an access path $A = \langle form, f_1, \ldots, f_d \rangle$ through which p_n has gained access to mem in execution E. Thus, by equation (2.3) $\exists$ access path $A' \in IRef/_\sim(method(p_n))$ such that the last field of both access paths equal and A' is an alias for mem.

b) For an actual-in parameter $A = \langle act, f_1, \ldots, f_n \rangle$ of a call statement p_n, where $A \in CRef(method(p_n), p_n)$, there must also be a parameter $form$ such that an access path $A' = \langle form, f'_1, \ldots, f'_{d'} \rangle @A$ is an alias for mem due to equation (2.9).

c) Finally, if p_n is a return statement, the use $A = \langle form, f_1, \ldots, f_d \rangle$ at p_n must be in $GMod(method(p_n))$. With equation (2.9), we get $A' \in GRef(method(p_n))$ with $A' = A$.

In all cases, with equation (2.6) we have an access path $C \in CRef($ $method(p_i), p_i)$ which corresponds to A', i.e. $C = \langle act, f'_1, \ldots, f'_{d'} \rangle$ (and $f'_{d'} = f_d$) which constitutes a use in $method(p_i)$. Now we can apply the induction hypothesis on the path $P' = \langle p_1, \ldots, p_i \rangle$ which yields a path $S = \langle p_1 = s_1, \ldots, s_m = p_i \rangle$ where $label(s_i, s_{i+1}) \in$

---

[9]A regular field assignment statement is a bytecode that actively manipulates the heap, in contrast to synthetic field assignments induced by parameter passing.

[10]Or static (global) variables, which are modeled as extra parameters in SDGs

$\{DD, PI, PO\}$. As the algorithm inserts a parameter-in edge (C, A'), and a data dependence edge (A', p_n), we get the claim.

The last interprocedural statement p_i in P is a return
There are two possibilities for $c = correspondingCall(p_i)$:

1. $c \in P$

There exists an access path $A = \langle v, f_1, \ldots, f_d \rangle$ via which p_n has gained access to mem in execution E. As $\langle p_i, \ldots, p_k \rangle$ does not contain any redefinition statements of memory mem, there are two possibilities:

(a) There is $A' \in GMod(method(p_i))$ which may be aliased to mem, and by definition $A \in GRef(method(p_i))$ corresponds to A'. This may be due to a regular modifying statement m in a method that is reachable from c in the call graph that modifies a memory cell which may be aliased to mem (but as the p_i contain no redefinition for $i = 2, \ldots, n-1$ it was not aliased or executed in this execution). Then there is, according to the induction hypothesis applied to the path $c, \ldots, p_i$ a path from A to A', as $c, \ldots, p_i$ does not redefine mem. With equations (2.6) and (2.7) we have $C \in CRef(method(c), c)$ and a corresponding $C' \in CMod(method(c), c)$ that are connected to A and A' with parameter-in and -out edges, respectively. C' represents a definition, thus we have a data dependence (C', p_n) and get the claim with the induction hypothesis applied to the path $\langle p_1, \ldots, c \rangle$, as C represents a use at c. The e SDG contains thus a path $p_1 \to^{dd} \cdots \to^{dd} C \to^{pi} A \to^{dd} \cdots \to^{dd} A' \to^{po} C' \to^{dd} p_n$.

(b) If there is no location in $GMod(method(p_i))$ which may be aliased to mem, then there is no definition C' where $C' \in CMod(method(c), c)$ is aliased to mem, therefore we can apply the induction hypothesis on the last interprocedural statement preceding c.

2. $c \notin P$: In this case, we show the claim in Lemma 2.3.

$\square$

Lemma 2.3. *For all runs of the program p whose SDG G was built according to section 2.5, if the execution E contains a path $P = \langle p_1, \ldots p_n \rangle$ where p_1 defines memory cell mem and p_n reads mem, where either $p_1 = correspondingCall(p_n)$ and both p_1 and p_n are synthetic field assignments due to parameter passing or p_1 is a regular field assignment. Moreover, $\forall p_i \in \{p_2, \ldots, p_n\}$ we have that p_i is not a regular field assignment statement to memory mem, and the last interprocedural statement in P is a return statement at p_j with $correspondingCall(p_j) = c \notin P$, then $\exists$ path $S \in G$ with $S = \langle p_1 = s_1, \ldots, s_m = p_n \rangle$ where $label(s_i, s_{i+1}) \in$*

$\{DD, PI, PO\}$. Furthermore, we assume the induction hypothesis of Theorem 2.2.

Proof. The proof is an induction over the number q of interprocedural statements in the execution trace P, where interprocedural statements are either `call`, `return`, or `throw` statements. Again, without loss of generality, we assume that we have no `throw` statements.

Base case: $q = 0$, **intra-procedural case** As the precondition of the claim is not satisfied, we vacuously get the claim.

Inductive step: $q \to q + 1$

The first interprocedural statement p_i in P is a `call` As p_i is the first interprocedural statement in P and the call corresponding to p_j happened before p_1 (as it is not in P), we get the following invocation structure:

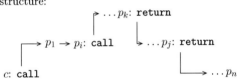

As invocation is nested in the execution, there must be a $k \in]i, j[$: $p_k = $ `return` $\land p_i = correspondingCall(p_k)$. There exists an access path $A = \langle v, f_1, \ldots, f_d \rangle$ via which p_1 has gained access to mem in execution E. As $\langle p_i, \ldots, p_k \rangle$ does not contain any redefinition statements of memory mem, there are two possibilities:

1. There is $A' \in GMod(method(p_k))$ which may be aliased to mem and a corresponding $A \in GRef(method(p_k))$. This may be due to a modifying statement in methods reachable from p_i in the call graph that access a memory cell that may be aliased to mem. Then there is, according to the induction hypothesis and the induction hypothesis of Theorem 2.2 applied to the path $\langle p_i, \ldots, p_k \rangle$ a path from A to A', as there is a path in CFG that does not redefine mem. With equations (2.6) and (2.7) we have $C \in CRef(method(p_i), p_i)$ and a corresponding $C' \in CMod(method(p_i), p_i)$ that are connected to A and A' with parameter-in and -out edges, respectively. C represents a use, thus we have a data dependences (p_1, C) and get the claim with the induction hypothesis of Theorem 2.2 applied to the path $\langle p_{i+1}, \ldots, p_n \rangle$, as A represents a definition at p_{i+1}.

2. If there is no location in $GMod(method(p_k))$ that may be aliased to mem, then there is no definition $C' \in CMod(method(p_i), p_i)$, therefore we can apply the induction hypothesis on the first interprocedural statement following p_k.

The first interprocedural statement p_i in P is a return
As statements in Java can – again – only access a memory cell via a parameter or local variable that is returned, we know that there exists an access path $A = \langle v, f_1, \ldots, f_d \rangle$ via which p_1 has gained access to mem in execution E.

a) For a regular field modification statement we know by equation (2.4) that there exists an access path $A' \in GMod(method(p_1))$ because p_1 is a definition.

b) For an actual-out parameter of a method call $A = \langle f_1, \ldots, f_d \rangle \in CMod(method(p_1), p_1)$ at p_1, we have with equation (2.10) $\exists$ access path $A' = \langle f_1', \ldots, f_{d'}' \rangle @ A \in GMod(method(p_1))$ for A to be visible after $method(p_1)$ returns.

c) For a formal-in parameter $A = \langle f_1, \ldots, f_d \rangle \in GRef(method(p_1))$ at p_1 (that also constitute definitions) A is corresponding to the access path $A' \in GMod(method(p_1))$ (which exists as p_1 is synthetic, so p_n is synthetic, too and $p_1 - correspondingCall(p_n)$) due to equation (2.9). Thus, with equation (2.7) we have an access path $C \in CMod(method(p_{i+1}), correspondingCall(p_i))$ with $C = \langle v', f_1', \ldots, f_{d'}' \rangle$ which constitutes a definition at p_{i+1}.

Thus we apply the induction hypothesis on the path $P' = \langle p_{i+1}, \ldots, p_n \rangle$. Then $\exists$ path $S = \langle C = s_1, \ldots, s_m = p_n \rangle$ where $label(s_i, s_{i+1}) \in \{DD, PI, PO\}$. As the algorithm inserts a parameter-out edge (A', C), and a data dependence edge (p_1, A'), we get the claim.

$\square$

Corollary 2.4 (Safety of Unfolding Criterion in Definition 2.5). *Using $IRef/_\sim$ and $IMod/_\sim$ instead of $IRef$ and $IMod$ is sound.*

Proof. The proofs of Theorem 2.2 and Lemma 2.3 do not rely on the actual access path A of the execution E, but on an abstraction A' that has (at least) the same aliasing relation and ends with the same field name. Thus, using the shortest location with the same field and aliasing relation, which is $IRef/_\sim$ or $IMod/_\sim$, is sufficient. $\square$

2.6 Related Work

Danicic et al. [DHHO07] present a lazy semantics for Weiser-style program slicing (i.e. without using intermediate representations like dependence graphs) of a simple *while* language. This semantics allows program slicing to introduce termination (i.e. a program slice may terminate while the original program does not, see [Wei84], so it is non-termination insensitive in the sense of Ranganath et al. [RAB+07].) Their semantics is consistent with program slicing and substitutive, thus allowing program transformations and software maintenance tasks like component reuse.

A formalization of program slicing that allows comparison of various variants of program slicing has been given in Binkley et al. [BDG+06]. This theory allows

classification of static slicing, dynamic slicing, both with or without counting
iterations, and their variants that additionally require the program and its slice
to follow identical paths[11]. Further, it formally defines what it means for one
slicing algorithm to be weaker than another, which gives a precise understanding
of what uncouth sentences like "Dynamic slices are smaller than static slices"
mean. Finally, simultaneous slices (i.e. involving a set of slicing criteria) and
conditioned slicing [CCL98] are related to other forms of slicing. Dependence
graph based slicing usually produces a non-executable slice[12], and it remains an
open question how these relate to the forms presented in this paper.

Binkley et al. [BDH+06] prove a formal relationship between (conditioned)
program slicing and partial evaluation [JGS93]. A combination of these techniques might allow construction of practical amorphous slicers [HBD03]. Parametric program slicing [FRT95] allows specification of constraints over the program's input. A term rewriting system extracts a program slice satisfying these
constraints. Conditioned program slicing [CCL98] is a similar technique that
slices based on a first order logic formula on the input variables. The conditioned
slice is based on deleting statements while preserving the program's behavior.
Amorphous program slicing [HBD03] is a different technique that does only
preserve the program's behavior with respect to the slicing criterion, but not
the original source code structure. This allows all kinds of semantics-preserving
program transformations.

Other Notions of Control Dependence The first rigorous examination
of control dependence was by Podurski and Clarke [PC90]. They define two
notions of control dependence, *strong control dependence* and *control dependence!weak*weak control dependence. The former is actually equivalent to the
transitive closure of the standard control dependence defined earlier. Weak control dependence generalizes control dependence to cases, where an infinite loop
may hinder statements reachable from this loop from execution, which represents another form of controlling whether another statement is executed. Apart
from the cases covered by standard control dependence, a statement is intuitively weakly control dependent on the predicate of the directly predecessing
possibly nonterminating loop.

This intuitive notion was coined *divergence dependence* by Hatcliff et al.
[HCD+99] but later divergence dependence together with standard control dependence was replaced by the more general definition of weak control dependence [RAB+07]. Cheng [Che93b] presents a generalization of control dependence for non-deterministic choice operators, called *selection dependence*.

Ranganath, Amtoft et al. [RAB+07,Amt08] present new forms of control dependence suitable for control flow graphs that do not satisfy the *unique end property*, i.e. which do not terminate (e.g. reactive systems) or have multiple points
of return (e.g. return and throw statements). They generalize standard control
dependence to *nontermination-insensitive control dependence* and weak control dependence to *control dependence!nontermination-sensitive*nontermination-

---

[11]Called Korel and Laski [KL88] style slicing in [BDG+06]
[12]Although most techniques can be extended to executable slices

sensitive control dependence. Nontermination-sensitivity guarantees that the standard program semantics (instead of a lazy semantics) is preserved by slicing, which plays an important role in their application, namely model checking. Furthermore they define various notions of *order dependence* which constitute ternary relations rather than traditional binary relations, allowing a rigorous definition of slicing with correctness proof even in the case of irreducible control flow graphs. Amtoft [Amt08] took on one of these, namely *weak order dependence*,[13] to verify the correctness of nontermination insensitive slicing without assuming a unique end node in the control flow graph. Slicing with this ternary relation $a \to (b, c)$ includes a into the slice, only if b and c are already contained. Currently, both works have no extension to interprocedural programs.

When programs contain `halt` statements in procedures, Sinha et al. [SHR01] found that intraprocedural control dependences together with call dependences do not suffice to guarantee semantic preservation during slicing. Based on Podurski and Clarke's work [PC90], they define *interprocedural control dependences* to capture the effects of non-terminating procedure calls. They prove that these guarantee semantic preservation, however, their approach captures context-insensitive slicing only. They propose a second algorithm that preserves context-sensitivity, but this algorithm is practically infeasible as it relies on method inlining even for recursive methods. Their approaches are claimed to extend to weak control dependence, however, without any proof.

Exception Handling Sinha and Harrold [SH00] take a different approach for modeling exception handling in Java: They add interprocedural control dependences from throw statements to possible catch blocks in methods above in the call graph. However, this approach does not handle implicit exceptions and requires non-standard interprocedural control dependence edges, which may render efficient context-sensitive slicing with summary edges infeasible. Allen and Horwitz [AH03] show that this problem may lead to incorrect slices for certain programs, where the call chain is greater than one. Further, Sinha and Harrold ignore data dependences due to exceptions, rendering their approach unsound.

Allen and Horwitz [AH03] model `try`, `throw` and `catch` statements – in analogy to jump statements of traditional language [BH93, CF94] – as synthetic predicates. Like in our approach, possibly excepting call statements are modeled as predicates that introduce control dependences on their successors, as these depend on whether the method terminates normally or abruptly, however, there may be multiple successors, one for each type of exception that may be thrown. Their modeling of interprocedural dependences for the returned or thrown values is non-standard, as they insist on having a control dependence path from a throw statement to all vertices whose execution may be affected. Thus they need summary edges between parameter-in nodes and non-parameter nodes. In contrast, our approach handles these values with traditional interprocedural data dependences (parameter-out edges); this induces the same transi-

---

[13]However, using an incompatible definition

tive dependences with standard techniques. In order to get more precise slices
for exception paths, they propose to split return parameter nodes, such that
each possible exception type that may be thrown has its own node. While this
requires an interprocedural uncaught exception analysis that is not discussed in
this paper, it also raises the problem that realistic programs already include a
high number of parameters due to object nesting, so splitting may dramatically
reduce scalability with only minor impact on precision. Further, it has been
shown [Tip95] that synthetic predicates are more conservative than necessary,
which may lead to imprecise slices.

Extensions for Object-oriented Languages Although program slicing and
dependence graphs are relatively old, extensions for object-oriented features
have not yet reached the degree of maturity of procedural analysis. One early
approach to object-oriented slicing was the work by Larsen and Harrold [LH96].
This approach represents fields of object parameters as extra (scalar) parameters
and thus merges all fields of different objects. This results in a more conservative approximation, as the approach is not object-sensitive. As already proposed
by Malloy [MMKM94], they include *membership dependences* and *inheritance
dependences*, which are only interesting for executable slices. Several authors
proposed Java implementations based on Larsen and Harrold's work: Kovács
et al. [KMG96] based their implementation of a Java slicer on that representation, with a slight adaption for Java. Zhao [Zha00] also bases his proposal on
the Larsen/Harrold work. Eventually Liang [LH98] pointed out that Larsen's
approach is insufficient: An object passed as a parameter to another object's
methods calls or being used as another object's field cannot be represented.
Apart from that, its model of polymorphic choice at invocation sites may give
incorrect results. It remains unclear how the approaches based on Larsen's work
circumvent these defects.

Tonella [TAFM97] proposed to use the results of a flow-insensitive points-to
analysis to resolve the runtime types of an object but represent an object as
a single vertex when an object is used as a parameter. Thus his approach is
field-insensitive and lacks precision.

Liang and Harrold [LH98] correct several flaws and imprecision of previous
approaches. They introduce full object-sensitivity in their SDG, and can handle
(polymorphic) objects that are passed as parameters or used as data members in
other objects. Further, they soundly represent polymorphism with its parameters and inheritance. They represent object parameters as tree structures, however, they propose limiting its depth to a fixed number and it remains unclear
how dependences due to deeper levels are approximated. This problem inspired
this work, which gives a precise condition for unrolling these trees together with
a soundness argument. Liang and Harrold discuss a language without exceptions, our work also integrates exception handling. Liang and Harrold do not
report an implementation of their approach.

Walkingshaw [WRW03] implemented a SDG generator for sequential Java
using the SOOT framework. Threads, exceptions and unstructured control flow
are not yet represented. Like our approach, it is object sensitive for field depen-

dences, but no algorithm to compute the object trees was given. In addition to our SDG, his graph contains membership dependences and inheritance dependences as proposed in [MMKM94]. For non-executable slices, the latter are not necessary as they do not increase the precision of the slice. Thus in our SDG membership and inheritance dependences are omitted.

Nanda's approach [NR03] models fields of objects as extra parameter nodes called *escape nodes*. The concept is similar to our approach but they build no trees which makes it harder to find the dependence between a field and the containing object.

CodeSurfer [AT01, ART03] contains a beta version slicer for C++. A Java version is planned. As of today, nothing is known about the precision of Codesurfer for C++.

The Bandera [HDZ00] project uses the Indus[14] Java slicer to automatically reduce the size of the transition system for model checking of Java source code [DHH+06]. The Bandera slicer is designed as a model checker frontend, not as a tool for program analysis. In contrast, the Kaveri Eclipse plugin [JRH05] offers a slicer for Java in a popular development environment. To our knowledge only the Indus slicer is—besides ours—fully implemented and can handle full Java bytecode. Indus is customizable, embedded into Eclipse, and has a very nice GUI, but is less precise than our slicer e.g. in terms of interprocedural data dependences of object fields. Like all implementations based on SOOT, they do not include all possible control flow based on implicit exceptions, which may lead to unsound results.

Many implementations of slicers for Java like [JRH05] pursue a relaxed notion of dependence graph[15], where data dependences are allowed to cross method boundaries. While this allows a more efficient implementation, one looses context-sensitivity for slicing and thus precision[16] As an example, Kaveri only offers k-limiting of contexts for precise slicing, while SDG slicing is precise even for recursive methods. Furthermore, applications like our precise information flow control algorithm (see section 4.6.1) require context-sensitive slicing and are thus not applicable to such relaxed graphs. Only the basic IFC algorithm can be leveraged in such a setting.

---

[14]http://indus.projects.cis.ksu.edu
[15]In comparison to the traditional system dependence graph of [HRB90].
[16]A more detailed study of slice sizes compared to our approach can be found in section 7.1.

Chapter 3

Concurrency

Both standard Java (J2SE) and Java for embedded devices (J2ME) support several threads of execution at the same time, either virtually dispatched to a single processor or running concurrently on multiple processors like in the current multicore architectures. All these threads share main memory, where the heap objects reside. Threads in Java are integrated into the programming language itself, whereas most languages need to include a multi-threading library that accesses native operating system routines. Therefore, threads in Java are much more system-independent than in other languages.

As Java is an object-oriented language, each thread running in the Java VM is associated an object of the `Thread` class. There is no other way for a user to create a thread but via a `Thread` object[1] whose `start` method is invoked. In such a case, a new thread is spawned and the `run` method of this thread object is executed. All threads share a single heap for storage of objects and their only interactions consist of synchronization and communication via shared variables (i.e. at least two threads share the reference to a heap memory cell).[2]

Making threads independent of the base operating system required the definition of a semantics for thread operations. Apart from that, the Java designers wanted to give compilers the ability to apply aggressive optimizations while at the same time giving programmers a certain kind of security. As a result, the *Java Memory Model* (*JMM*) was released based on JSR-133 and incorporated into Java 1.5 [GJSB05].

3.1 The New Java Memory Model

A memory model answers the question on which conditions a thread will see the value of a shared variable that has been previously (re)defined in another thread. With multicores having separate caches, it is no longer the case that one thread might ever, let alone immediately, see the results of an operation

---

[1] In analogy to previous work, the term *thread* will mean a thread of execution in the operating system, while an instance of the class `thread` will be called a *thread object*.

[2] If one thread $t1$ calls a (non-synchronization) method of the thread object $t2$ (where $t2$ corresponds to a thread executing in parallel to $t1$), this call is nevertheless executed in $t1$'s thread of execution, thus will only interact with $t2$'s thread in terms of shared memory.

in another thread. Defining a precise memory model has several advantages: First, describing the behaviors that multithreaded programs are allowed to exhibit allows all kinds of compiler optimizations, even if such an optimization is not yet known or implemented by the time the memory model is defined. To remain consistent, the Java Language Specification requires an *as-if-serial* semantics within thread boundaries that programmers are used to from sequential programming. And second, the specification committee wanted to guarantee a certain level of security, even if the program is insufficiently synchronized: The result of an improperly synchronized field access is not undefined as in traditional programming languages, which might lead to reading an arbitrary value from memory (e.g. a secret password). Instead, the JMM defines that only a value written to that field in this or another thread before the read instruction may ever be seen, even in the case of race conditions.[3]

Requiring that every processor in a shared-memory multiprocessor environment immediately sees what all the other processors are doing is prohibitively expensive in contemporary architectures, that only appear to adhere to the von Neumann computing model. In practice, this requirement would abandon nearly all recent achievements in speeding up processors, like pipelining, caches or speculative execution. Therefore, all contemporary architectures use a more or less relaxed notion of *memory-coherence* and require the operating system, compilers and sometimes even the program to insert special instructions (*fences*) to guarantee safe sharing of data. Java's write once, run everywhere philosophy thus required the definition of a common memory model, which is enforced by the JVM in terms of the platform's memory model.

The JMM describes, based on a program and a corresponding execution trace, whether the trace is a legal execution of the program. To this end, it validates for each read, that the observed write follows certain rules. Implementations of the JMM need only make sure that the execution produces a result that can be derived from the rules in the JMM, but are free in all other details. In particular, all present and future compiler optimizations are legal, if they adhere to those rules.

The actions of each thread in isolation must obey an *as-if-serial semantics* also called *intra-thread semantics*, i.e. all actions must appear to execute in the same order that the thread's statements are ordered in the program, with the additional restriction that the observed values of shared variables must adhere to the rest of the memory model. As-if-serial semantics does, however, not restrict optimizations that change a thread's semantics but preserve that appearance (e.g. loop invariant code motion).

In Java, all instance and static fields and arrays are stored in shared heap memory and are therefore affected by the memory model. In contrast, local variables in methods or formal method or exception handler parameters are not shared and thus need only adhere to intra-thread semantics. For the rest of the memory model, the term *variable* will denote a shared variable. Two

---

[3]An exception to this rule exists for 64 bit values, where access may be split into two accesses of 32 bit length, so an inconsistent value might be observed in case of insufficient synchronization.

accesses (reads or writes) to the same variable are said to be *conflicting*, if at least one is a write. An *inter-thread action* is an action by one thread, that can be detected or directly influenced by another thread. The inter-thread actions include reads and writes to variables, locks and unlocks of monitors [Hoa74] as short-term scheduling means, and starting and joining of threads. Mid-term scheduling is provided via Brinch-Hansen style [BH73] signal-and-continue [How76] wait/notify/notifyAll primitives.

The JMM guarantees visibility of results between two inter-thread actions only if they are ordered by a partial ordering called *happens-before*. If two actions are not ordered by happens-before, the JVM may reorder them arbitrarily which allows compiler optimizations. Two conflicting accesses are said to form a *data race* (aka. *race condition*), if they are not ordered by happens-before. A correctly synchronized program in Java exhibits no data races.

Happens-before is defined by the following rules [GJSB05, GPB+06]:

Program order defines that each action in a thread happens-before every action in that same thread that follows in the program order.

Monitor lock An unlock on a monitor lock happens-before every subsequent lock on the same monitor.[4]

Volatile variable A write to a volatile variable happens before every subsequent read on that same variable.

Thread start A call to Thread.start happens-before every action in the started thread.

Thread termination Any action in a thread happens-before any other thread detects that the thread has terminated through join or isAlive of class Thread.

Interruption A thread calling interrupt on another thread happens-before the interrupted thread detects the interrupt through an InterruptedException or isInterrupted or interrupted.

Finalizer The end of a constructor happens-before the start of a finalizer for that object.

Transitivity Happens-before is transitive.

The transitivity rule together with program order makes synchronization on the same variable effectively a *fence instruction*, i.e. *all* actions in one thread before a lock release are visible in the other thread after its subsequent acquisition. The same holds for a write and a read of a volatile variable. However, if two threads synchronize on different locks, there is no happens-before relation and therefore no ordering required.

---

[4]This rule includes wait/notify synchronization, due to the implicit unlocking of wait.

3.2 Slicing Concurrent Java

The JMM defines the inter-tread semantics for accessing shared variables and therefore forms the basis for intra-thread slicing. The program order rule's intra-thread semantics effectively requires that program transformations must adhere to the topological ordering imposed by data and control dependences (see definitions in the last chapter). Statements that are not ordered by these dependences can safely be reordered.[5] Therefore, a more precise data and control dependence analysis may enable more aggressive compiler optimizations. Additionally, the memory model requires that values written to shared variables in other threads are visible to a read of that variables, if they are ordered by happens-before. Therefore, the SDG needs to be extended to a *concurrent system dependence graph (cSDG)*, a representation of concurrent programs where threads communicate via shared variables. These communications are represented as a special kind of data dependence for shared variables that is traditionally called *interference dependence*. The most basic form just requires that the involved accesses are conflicting:

Definition 3.1 (Interference Dependence). *A node m is interference dependent [Kri98, HCD$^+$99] on node n ($n \rightarrow_{ir} m$), if*

1. *there is a variable v, such that $v \in \mathrm{Def}(n)$ and $v \in \mathrm{Ref}(m)$,*

2. *n and m might execute in different threads[6] at runtime ($\theta(n) \neq \theta(m)$),*

where a thread map θ maps a CFG node n to a thread identifier to which n belongs.

This definition is very conservative and we will see in the subsequent sections, how to refine this definition to prune many of the spurious cases that many previous approaches [HCD$^+$99, Zha99, RH04] suffer from.

Thread invocation is traditionally modeled in analogy to procedure calls, i.e *fork sites* are connected via *fork edges* to the corresponding run() methods. As Java only supports thread invocation via calling Thread.start(), which spawns a new thread executing its run() method, and both do not have explicit parameters, such a fork site can only have one parameter for the implicit this pointer, as well as synthetic parameters for static variables. This parameter passing is modeled as *fork-in* edges, in analogy to parameter-in edges of method invocations. Changes in parameters are already modeled with interference edges[7], so separate parameter-out edges are not needed.

As an example, consider Figure 3.1, where a program fragment is depicted alongside its cSDG. The variables x and y are global, and thus added as extra parameters at the thread's fork point. Note the fork edge between nodes 4 and 10 and the fork-in edges between nodes 5 and 11, and 6 and 12. Node 15 defines the shared variable x, which is used at node 7 in the main thread, therefore an interference dependence is included from 15 to 7. The same goes for nodes 9 and 13, where the shared variable y is redefined.

---

[5]Unless they are subject to another rule of the memory model.
[6]It may also be the case that two threads are different objects of the same class
[7]This is due to the obliviousness of Thread.join() of our model.

```
int x,y;

main() {
    x = 0;
    y = 1;
    fork(thread_1);
    int p = x - 2;
    int q = p + 1;
    y = q * 3;
}

thread_1() {
    int a = y + 1;
    int b = a * 4;
    x = b / 2;
}
```

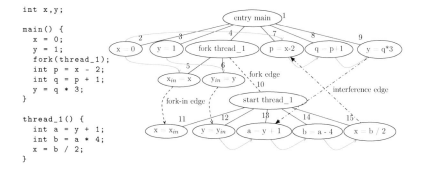

Figure 3.1: An example cSDG

3.2.1 Undecidability of Slicing

Precise slicing is undecidable in general. Several undecidability results have impact on the slicing technique for concurrent programs:

1. Whether a condition becomes *true* or *false* in the run of a program cannot be statically decided. To circumvent this, one generally assumes non-deterministic choice operators at conditionals during static analysis, with the consequence that every path in the intraprocedural CFG is assumed to be feasible (see chapter 2, page 27).

2. Precise slicing of languages with respect to synchronization and recursion is undecidable [Ram00].

3. In combination with interference dependence, data dependence is no longer transitive [MOS01], rendering parallel interprocedural slicing undecidable altogether.

4. In the following, we will present another source of undecidability: Precise intraprocedural slicing [Kri98] in combination with dynamic thread creation is undecidable.

To illustrate the results (2) and (3), consider Figure 3.2, which shows small example programs. The program on the left demonstrates how synchronization can induce an ordering on the execution sequence: first a is set to 1, after notification the other thread can proceed and will thus kill the first definition assigning 0 to a. So the dependence between a:=1 and write(a) could be removed.

In the example on the right (taken from [MOS01]), the value of a will not have an influence on write(c) in any possible execution sequence. The statement in the right thread might either be scheduled before b:=0 or after. If it executes before, then c will be redefined in the first thread before the join. If not, b will already be redefined to 0, and thus independent from the value of a. The works cited above show that the effects presented in these examples

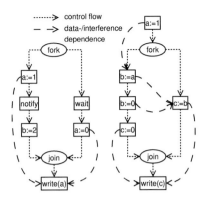

Figure 3.2: Examples for imprecise slices

combined with context-sensitive slicing of procedure calls make precise slicing undecidable, so conservative approximations need to be leveraged.

3.2.2 Dynamic Thread Creation

Threads in Java are — in contrast to several previous languages like Ada — totally dynamic. In general, static detection of the number of threads running in a program's execution is undecidable. A thread object can be created like any other object calling one of java.lang.Thread's constructors, and a subsequent invocation of its start() method will create a new thread of execution in the operating system executing its run() method. All this may happen in loops or recursion, so there is no static bound on the number of threads.

When a language offers threads that can be created and destroyed dynamically, and when thread creation may occur in a control flow cycle one gets another source of undecidability even if the language offers no procedures. In this case, the undecidability result from sequential intraprocedural slicing causes another undecidability: One cannot determine if, or how often, the cycle is executed and thus a new thread instance is created. For program analysis one therefore has to conservatively assume that an indefinite number of thread instances will be created. Hence, the question if there may exist two threads during program execution where one is at a given statement s_1 and the other at a given statement s_2 must be conservatively answered 'yes', for there may always be *another* thread that is currently at statement s_2.

As an example, consider Figure 3.3, where the main thread forks an unknown number of threads t, and t exposes no classical data dependence due to control flow. However, interference is possible to other instances of t. The graph on the right illustrates, that a feasible interference path can only be found if at least three instances of t have been created. However, since it is undecidable if the loop executes at least thrice, precise slicing is undecidable here as well.

This dynamic characteristic make static analysis of threads in Java more challenging than in languages with a statically bounded number of threads,

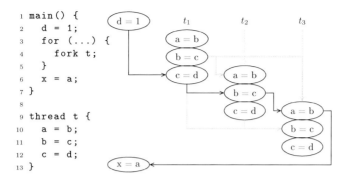

```
 1  main () {
 2     d = 1;
 3     for (...) {
 4        fork t;
 5     }
 6     x = a;
 7  }
 8
 9  thread t {
10     a = b;
11     b = c;
12     c = d;
13  }
```

Figure 3.3: Example program for undecidability

and means that for most cases one needs to become more conservative. For determining interference, it is crucial to know if more than one instance of a given thread class might ever execute in parallel, as in this case different instances of this thread class could interfere. If only a single instance of a given thread class will ever be created or executed, then no interference between two instances of this class is possible, and we can only have interference between this thread and threads of another class. For a specific code this can be easily determined: The thread executing the main method is a singleton, provided its class does not extend Thread or implement Runnable; however, in general determining threads that may ever only be created once in a program's execution is undecidable. But similarly to must-aliasing as described in section 2.3.3, if a Thread allocation statement a is not contained in a cycle of the interprocedural control flow graph, then we know that a's equivalence class represents actually a singleton set, thus if there is no other allocation site of a's type, we know that there cannot be interference from a to another instance of a. A similar idea was presented in [RH04], where singleton sets of thread allocations are determined not to have thread-local data escaping.

To get a dependence graph which is most similar to the sequential SDG-variants, many approaches [Kri03b, Zha99, NR06] propose to build one sequential dependence graph for each thread of execution and connect those with inter-thread dependences. This may reduce the number of spurious interference dependence edges, but in a highly dynamical language, where (at least theoretically) an unbounded number of threads can be started during program execution, this approach is no longer feasible. Another reason against this approach is that class libraries like Java's are so large that one needs to share their dependence graphs.

For these reasons, our approach includes every method into the cSDG only once. Yet, this complicates the determination of the θ function for Definition 3.1, which in the other approaches simply returns the enclosing thread for a given node n. In our setting it must return a set of enclosing threads. But as the number of threads generated at runtime is not fixed we have to conservatively

---

Algorithm 4 Virtual thread numbers

Input: The call graph

Output: A map $\theta : method \rightarrow set\ of\ numbers$ and
the maximal number of virtual threads $maxThreads$

$maxThreads = 0$
assign $\{0\}$ to all root methods of the call graph
add all methods in the cSDG into the worklist *changed*
while *changed* is not empty **do**
  remove method m from worklist
  for all $c \in caller(m)$ **do**
    if m is redefinition of Thread.run() and
       c is Thread.start() **then**
      if m's thread may be started more than once **then**
        $\theta(m)\ \cup= \{maxThreads + 1, maxThreads + 2\}$
        $maxThreads\ += 2$
      else
        $\theta(m)\ \cup= \{maxThreads + 1\}$
        $maxThreads\ += 1$
      end if
    else
      $\theta(m)\ \cup= method(\theta(c))$
    end if
    if $\theta(m)$ has changed **then**
      add all callees of m to worklist
    end if
  end for
end while

---

approximate the effects. If we do not know for sure that a thread is only started once, we assume that there are at least two instances of the given thread class. Thus we will include interference dependence, whenever one instance of the thread class defines a field which another instance reads. Our approach is thus similar to Lee et al's [LPM99] analysis of `parallel do` which summarizes conflict and synchronization information between all dynamically created threads of the `parallel do`.

Unfortunately, determining whether a thread class (!) is only started once is undecidable in general; A precise answer is feasible only in very special cases. For example, if there is only one calling context for the redefined `run()` method where the points-to set of the `this` pointer is a singleton $\{a\}$ and one can establish that the allocation site a is only executed once. Finding these cases requires a special whole program analysis, e.g. based on Ruf [Ruf00], which is beyond the scope of this thesis, but has been integrated into our framework [GH09].

For analysis purposes, we model this distinction between singleton and general threads by so-called *virtual thread numbers*. The prefix 'virtual' represents that the dynamic number of threads created at runtime is unknown. Virtual thread numbers are determined according to the call graph we get from a points-to analysis. Algorithm 4 describes how to compute the θ function: There is one thread that we know for sure is dynamically only created once: The thread executing the `main`-method[8]. We assign the set containing only the virtual thread number 0 to all the root methods (including `main` and class initializers).

Then we iterate over all methods in the call graph: if a new thread has been started, i.e. the method m we are currently working on is a redefinition of `Thread.run()` and it has been called by `Thread.start()` (in all the other cases the `run()` method behaves like a normal method) then we add new numbers to the set of virtual thread numbers. Otherwise the set of virtual thread numbers of the caller is included into the set of m. A singleton thread class will be assigned a single thread number, such that it will not exhibit interference to itself, while general thread classes are assigned two distinct thread numbers. As interference is determined between statements with different numbers, interference arises for singleton threads only from and to threads of a different class.

When the set of virtual thread numbers has changed, all the methods called by the analyzed method have to be (re-)analyzed, too. This fixed point iteration ends when no more changes in these sets have been found. Thread numbers are bounded by the number of thread classes, so this monotonic iteration is guaranteed to terminate with a minimal fixed point. Finally, all statements in each method are assigned the thread numbers of their method.

As an example, consider the program in Figure 3.4 together with its bipartite callgraph in Figure 3.5. Boxes represent methods and ellipses callsites in the call graph. Note that we omitted native and library methods as they do not contribute interference dependences in this example. The root method `main` is assigned the virtual thread number 0 according to Algorithm 4. Then, all methods in the callgraph are added to the worklist. For all methods ex-

---

[8]If the `main` class is an instance of Thread then its forked instances receive new virtual thread numbers

```
1  public class FacThreads extends Thread {
2    static int i;
3    static final Int[] facs = new Int[10];
4
5    public static void main(String[] args) {
6      new FacThreads().start();
7      for (int i = 0; i < facs.length; i++) {
8        fac(i);
9      }
10   }
11
12   static void fac(int n) {
13     if (n <= 1)
14       return setValue(n, 1);
15     return setValue(n, n * fac(n - 1));
16   }
17
18   static int setValue(int n, int i) {
19     synchronized (facs) {
20       if (facs[n] == null) {
21         facs[n] = new Int(i);
22         facs.notify();
23       }
24     }
25     return i;
26   }
27
28   public void run() {
29     for (int i = 0; i < facs.length; i++) {
30       synchronized (facs) {
31         while (facs[i] == null) {
32           try {
33             facs.wait();
34           } catch (InterruptedException e) {}
35         }
36         System.out.println(facs[i].value);
37       }
38     }
39   }
40
41   static class Int {
42     int value;
43     public Int(int i) {
44       value = i;
45     }
46   }
47 }
```

Figure 3.4: Example program with multiple threads

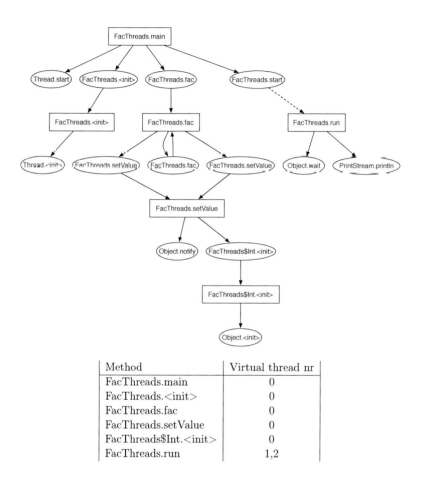

Method	Virtual thread nr
FacThreads.main	0
FacThreads.<init>	0
FacThreads.fac	0
FacThreads.setValue	0
FacThreads$Int.<init>	0
FacThreads.run	1,2

Figure 3.5: Call graph and virtual thread numbers for the example program 3.4

cept `FacThreads.run` the algorithm will branch to $\theta(n)$ $\cup=$ $method(\theta(c))$, thus they will be assigned thread number 0, which eventually reaches a fixed point. `FacThreads.run` is forked from a callsite `FacThreads.start`, a redefinition of `Thread.start`. Therefore the first branch is executed which determines that there may be several threads spawned from that callsite, as a consequence of being invoked in a loop. Thus, `FacThreads.run` is assigned two virtual thread numbers, 1 and 2.

We use virtual thread numbers as an approximation of θ when computing interference dependence. Thus, using thread numbers prunes interference dependence for cases violating the second requirement of Definition 3.1.

3.3 Dependence Analysis for Concurrent Programs

Thread numbers give an initial conservative approximation which threads may execute in parallel. With these numbers, we follow the spirit of Krinke [Kri98, Kri03b] who assumes all threads executing concurrently from the start to the program's termination. But in contrast to previous works, we generalize to dynamic thread creation instead of working with a statically fixed set of 'tasks'.

3.3.1 Interference Dependence

One main requirement of analyzing threaded software is to find possible dependences due to shared data being changed by a concurrently executing thread as presented in Definition 3.1. However, this definition needs refinement to apply to Java's memory model:

Definition 3.2. *A node r is* interference dependent *on node d, if $\theta(d) \neq \theta(r)$ (d and r may potentially be executed in parallel) and*

1. *either there is a static field f, such that d defines f and r references f,*

2. *or there is a (non-static) field f, such that d defines f of variable v and r references f of variable w, and v and w are potential aliases.*

While this definition is still fairly imprecise when compared to the Java memory model as previously presented, it improves significantly over previous works, which did not introduce interference based on aliasing of the base variables, but on either typing [Zha99, HCD+99] (i.e. all reads of a given field f are interference dependent on all writes to f, ignoring the base variables) or escape analysis [RH04] (accesses to a given field f of object o have interference if o is found to be possibly escaping its thread.[9])

Definition 3.2 gives rise to Algorithm 5:

Coming back to our example in Figure 3.4 with the virtual thread numbers in the table of Figure 3.5, Algorithm 5 can only find interference between the methods with number 0 and `FacThreads.run` and from the latter to itself. However, `FacThreads.run` does not contain definitions of shared variables, so

---

[9]Ranganath uses a highly efficient but admittedly imprecise unification based escape analysis based on Ruf's approach [Ruf00].

Algorithm 5 computeInterference()

---

1 **foreach** $(i, j) \in \{(i, j) : 0 \leq i, j \leq maxThreadNumber : i \neq j\}$
2   **foreach** field f where f is used in thread i and defined in j
3   **foreach** statement $g \in thread(i) : f \in \mathrm{Ref}(s)$
4   **foreach** statement $s \in thread(j) : f \in \mathrm{Def}(s)$
5   **if** f is static or s and g are aliased
6   addInterference(s, g);

---

only methods with thread number 0 can be the source of interference to other threads. In line (21), an entry of the `facs` array is written, therefore all reads to that array in `FacThreads.run` are interference dependent on it, namely the condition in line (31) and line (36). Another definition can be found in line (44) for the field `value`. Again, this statement has interference dependence to line (36).

Other more refined definitions of interference for Java can be imagined, and Ranganath presents the following:

Definition 3.3 (Interference Dependence [RH04]). *Let P be a program, o be an object with field f, and t_1 and t_2 be threads such that $t_1 \neq t_2$. If there exists an execution trace of P such that f is written at trace state s_m by a statement at program point m executed by thread t_1 and read at state s_n by a statement at program point n executed by t_2 (with s_n occurring after s_m) and no write to $o.f$ occurs between s_m and s_n, then n is interference dependent on m.*

However, it is immediately clear from the undecidability results for concurrent programs that such a definition can only be conservatively approximated. Note that even though this definition was given before the specification of the new Java memory model, this definition must not contain a clause requiring that s_m and s_n are ordered by happens-before, because the Java memory model *allows* values to be seen without ordering, it just does not *guarantee* them to be seen. So to remain conservative, such a clause must not be included.

3.3.2 Other Concurrency-Related Dependences

Apart from interference, other inter-thread dependences have been found relevant for slicing of multi-threaded Java programs. Cheng [Che93b] proposed *synchronization dependence* to reflect if the start or termination of one statement depends on the start or termination of another statement. For a JVM-like language, Hatcliff et al. [HCD+99] define synchronization dependence from an access to a shared variable to both the monitor acquisition and release statements of the directly enclosing critical region. Apart from that Hatcliff et al. introduce *ready dependence* modeling that a monitor or wait/notify statement may delay the execution of another such statement indefinitely.

Both works combine concurrency-related dependences with weak control dependence [PC90] (which Hatcliff et al. [HCD+99] decompose into standard control dependence and *divergence dependence*; for the latter they only provide an intuitive definition). Hatcliff et al. state (however without correctness proof) that this set of dependences is guaranteed to produce a correct slice in the sense

```
int x;

main() {
  cons() || prod();
}

prod() {
  set();
}

void set() {
  x = ...;
}

cons() {
  int y = get();
  print(y);
}

int get() {
  return x;
}
```

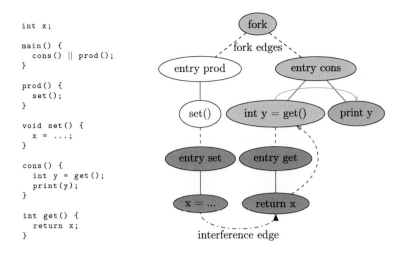

Figure 3.6: A counter example to Zhao's approach

of a bisimulation-based correctness criterion that extends the classic notion of projection in the single-threaded case, as originally presented by Weiser [Wei84].

3.4 Slicing the cSDG

Several algorithms have been proposed to slice concurrent SDGs. The most general and thus trivially correct algorithm is building the transitive closure of dependences.[10] This classical context-insensitive slicing algorithm is, however, far too conservative, as calling contexts are not taken into account.

Zhao [Zha99, ZL04] proposed leveraging the standard context-sensitive two-phase slicing algorithm [HRB90] for slicing concurrent SDGs. However, this may yield incorrect slices, which was first noticed by Nanda [Nan01, NR06]. Figure 3.6 shows a minimalist producer-consumer example with interference between the producer and the consumer. Two-phase slicing of the print node misses the invocation of prod.run: In the first phase, all light gray nodes are traversed starting from print x. The second phase starts at the omitted parameter-out edge to the return statement and marks this statement and the header get as part of the slice. As Zhao's algorithm traverses interference as if it were a standard dependence edge, it also marks both nodes in the set method in the second phase. However, since the second phase must not ascend into calling methods, the invocation of set will not be included, even though it clearly belongs to the slice of the print statement.

Algorithm 6 Iterative two-phase SummarySlicer

1 **Input**: The cSDG G, a slicing criterion s.
2 **Output**: The slice S for s.
3
4 $W = \{s\}$ // , a worklist
5 $M = \{s \mapsto true\}$ // , a map for marking the contents of W
6 // (true represents phase 1, false phase 2)
7
8 **repeat**
9    $W = W \setminus \{n\}$ // , remove next node n from W
10
11   **foreach** $m \rightarrow_e n$ // , handle all incoming edges of n
12   // If m wasn't visited yet or m was visited in phase 2 and we are in phase 1 ...
13   // or traversing an interference edge,
14   **if** $m \notin \text{dom } M \vee (\neg M(m) \wedge (M(n) \vee e = id))$
15   // if we are in phase 1 or if e is not a call or param−in edge, add m to W
16   **if** $M(n) \vee e \notin \{pi, c\}$
17          $W = W \cup \{m\}$
18
19   /* Now we determine how to mark m: */
20
21   //If we are in phase 1 and e is a param−out edge, mark m with phase 2
22   **if** $M(n) \wedge e = po$
23        $M = M \cup \{m \mapsto false\}$
24   //If we are in phase 2 and e is an interference edge, mark m with phase 1
25   **elseif** $\neg M(n) \wedge e = id$
26        $M = M \cup \{m \mapsto true\}$
27   //Else mark m with the same phase as n
28   **else**
29        $M = M \cup \{m \mapsto M(n)\}$
30
31 **until** $W = \varnothing$
32 **return** dom M

3.4.1 Iterative two-phase SummarySlicer

A straightforward extension of two-phase slicing makes this algorithm correct for slicing cSDGs. As a remedy, each time an interference edge is traversed, its source node (i.e. the node in the other thread) is marked as another synthetic slicing criterion, which means that it will be processed in the first phase of the slicing algorithm again, even if the target node of the interference edge was processed in the second phase. Therefore this algorithm is called *iterative two-phase slicing*. A highly optimized pseudocode for it is given in Algorithm 6. The iterated two-phase slicing traverses each node and edge in the SDG at most twice, and thus has the same worst case complexity as the original two-phase slicing algorithm by Horwitz et al. [HRB90]. Its running time can be minimized, if all nodes that are to be traversed in the first phase are removed from the worklist before those of phase two, as nodes found in the first phase will not need to be checked again.

Applied to the example program in Figure 3.6, it initializes its worklist W to the print node. This node is also included into a map M where it maps to *true*, meaning that it has been traversed in phase 1. As nodes for phase 1 are prioritized, it first marks the same light gray nodes as Zhao's algorithm. When traversing the parameter-out edge to the return statement of set, the return node is marked with *false* to indicate phase 2. Now no more nodes in phase 1 are available, so this return node is taken from the worklist. Its incoming edges mark the method header get for phase 2 and the assignment to a.x for phase 1, as it is reached via interference. So this assignment node comes next, and its header node set is included into the slice marked with phase 1. Now we may ascend into its calling method and mark prod.run with phase 2. All remaining nodes in the worklist do not change the slice or marking. So the slice for the print statement is the whole graph, as expected.

Nanda had presented the first algorithm for iterative two-phase slicing in [Nan01, NR06]. However, they used an unoptimized version, consisting of two nested while loops. Iterative two-phase slicing preserves context-sensitivity in each thread in isolation but breaks the calling contexts when crossing thread boundaries via interference dependence, thus it is sound but not precise.

3.4.2 Time Travel

Krinke [Kri98] first noticed that interference dependence is not transitive, in contrast to standard data dependence. With iterated two-phase slicing, it is possible to reenter a thread via interference that was previously left via interference. However, as interference is determined without taking possible control flow into account, traversing interference several times may correspond to control flow that is impossible in any valid program execution. In practice, the node of reentrance must execute before the node where that thread was previously left. Otherwise, this would correspond to a so-called "time travel" situation, where a value is dependent on a statement that will be executed in the future.

---

[10]Provided all necessary dependence types are included.

```
int x,y;

main() {
    x = 0;
    y = 1;
    fork(thread_1);
    int p = x - 2;
    int q = p + 1;
    y = q * 3;
}

thread_1() {
    int a = y + 1;
    int b = a * 4;
    x = b / 2;
}
```

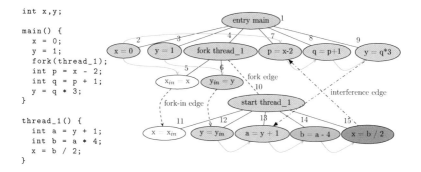

Figure 3.7: Slicing an example cSDG

As an example, consider the program and corresponding graph in Figure 3.7, where the shaded nodes are the slice for node 14 computed by the iterated two-phase slicer. The computation leaves thread_1 at node 13 towards node 9 and later returns to node 15 via the interference edge from node 7. Obviously, node 15 cannot influence the slicing criterion 14, because it cannot execute before 14.

As the exact execution order between threads is undecidable [Ram00,MOS01], this order cannot be taken into account when computing interference dependence. In contrast, intra-thread dependences like data or control dependence take control flow into account, making them transitive.

Slicing other Concurrency-Related Dependences Intransitivity has been regarded for interference only, mainly due to incompatible programming models. Krinke's and Nanda's models do not consider synchronization primitives, thus they can only argue about interference dependence. Approaches with a finer-grained concurrency model like those by Cheng and by Hatcliff [Che93b, HCD+99,RH04] leverage context-insensitive slicing, which ignores intransitivity issues anyway and thus is oblivious of precision. Dwyer et al. [DCH+99] argue that it remains unclear whether the gain in precision of context-sensitivity outweighs the additional cost.

However, taking all concurrency-related dependences into account, time travel may occur for all kinds of dependences that cross thread boundaries, if control flow is ignored during dependence computation. In particular, ready dependence [HCD+99, RH04] is intransitive when crossing thread boundaries. Accordingly, the same algorithms that prune time travel situations for interference dependence must be applied to get precise slices with ready dependence. The author is not aware of any work that identifies or targets this problem.

3.4.3 Slicers Disallowing Time Travel

To prune interference traversals that correspond to time travel situations, Krinke and Nanda [Kri03b, NR06] defined which paths in each thread's control flow graph correspond to a valid program execution. Their slicing algorithms are effectively exponential symbolic executions that marks all other paths as invalid such that they are not traversed during slicing.

The threaded control flow graph (TCFG) consists of the ICFGs of each thread that are connected at fork and join nodes, respectively. Note that Krinke [Kri03b] and Nanda [NR06] require threads to be disjoint, which is in general not the case for Java threads. However, one can always duplicate shared parts of the graph to achieve disjointness, which will be assumed in the sequel.

A *threaded interprocedural realizable path* $P =< n_1, \ldots, n_k >$ is an ordered sequence of nodes in the TCFG G such that every projection of P to a thread θ_i created in P is either empty or corresponds to an interprocedural realizable path in the ICFG of θ_i.

The *slice* of a cSDG w.r.t. the criterion p, denoted by $S(p)$, consists of all nodes q on which p transitively depends and there exists an interprocedural trace witness W in the TCFG G for each such q.

$$
S(p) = \left\{ q \left| \begin{array}{l} W =< n_1, \ldots, n_k >, \\ q = n_1 \to^{d_1} \cdots \to^{d_{k-1}} n_k, = p, d_i \in \{cd, dd, id\}, 1 \le i \le k, \\ \exists P \text{ is a threaded interprocedural realizable path in G} \\ \text{where each } n_i \text{ is contained in } P \text{ in the same order as in } W \end{array} \right. \right\}
$$

Krinke's algorithm [Kri98] was the first to solve the transitivity problem for programs without method calls[11]. The effects of synchronization are ignored in this approach. The idea of his slicing algorithm is to keep track of control flow that is necessary for an execution to be valid. To this end, each visited node is annotated with a state tuple Γ containing as many entries as threads. For each thread, the entry in such a state tuple is its last node on the path from the slicing criterion to the currently visited node. Initially, the state tuple for the slicing criterion is empty except for the criterion's thread, which contains the slicing criterion s. Empty slots in the tuple are usually denoted $\perp$, and do not impose any restriction on that thread's control flow.

With each traversal of an dependence edge $m \to n$, m is annotated with a clone of n's state tuple, where the entry of m's thread is replaced by m. When thread boundaries are crossed via interference, one must check whether intra-thread control flow from the source of the interference dependence to the statement last visited in this thread (i.e. the entry in m's slot of the state tuple at m) is actually possible. Krinke calls a feasible state tuple a *threaded witness*.

In our example program of Figure 3.7, this situation arises when the algorithm traverses from node 7 to node 15. As thread_1 had previously been left via interference dependence from node 13, it is checked whether node 13 is reachable from node 15 via an interprocedual realizable path in the control flow graph. This is not the case, so the traversal is rejected due to resulting in an invalid execution trace, which means that node 15 is not included in the slice from node 14.

---

[11]When methods are inlined, this approach may also be used for programs with method calls, but may require exponential space, and inlining is not possible for programs with recursion

3.5 Related Work

Nanda [NR00] adapted this approach for programs where threads are interleaved with loops. This paper targets `cobegin/coend` style thread spawning which allows an optimization that may improve precision but only allows a fixed number of threads. Thus, an adaption to Java's dynamic creation scheme cannot be easily done.

Chen and Xu [CX01a] propose another exponential symbolic execution, but this algorithm, although proposed for Java, suffers from the same deficiencies, as it, too, was originally [CXY+00] proposed for Ada with a fixed number of threads and inlining of method calls accessing shared variables. Again this cannot be done for recursive programs. It remains unclear how their Java version models threads which may be started an unbounded number of times.

In [Kri03b], Krinke extended his approach to procedural programs. Whilst this algorithm can handle method calls, it still uses a fixed number of threads which cannot be applied to Java.

In her thesis [Nan01], Nanda, too, extended her approach to programs with method calls and fork-join threading. Like all approaches using a fixed number of threads she duplicates a procedure for every thread from which it is called. Furthermore she presented a version of her iterative two-phase algorithm which is context-sensitive and does not allow time travel.

A detailed discussion and evaluation of Krinke's [Kri03b] and Nanda's [Nan01, NR06] precise algorithms can be found in [GH09]. The authors present solutions to several shortcomings of the previous algorithms, most prominently dynamic thread creation in loops and recursion, which Krinke and Nanda did not fully support. In spite of new optimization techniques, precise slicing remains very expensive (exponential in the number of threads), and the experiments in [GH09] indicate that preventing time travel should only be applied as a post-processing step, when cheaper methods like the iterative two-phase slicer fail at establishing a desired property.

Zhao and Li [ZL04] present the concurrent program dependence graph (CPDG), featuring the traditional data, control, call and parameter dependences as well as class membership and class inheritance dependences. Furthermore, they introduce interface-membership, package-membership and interface-inheritance dependences for the intra-thread case. As inter-thread dependences, they use synchronization and communication dependences of Cheng [Che93b, Che93a] and introduce synchronized-membership dependence for methods as opposed to usual membership dependence. Yet, it is unclear how they model dependences due to field access, and their example program and CPDG clearly miss these dependences[12]. Furthermore, they propose to use the two-pass slicing algorithm proposed in [HRB90] which has been shown incorrect (cf. section 3.4)

Naumovich's work on *may happen in parallel analysis* [NAC99] may significantly improve computation of interference and ready dependence: Their definitions require two dependent statements to execute in parallel. Ready dependence itself is completely equal to Naumovich's notify-edges. However, MHP

---

[12]For example there is no data dependence from line s30 to s32 in [ZL04]

analysis currently has no extension for programs with recursive method calls and synchronization.

Another approach for eliminating spurious interference and ready dependences is the work on Concurrent Static Single Assignment form in the presence of Mutual Exclusion based on the work of [NUS98, LPM99].

Chapter 4

Information Flow Control

Information flow control (IFC) is a technique that asserts the security of a software system with respect to a security specification. Research on IFC is on the rise due to the ubiquity of mobile code and security-relevant applications. Information flow control is often verified with special type systems [SM03] However, type systems do not exploit the whole repertoire of contemporary program analysis, thus suffer from restrictive languages and a high annotation burden. This chapter will present a new approach for information flow control based on program slicing and the system dependence graph as defined in the last chapters. Contrary to type systems, the presented algorithm is flow-, context-, and object-sensitive as a result of the underlying slicing technology, reducing false alarms. Recent advances in program analysis render this technique feasible and scalable even for realistic languages like full Java bytecode.

Previous results from this effort were published in [HKS06, HKN06, HS08].

4.1 Computer Security

Security in the technical sense is defined as the condition of being protected against danger or loss, with an emphasis on the protection from dangers that originate from the outside. In terms of computer science, three main dimensions of security can be identified, which are commonly depicted in the CIA-triad:

Confidentiality is the assurance of data privacy. Only the intended and authorized recipients — individuals, processes or devices — may read confidential data.

Integrity is assurance of data non-alteration. Data integrity asserts that the information has not been altered in transmission, from origin to reception, and includes checks of untrustworthy inputs for validity.

Availability is assurance in the timely and reliable access to data services for authorized users. It ensures that information or resources are available when required.

Language-based security derives security properties from the source or intermediate code. To this end, it leverages programming languages technology, typically a part of compiler technology. As temporal properties cannot be validated with language-based technologies, they only target confidentiality and/or integrity.

4.1.1 Information Flow

Information security has traditionally only considered the identity and origin of a software artifact and its user. An example is Bell and LaPadula [BL73, BL96] style access control, which has become mandatory in all major operating systems. Other "classical" means include encryption, code signing, virus scanners, firewalls, automatic updates. However, all these means cannot assert security on the whole processing path of data (*end-to-end security*), but only check for violations at a certain point in the computation. The problem is that these classical means only verify the identity and origin, but ignore the semantics of a piece of software. As an example, access control may only verify whether a user has the right to access a certain service or confidential data. After releasing that data, it can no longer control if a program makes confidential data public, because this would require to analyze the program's semantics. So with traditional means, a user must *hope* that a piece of software does not maliciously use its data, usually based on a company's identity and reputation. However, in the past several incidents have become public, where even renown software producers have collected data on their users and sent that data back to their servers.

As a remedy, language based security can verify a certain security policy for a program's information flow. An *information flow policy* defines the security requirements for a given system, e.g. rights and restrictions how data may be used in a computation. The most desirable property is *end-to-end security*, where sensitive data is protected along the complete processing path [SRC84], e.g. from the file system (with access control), through data processing in a program, until it is finally presented to an authorized user. Since access control is integrated in all major operating systems, controlling the information flow during data processing remains the grand challenge.

4.1.2 Channels and Information Flow

Lampson [Lam73] has identified three so called *channels* by which a program can transmit information to its environment: *Legitimate channels* are the declared formal outputs of the program, *storage channels* is other storage in the program's non-local environment, and *covert channels* are any other means of transmitting information (i.e. not involving values in any of the system's stores). A *timing channel* is an example of a covert channel where an attacker can retrieve information from measuring a program's execution time. Timing channels have been successively exploited, e.g. for RSA using the Chinese Remainder Theorem, to crack encryption in smart cards [Sch00].

When it comes to transmitting information from a source to a channel, there are two major means for information flow:

Explicit Flow from x to y occurs, when y is assigned a value whose computation contains a reference to x. `y = f(x)` is an example of explicit flow.

Implicit Flow from x to y emerges from control flow, where the execution of y depends on the value of x. For example the program `if (x==0) y=0 else y=1;` contains implicit flow from x to y. Historically, some authors regarded implicit flow as a covert channel, however, today, this classification is no longer found, as implicit flow can easily be checked with language-based techniques.

4.2 Information Flow Control

A means to control how information flows through the channels of a program is called *information flow control* (*IFC*). Of the three dimension described in the CIA-triad, information flow control avers confidentiality and/or integrity. Often integrity is assumed dual to confidentiality (based on an observation of Biba [Bib77]), so generally one describes only how to assert confidentiality. Information flow control can be done online (during program execution) or offline (often at compile time). Both approaches have different advantages and disadvantages:

The major advantage of online (dynamic) IFC is that it does not spuriously reject secure program execution, so it is precise. Its classification of information may be static (each variable has a fixed security level for the whole execution) or dynamic (the security level is determined at each assignment). But like most dynamic program analyses, it cannot show the general security of the program, and it slows down program execution with runtime tests. Also, dynamic checking can at best prevent illicit flow that is about to happen, but a malicious adversary might gain the information that the program was terminated due to a violation of the security policy, so the program leaks at least boolean information. Some systems like Fenton's Data Mark Machine [Fen74] employ special techniques to avoid this information leak, but these may not be effective in the presence of side-effects. The most limiting property of runtime IFC arise in detecting implicit flows. To detect information flow by control structures, a synthetic variable, called *program counter* (*PC*) (also called *process sensitivity label* in [ora85]) keeps track of the security of data in control flow constructs. However, the security label of a control predicate p does not only restrict the security level of statements that are controlled by the predicate in a given program execution, but also of variables that *might* change as a consequence of the predicate p in another execution. But dynamic analysis is characterized by only analyzing one path of execution, not all possible paths. One approach to detect all possible implicit flows is to keep the PC at the security level of p for the rest of the program (and increase with subsequent control structures, an effect which is called *label creep* in [SM03]), making dynamic analysis too restrictive in practice.

By contrast, static (offline) IFC needs to be done only once (usually at compile time.) If the program can be verified, no program execution can exhibit illegal information flow, avoiding the overhead of runtime checks. However,

Figure 4.1: A lattice with incomparable elements

precise static IFC analysis is undecidable [SM03], so all static analyses need to be conservative. Consequently, there is always a class of secure programs that will be spuriously rejected.

As a remedy, some IFC systems like Jif [MCN$^+$] offer a hybrid approach: the compiler certifies as much as is statically possible to limit the number of necessary runtime checks and only inserts dynamic checks at user-specified program points that cannot be statically verified.

4.2.1   The Lattice Model of Information Flow

Usually, data is classified into a finite set of *security domains* (also called *security levels* or *security classes*) $L = \{l_1, \ldots, l_n\}$. A transitive, reflexive and antisymmetric *interference relation* (i.e. a partial order) $\rightsquigarrow: L \times L$ denotes $x \rightsquigarrow y$ iff information in class x is permitted to flow into class y. The complement relation, called *noninterference relation*, defined by $\not\rightsquigarrow := L^2 \backslash \rightsquigarrow$ means that information flow between security levels must be prevented. Frequently the security levels are arranged in a lattice $\mathcal{L}$, in which case $\rightsquigarrow$ is equivalent to $\leq$. If the interference relation does not form a lattice, it can always be extended to a complete lattice, so we assume a complete bounded lattice $\mathcal{L} = (L, \leq, \bot, \top, \sqcup, \sqcap)$ of security levels in the sequel for convenience. The most trivial lattices are given by linear priority lattices that can be represented as a sequence $0 \ldots n$, like LOW (L) $\leq$ HIGH (H) which can also be written as $0 \leq 1$, or like the well-known military classification levels Unclassified (0), Confidential (1), Secret (2) and Top Secret (3). More complex lattices contain incomparable elements where neither $x < y$ nor $y < x$ as shown in Figure 4.1. Lattices have been found to naturally represent the semantics of information flow [Den76]: When information is composed of pieces with different security levels, the supremum operator $\sqcup$ specifies which security class results for the combined information. The operands' security levels are joined using the supremum operator, e.g. if information of the security levels Confidential and Secret is merged, the result must at least be Secret again.

4.2.2   Language-Based Information Flow Control

Security lattices are used for both static and dynamic analyses. In this thesis, we focus on static information flow control in a language-based setting. *Language-based information flow control* [SM03] offers compile-time certification of a program that guarantees some information flow policy. It can exploit a long history of research on program analysis; for example, type systems, abstract interpretation, dataflow analysis, etc. A correct language based IFC will discover any security leak caused by software alone (but typically does not consider physical side channels). It is generally undecidable, if an allegedly illegal execution in a program may actually happen, so correct language based information flow control must be conservative and thus may reject secure programs. Denning and Denning [DD77] were the first to present a static (language-based) information flow control mechanism. It addresses confidentiality, which is also known as the *confinement problem*, i.e it's goal is to certify that a program's non-confidential outputs cannot depend on confidential input data. It comprises explicit and implicit information flow but no rigorous proof of correctness was given. Its information flow policy is represented by a lattice of security levels, where information flow is only allowed to higher security classes. Each storage object — constant, variable, array or file — is labeled in the source with a security class that does not change during program execution. All unlabeled program constants are implicitly assumed to be labeled with $\perp$.

Language-based IFC can be done with various forms of analyses (see Sabelfeld and Myer's overview article [SM03] and the related work section for a more detailed overview). The predominant kind of analysis was, until recently, type based information flow control. Type checking goes back to Volpano, Smith and Irvine [VIS96, VS97, SV98], who rewrote Denning's analysis as a type system to gain a more rigorous system for proving that this mechanism guarantees confidentiality. The type system offers a formal specification that separates the security policy from the enforcement mechanism. Type-based IFC is efficient, compositional, and correctness proofs are not too difficult. Thus, type system have been a success story, opening the door for the whole field of language-based IFC. For type-based IFC, the elements of Denning's security lattice becomes a set of additional[1] types where the interference relation $\leq$ between security levels is represented by suptyping. Therefore legal upward information flow is accommodated. The information flow policy enforces that a program is well-typed, iff variables do not interfere with variables of a lower type, which guarantees confidentiality. Typing rules propagate security levels through the expressions and statements of a program, guaranteeing to catch illegal information flow.

Most contemporary IFC approaches [SM03] are based on extensions of Volpano's type system. There was an abundant number of systems proposed to extend that initial type system to realistic languages with procedures, object-oriented features like dynamic dispatch, concurrency or even timing leaks [Aga00], most approaches *define* a language that the system can provably certify, instead of defining a type system for a realistic language. There exist very few implementations of type systems and their underlying languages, thus these works present only theoretic results with no impact on security engineering [Zda04]. Only two implementations for realistic core languages have been presented: Flow Caml [PS03] and Jif [MCN+, ML00]. But even Jif is a special-purpose language based on Java's syntax, but significantly different (e.g. there are no static vari-

---

[1]in addition to the standard variable types like int

```
1 if (confidential==1)
2    public = 42
3 else
4    public = 17;
5 ... // no output of public
6 public = 0;
```

Figure 4.2: A secure program fragment

ables nor implicit exceptions). So lifting Java programs to Jif may become intricate [AS05].

Apart from that, type-based analysis is usually not flow-sensitive, context-sensitive, nor object-sensitive, leading to false alarms: For example, the well-known program fragment in Figure 4.2 is considered insecure by type-based IFC, as type-based IFC is not flow-sensitive. It does not see that the potential information flow from confidential to public in the if-statement is guaranteed to be killed[2] by the following assignment and thus declares the fragment to be untypeable.

Classical noninterference [GM82, GM84] however only demands that two streams of public output of the same program must be indistinguishable even if they differentiate on secret variables, which is true for this program. Thus secret data in a public variable is perfectly eligible as long as its content does not flow to output. Note that the killing statement may be far away from the supposed illegal flow.

Type-based IFC performs even worse in the presence of unstructured control flow or exceptions. Therefore, type systems over-approximate information flow control, resulting in too many secure programs rejected (false positives). First steps towards flow-sensitive type systems have been proposed, but are restricted to rudimentary languages like While-languages [HS06], or languages with no support for unstructured control flow [ABB06].

4.2.3   Dependence Graphs for Information Flow Control

Fortunately, program analysis has much more to offer than just sophisticated type systems. In particular, the system dependence graph as presented in chapter 2 has become, after 20 years of research, a standard data structure allowing various kinds of powerful program analyses – in particular, efficient program slicing [Wei84]. Apart from that, commercial SDG tools for full C are available [ART03], which have been used in a large number of real applications. We present a novel IFC algorithms based on the dependence graph defined in this thesis.

The first IFC algorithm based on SDGs was presented by Snelting in 1996 [Sne96]. But more elaborate algorithms were needed to make the approach work and scale for full C and realistic programs [RS02,SRK06]. The latter article contains a theorem connecting dependence graphs to the classical noninterference

---

[2]For a definition see section 2.1.2

criterion (see also section 4.3). Later, we developed a precise SDG for full Java bytecode as described in chapter 2, which is much more difficult than constructing the SDG for C due to the effects of inheritance and dynamic dispatch, and due to the concurrency caused by thread programming. Today, we can handle realistic C and Java programs and thus have a powerful tool for IFC available that is more precise than conventional approaches. In particular, it handles Java's exceptions and unstructured control flow precisely.

In this chapter, we augment PDGs and SDGs with Denning-style security level lattices and explain the equations which propagate security levels through the program in details. When declassification is introduced in called methods, the original slicing-based approach only yields conservative results, which may result in false positives. Therefore, this thesis contains a precise interprocedural analysis for declassification in called methods, which generates precise results.

4.3 Dependence Graphs and Noninterference

The soundness of our PDG construction guarantees that a missing path from a to b in a PDG implies that there is no influence from a to b. This asserts that information flow which is not caused by hidden physical side channels such as timing or termination leaks is impossible. It is therefore not surprising that traditional technical definitions for secure information flow such as *noninterference* are related to PDGs.

Noninterference as presented by Goguen and Meseguer [GM82, GM84] is defined with respect to an abstract automaton[3] $\mathcal{M} = (S, A, O, step, output, s_0)$ representing state transitions of a program. The generally infinite set of program states S contains an initial state $s_0 \in S$, the set of actions A can be thought of as the program's instructions, and the set of outputs O represent all possible outputs. $step : S \times A \to S$ is the state transition function, which in our case is induced by the program semantics, and $output : S \times A \to O$ is the output function. We derive the function $run : S \times A^* \to S$ as the natural extension of $step$ to sequences of actions in A^* in the standard manner: $run(s, \epsilon) = s; run(s, a \cdot \alpha) = run(step(s, a), \alpha)$.

The security level of action $a \in A$ is $dom(a) \in L$. Given a statement sequence α and a security domain d, the function $purge : A^* \times L \to A^*$ removes from α all statements which must not influence security level d: $purge(\alpha, d) = \langle a \in \alpha | dom(a) \rightsquigarrow d \rangle$.

A system is considered safe according to the Goguen/Meseguer noninterference criterion if, for all statement sequences α that are possible according to the control flow graph and all final statements a (executed after α has been processed),

$$output(run(s_0, \alpha), a) = output(run(s_0, purge(\alpha, dom(a))), a) \qquad (4.1)$$

Thus noninterference requires that the final program output must be unchanged if every statement is deleted which – according to its security level – must not influence the final program state.

---

[3]We will use the notation of Rushby [Rus92] instead of the original notation.

If the criterion is not satisfied, then the outputs for the final statement a differ between the actual run α and α with all supposedly non-influential statements removed – thus there is an influence from a statement s in α to a even though this is forbidden due to $dom(s) \not\rightsquigarrow dom(a)$. We see that the notion of security is based on observational behavior and not on the source code.

Type systems based approaches usually define the notion of noninterference in a more compact form. In its simplest variant – which assumes only security levels Low and $High$ – it reads

$$s \cong_{Low} s' \implies [\![c]\!]s \cong_{Low} [\![c]\!]s' \qquad (4.2)$$

where c is a statement or program, s, s' are two initial program states, and $[\![c]\!]s, [\![c]\!]s'$ are the corresponding final states after executing c. $s \cong_{Low} s'$ means that s and s' are Low equivalent: they must coincide on variables which have Low security, but not on variables with $High$ security. Thus variation in the high input variables does not affect low output, and hence confidentiality is assured. Note that various extensions of elementary noninterference have been defined, such as possibilistic or probabilistic noninterference; some of them based on PER relations [SS01]. Pistoia et al. [PCFY07] already noted that Goguen/Meseguer noninterference is more general than the criterion of secure information flow of equation 4.2 and its descendants, because the former only considers observational behavior and does not constrain implicit and explicit flow at each statement. The approach presented in the sequel only considers observational behavior, and thus adheres to the original Goguen/Meseguer definition.

The following theorem connects PDGs to the original Goguen/Meseguer definition and demonstrates how PDGs can be used to check for noninterference.

Theorem 4.1. *If*

$$s \in BS(a) \implies dom(s) \rightsquigarrow dom(a) \qquad (4.3)$$

then the noninterference criterion is satisfied for a.
Proof. *See [SRK06].* $\qquad \qquad \square$

Thus if $dom(s) \not\rightsquigarrow dom(a)$ (s and a have noninterfering security levels), there must be *no PDG path* $s \rightarrow^* a$, otherwise a security leak has been discovered.

The generality of the theorem stems from the fact that it is independent of specific languages or slicing algorithms; it just exploits a fundamental property of any correct slice. The theorem is valid even for imprecise PDGs and slices, as long as they are correct. Applying the theorem results in a linear-time noninterference test for a, as all $s \in BS(a)$ must be traversed once. More precise slices result in less false alarms. However, as we will see later, it is not possible to use declassification in a purely slicing based approach, thus later we will present extended versions of Theorem 4.1.

4.4 Examples for Slicing-based IFC

In the following, we assume some familiarity with slicing technology, as presented in chapter 2. Our Java PDG is based on bytecode rather than source text for the following reasons:

```
 1 class PasswordFile {
 2 private String[] names;
 3             /*P: confidential*/
 4 private String[] passwords;
 5             /*P: secret*/
 6 // Pre:all strings are interned
 7 public boolean check(String user,
 8   String password /*P: confidential*/) {
 9   boolean match = false;
10   try {
11   for (int i=0; i<names.length; i++) {
12     if (names[i]==user
13     && passwords[i]==password) {
14       match = true;
15       break;
16     }
17   }
18   }
19   catch (NullPointerException e) {}
20   catch (IndexOutOfBoundsException e) {};
21   return match;  /*R: public*/
22   }
23 }
```

Figure 4.3: A Java password checker

- Bytecode must be considered the ultimate definition of a program's meaning and potential flows.

- The bytecode is much more stable than the source language (see e.g. generics in Java 5, which did not change the bytecode instructions).

- the bytecode is already optimized, and artifacts such as dead code are removed and cannot generate spurious flow.

4.4.1 Exceptions

As presented in section 2.4.2, our dependence graphs contain a sound model of control flow due to implicit and explicit exceptions. For security, such a model is of the utmost importance. Figure 4.3 shows a fragment of a Java class for checking a password (taken from [MCN+]) which uses fields and exceptions. The P and R annotations will be explained in section 4.5. The initial PDG for the check method is shown in Figure 4.4. Solid lines represent control dependence and dashed lines represent data dependence. Node 0 is the method entry with its parameters in nodes 1 and 2 (we use "pw" and "pws" as a shorthand for "password" and "passwords"). Nodes 3 – 6 represent the fields of the class, note that because the fields are arrays, the reference and the elements are distinguished[4].

---

[4]See section 2.4.3

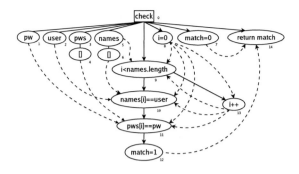

Figure 4.4: PDG for check in Figure 4.3

Nodes 7 and 8 represent the initializations of the local variables match and i in lines (9) and (11). All these nodes are immediately control dependent on the method entry. The other nodes represent the statements (nodes 12, 13, and 14) and the predicates (nodes 9, 10, and 11).

This PDG is still incomplete, as it does not include exceptions. Dynamic runtime exceptions can alter the control flow of a program and thus may lead to implicit flow, in case the exception is caught by some handler on the call-stack, or else represent a covert channel in case the exception is propagated to the top of the stack yielding a program termination with stack trace. This is why many type-based approaches disallow (or even ignore) implicit exceptions. Our analysis conservatively adds control flow edges from bytecode instructions which might throw unchecked exceptions to an appropriate exception handler [CPS+99], or percolates the exception to the callee which in turn receives such a conservative control flow edge. Thus, our analysis does not miss implicit flow caused by these exceptions, hence even the covert channel of uncaught exceptions is checked. The resulting final PDG is shown in Figure 4.5. (For better readability, the following examples will not show the effects of exceptions.)

4.4.2 Context-Sensitivity and Object-Sensitivity in Action

To improve precision, we made the SDG *object-sensitive* by representing nested parameter objects as trees. Unfolding object trees stops once a fixed point with respect to the points-to situation of the containing object is reached, as presented in chapter 2.

Figure 4.6 shows another small example program, and Figure 4.7 shows its SDG. Note that we (again) identify node numbers by the statement's line number. For brevity we omitted the PDGs of the set and get methods. The effects of method calls are reflected by *summary edges* (shown as dashed edges in Figure 4.6) between actual-in and actual-out parameter nodes, which represent a transitive dependence between the corresponding formal-in and formal-out node pair. For example, the call to o.set(sec) contains two summary edges, one from the target object o and one from sec to the field x of o; representing

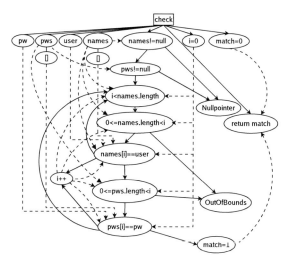

Figure 4.5: PDG with exceptions for Figure 4.3

the side-effect that the value of sec is written to the field x of the this-pointer in set. Summary edges enable context-sensitive slicing in SDGs in time linear to the number of nodes [HRB90].

In the program, the variable sec is assumed to contain a secret value, which must not influence printed output. First a new A object is created where field x is initialized to sec. However, this object is no longer used afterward as the variable is overwritten ("killed") with a new object whose x field is set to pub. Now context-sensitive analysis of set discovers that x of the new object is *not* influenced by sec. Thus there is no SDG path (13) $\to^*$ (19) from the initialization of sec to the first print statement (i.e. the leftmost println node). Instead, we have a path from the initialization of pub to this output node. Hence the sec variable does not influence the output. This example demonstrates that the x fields in the two A objects are distinguished (object-sensitivity), the side-effects of different calls to set are not merged (context-sensitivity), and flow-sensitivity kills any influence from the sec variable to the first println.

The next statements show an illegal flow of information: Line (21) checks whether sec is zero and creates an object of class B in this case. The invocation of o.set is dynamically dispatched: If the target object is an instance of A then x is set to zero; if it has type B, x receives the value one. (21) - (23) are analogous to the following implicit flow:

                    if (sec==0 && ...) o.x = 0 else o.x = 1;

In the PDG we have a path from sec to the predicate testing sec to o.set() and its target object o. Following the summary edge one reaches the x field and the second output node. Thus the PDG discovers that the printed value in line 24 depends on the value of sec. In the next section, we will formally introduce security levels and demonstrate that this example contains an illegal flow.

```
1  class A {
2   int x;
3   void set() { x = 0; }
4   void set(int i) { x = i;}
5   int get() { return x; }
6  }
7  class B extends A {
8   void set() { x = 1; }
9  }
10 class InfFlow {
11  void main(String[] a){
12   //1. no information flow
13   int sec = 0 /*P:High*/;
14   int pub = 1 /*P:Low*/;
15   A o = new A();
16   o.set(sec);
17   o = new A();
18   o.set(pub);
19   System.out.println(o.get());
20   //2. dynamic dispatch
21   if (sec==0 && a[0].equals("007"))
22     o = new B();
23   o.set();
24   System.out.println(o.get());
25   //3. instanceof
26   o.set(42);
27   System.out.println(o instanceof B);
28  }
29 }
```

Figure 4.6: Another Java program

But even if the value of x was not dependent on sec (after statement 26) an attacker could exploit the runtime type of o to gain information about the value of sec in line 27. This implicit information flow is detected by our analysis as well, since there is a PDG path (13) →* (27).

4.5 Analyzing Information Flow

The noninterference criterion prevents illegal flow, but in practice one wants more detailed information about security levels of individual statements. Thus theoretical models for IFC such as Bell-LaPadula [BL96] or Noninterference [GM84] utilize a *lattice* $\mathcal{L} = (L; \leq, \sqcup, \sqcap, \bot, \top)$ of security levels, the simplest consisting just of two security levels *High* and *Low*. The programmer needs to specify a lattice, as well as annotations defining the security level for some (or all) statements. In practice, only input and output channels need such annotations.

Arguing about security also requires an explicit attacker model. For our approach, we assume:

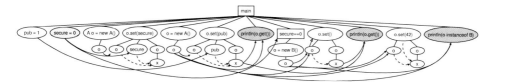

Figure 4.7: SDG for the program in Figure 4.6

- Attackers cannot control the execution of the JVM including its security settings.

- The code generated from source (e.g. bytecode) is known to the attacker (maybe through disassembling), but cannot be altered (e.g. via code signing)

- Therefore, the content of variables (local as well as in the heap) is not directly available to the attacker. Such an assumption would allow to learn all secrets as soon as they are stored.

- As a consequence, only input and output of the system with a certain security level (e.g. assigned by the OS) can be controlled (resp. observed).

4.5.1 Fundamental Flow equations

For a correct IFC, the actual security level of every statement must be computed, and this computation must respect the programmer-specified levels as well as propagation rules along program constructs. The huge advantage of PDG-based IFC is that the PDG already defines the edges between statements or expressions, where a flow can happen; as explained, explicit and implicit flow between unconnected PDG nodes is impossible. Thus it suffices to provide propagation rules along PDG edges. We begin with the intraprocedural case.

The security level of a statement resp. its PDG node x is written $S(x)$, where $S : N \to L$.[5] Confidentiality requires that an information receiver x must have at least the security level of any sender y [BL96]. In a PDG G, where $pred$ and $succ$ are the predecessor and successor functions induced by $\to$, resp., this fundamental property is easily stated as

$$y \to x \in G \implies S(x) \geq S(y) \tag{4.4}$$

and thus by the definition of a supremum

$$S(x) \geq \bigsqcup_{y \in pred(x)} S(y) \tag{4.5}$$

---

[5]Remember that N is the set of PDG nodes. Note that our S is called *dom* in the original Goguen/Meseguer noninterference definition, but we need *dom* for partial functions.

101

This fundamental constraint ensures $S(y) \rightsquigarrow S(x)$.[6] Remember that confidentiality and integrity are dual to each other [Bib77], hence the dual condition for integrity is

$$S(x) \leq \bigsqcap_{y \in pred(x)} S(y) \tag{4.6}$$

In the following, we concentrate on confidentiality, as all equations for integrity are obtained by duality.

Equation (4.5) assumes that every statement resp. node has a security level specified, which is not realistic. In practical applications, one wants to specify security levels not for all statements, but for certain selected statements only.[7] The *provided* security level specifies that a statement sends information with the provided security level, i.e. represents an input channel. The *required* security level requires that only information with a *smaller* or equal security level may reach that statement,[8] i.e. it represents an output channel of the specified security level. From these values the *actual* security levels can be computed.

Provided security levels are defined by a partial function $P : N \nrightarrow L$. The required security levels are defined similarly as a partial function $R : N \nrightarrow L$. Thus, $P(s)$ specifies the security level of the information generated at s (also called "the security level of s"), and $R(s)$ specifies the maximal allowed security level of the information reaching s.

The actual security level $S(x)$ for a node x must thus not only be greater than the levels of its predecessors, but also greater than its own provided security level. Thus equation (4.5) refines to

$$S(x) \geq \begin{cases} P(x) \sqcup \displaystyle\bigsqcup_{y \in pred(x)} S(y), & \text{if } x \in dom(P) \\ \displaystyle\bigsqcup_{y \in pred(x)} S(y), & \text{otherwise} \end{cases} \tag{4.7}$$

Note that R does not occur in this constraint for S. We need an additional constraint to specify that incoming levels must not exceed a node's required level:

$$\forall x \in dom(R) : R(x) \geq S(x) \tag{4.8}$$

We can now formally define confidentiality:

Definition 4.1. *Let a program's PDG be given. The program maintains confidentiality, if for all PDG nodes equations* (4.7) *and* (4.8) *are satisfied.*

As mentioned earlier, we are preparing a machine-checked proof [qui] that Definition 4.1 implies noninterference. For the time being, Definition 4.1 is treated as an axiom, which however, as discussed above, is well-founded in correctness properties of PDGs and classical definitions of confidentiality.

---

[6]In fact, the Goguen/Meseguer notion $S(y) \rightsquigarrow S(x)$ is the same as $S(y) \leq S(x)$ in modern terminology.

[7]For practicability of an analysis, it is important that the number of such annotations is as small as possible.

[8]The term "required" may be misleading here—it is actually more like a limit or maximum

Later, we will provide an interprocedural generalization of this definition (Definition 4.2 in section 4.6), which additionally exploits the fact that it is sufficient to consider the backward slices of all output ports instead of the whole PDG; this observation again reduces spurious flow and the risk for false alarms. For the time being, we demand (4.7) and (4.8) for the whole PDG, which is still a correct (if slightly less precise) definition.

For simplicity in presentation, we extend P and R to total functions P' and R' such that all nodes have a provided and required security level:

$$P'(x) = \begin{cases} P(x), & \text{if } x \in dom(P) \\ \bot, & \text{otherwise} \end{cases} \tag{4.9}$$

$$R'(x) = \begin{cases} R(x), & \text{if } x \in dom(R) \\ \top, & \text{otherwise} \end{cases} \tag{4.10}$$

Note that $\bot$ is the neutral element for $\sqcup$, and $\top$ is the neutral element for $\sqcap$. Now equation (4.7) simplifies to

$$S(x) \succeq P'(x) \sqcup \bigsqcup_{y \in pred(x)} S(y) \tag{4.11}$$

and equation (4.8) simplifies to

$$R'(x) \geq S(x) \tag{4.12}$$

4.5.2 Solving Flow equations

Equation (4.11) is satisfied in the most precise way, and hence the risk that equation (4.8) is violated is minimized, if the inequality for S turns into equality:

$$S(x) = P'(x) \sqcup \bigsqcup_{y \in pred(x)} S(y) \tag{4.13}$$

Of course (4.13) also satisfies (4.11), and can be read as an algorithm which computes $S(x)$ from $P(x)$ and x's predecessors S values. Thus equation (4.13) defines a *forward propagation*: it shows what happens if all the P values are propagated through the PDG (while ignoring R).

We will now show that equation (4.13) corresponds to a well-known concept in program analysis, namely a *monotone dataflow analysis framework* [KU77] as presented in section 2.1.1, which allows efficient fixpoint computation. Such frameworks start with a lattice of abstract values, which in our case is $\mathcal{L}$. For every $x \in N$, a so-called *transfer function* $f_x : L \to L$ must be defined, which typically has the form $f_x(l) = g_x \sqcup (l \sqcap \overline{k_x})$.[9] In our case, $g_x = P'(x)$ and $k_x = \bot$, thus $f_x(l) = P'(x) \sqcup l$. Furthermore, for every $x \in N$, the framework defines $out(x) = f_x(in(x))$ and $in(x) = \bigsqcup_{y \in pred(x)} out(y)$. In our case,

$$out(x) = f_x(in(x)) = P'(x) \sqcup \bigsqcup_{y \in pred(x)} S(y) = S(x)$$

---

[9]where $g_x, k_x \in L$. $\overline{k_x}$ denotes boolean complement, as many dataflow methods run over a *powerset* $\mathcal{L}$; in our case we have just a lattice but all we need is $\overline{\bot} = \top$.

The theory demands that all f_x are monotone, which in our case is trivial. The theory also states that if the f_x are distributive, the analysis is more precise. In our case $f_x(l_1 \sqcup l_2) = P'(x) \sqcup (l_1 \sqcup l_2) = (P'(x) \sqcup l_1) \sqcup (P'(x) \sqcup l_2) = f_x(l_1) \sqcup f_x(l_2)$, hence distributivity holds. The theory finally states that the set of equations for S (resp out) always has a solution in form of a minimal fixpoint, that this solution is correct, and in case of distributive transfer functions it is precise. This is another reason why our IFC is more precise than other approaches.[10] Efficient algorithms to compute this fixed point are well known. We will show examples for fixpoints later; here it suffices to say that it defines values for $S(x) \in L$ which simultaneously satisfy equations (4.13) and thus (4.5) for all $x \in N$.

Thus the computed fixpoint for S, together with equation (4.8), ensures confidentiality. If a fixpoint for S exists, but the condition for R cannot be satisfied, then a confidentiality violation has been discovered: For any $l = R(x)$ such that $l \not\geq S(x)$ we have a violation at x because $S(x) \not\rightsquigarrow l$ (the security level of $S(x)$ is not allowed to influence level l). Note that it is $\not\geq$ and not $<$ because l and $S(x)$ might not be comparable.

From a program analysis viewpoint, our transfer functions f_x are quite simple; in fact they are so simple that an explicit solution for the fixpoint can be given which will be exploited later:

Theorem 4.2. *For all $x \in N$, let $S(x)$ be the least fixpoint of equation* (4.13). *Then*

$$S(x) = \bigsqcup_{y \in BS(x)} P'(y) \tag{4.14}$$

Proof. Let $x \in N$. (4.13) implies $S(x) \geq P'(x)$ and $S(x) \geq S(y)$ for all $y \in pred(x)$. By induction, this implies for any path $y \rightarrow^* x$ (i.e. $y \in BS(x)$): $P'(y) \leq S(x)$. By definition of a supremum, $S(x) \geq \bigsqcup_{y \in BS(x)} P'(y)$.

On the other hand, (4.14) is a solution of (4.13):

$$\bigsqcup_{y \in BS(x)} P'(y) = P'(x) \sqcup \bigsqcup_{\substack{y \in pred(x) \\ z \in BS(y)}} P'(z)$$

$$= P'(x) \sqcup \bigsqcup_{y \in pred(x)} \bigsqcup_{z \in BS(y)} P'(z)$$

and since S is the least fixpoint we have $S(x) \leq \bigsqcup_{y \in BS(x)} P'(y)$. Thus equality, as stated in the theorem, follows. $\qquad\square$

4.5.3 The PDG-Based Noninterference Test

We will now exploit this intermediate result to prove the correctness of our PDG-based confidentiality check. The following statement is a restatement of Theorem 4.1 in terms of P and R:

---

[10]Note that we thus have total precision for the S solutions, but not for the underlying PDG.

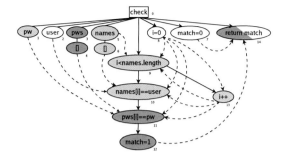

Figure 4.8: PDG for Figure 4.3 with computed security levels

Theorem 4.3. *If*

$$\forall a \in \mathrm{dom}(R) . \forall x \in BS(a) \cap \mathrm{dom}(P) : P(x) \leq R(a) \qquad (4.15)$$

then confidentiality is maintained for all $x \in N$.

That is, the backward slice from a node a with a required security level $R(a)$ must not contain a node x that has a higher security level $P(x)$.

Proof. Let $x \in N$. We need to show that (4.7) and (4.8) are valid for x. From the premise we know $\forall x \in BS(a) : P'(x) \leq R(a)$, as $P'(x) \leq P(x)$ if $x \in dom(P)$. Thus $R(a) \geq \bigsqcup_{x \in BS(a)} P'(x)$, hence $R(a) \geq S(x)$ by theorem 4.2. Hence (4.8) is satisfied. Furthermore, by definition of the fixpoint for S, S satisfies (4.13) and thus (4.11) and (4.7). $\square$

The theorem can easily be transformed into an algorithm that checks a program for confidentiality:

PDG-Based Confidentiality Check. *For every node in the dependence graph that has a required security level specified, compute the backward slice, and check that all nodes in the slice have lower or equal provided security levels specified.*

Once the PDG has been computed, each backward slice and thus confidentiality check has worst case complexity $O(|N|)$. Usually, the number of nodes that have a specified security level $R(a)$ is bounded and not related to $|N|$; typically just a few output statements have $R(a)$ defined. Thus overall complexity can be expected to be $O(|N|)$ as well.

Checking each node separately allows a simple yet powerful diagnosis in the case of a security violation: If a node x in the backward slice $BS(a)$ has a provided security level that is too large or incomparable ($P(x) \not\leq R(a)$), the responsible nodes can be computed by a so-called *chop* $CH(x,a) = FS(x) \cap BS(a)$.[11] The chop computes all nodes that are on a path from x to a, thus it contains all nodes that may be involved in the propagation from x's security level to a.

As an example, consider again the PDG for the password program (Figure 4.4). We choose a three-level security lattice: *public, confidential,* and *secret* where *public $\leq$ confidential $\leq$ secret*

---

[11] FS, the *forward slice* is defined as $FS(x) = \{y \mid x \to^* y\}$.

The program contains P-annotations for input variables, and an R-annotation for the result value. Thus the list of passwords is *secret*, i.e. $P(3) = secret \wedge P(4) = secret$. The list of names and the parameter `password` is *confidential*, because they should never be visible to a user. Thus, $P(1) = confidential \wedge P(5) = confidential \wedge P(6) = confidential$.

No *confidential* or *secret* information must flow out of `check`, thus we require $R(14) = public$. Remember that the PDG has additional dependences for exceptions (see Figure 4.5). In order to prevent an implicit flow from `check` to the calling method via uncaught exceptions, the node of the calling method representing any uncaught exception, m, is annotated with $R(m) = public$. Thus an implicit flow via an uncaught exception, where the exception is dependent on a *secret* variable, will be detected at m.

Starting with these specifications for R and P, the actual security levels $S(x)$, as computed according to equation (4.13), are depicted in Figure 4.8 (white for *public*, light gray for *confidential*, and gray for *secret*[12]). Let us now apply the PDG-based confidentiality check. It turns out that $3 \in BS(14)$ where $R(14) = public, P(3) = secret$. Thus the criterion fails. Indeed a security violation is revealed: $S(14) = secret \not\leq public = R(14)$, thus equation (4.8) is violated. The chop $CH(3, 14)$ contains all nodes contributing to the illegal flow.

It is however unavoidable that `match` has to be computed from *secret* information. Declassification was invented to handle such situations, and will be discussed later.

4.6 Inter-procedural propagation of security levels

Let us now discuss *interprocedural IFC*. To understand the problem of context-sensitivity, consider the program fragment and its SDG in Figure 4.9. In this fragment, $P(\texttt{secret}) = P(1) = High$, $P(\texttt{public}) = P(2) = Low$, and $R(\texttt{p}) = R(5) = Low$. Let us first assume that backward slices are computed just as in the intraprocedural case, that is, all nodes which have a path to the point of interest are in the slice. This naive approach treats interprocedural SDG edges like data or control dependence edges, and as a result will ignore the calling context. In the example, $3 \in BS(5)$ due to the SDG path $3 \rightarrow 3i \rightarrow a \rightarrow b \rightarrow 4o \rightarrow 5$ (where $3i$ is the actual parameter of the first call, and $4o$ is the return value of the second call). By equation (4.13), $S(4o) = S(5) = S(p) = High$, and $R(p) \not\geq S(p)$. However, semantically `secret` cannot influence `p`.

4.6.1 Context-Sensitive Slicing

To avoid such false alarms, an approach based on context-sensitive slicing (see section 2.2.2) must be used: not every SDG path is allowed in a slice, but only *realizable* paths. Realizable paths require that the actual parameter nodes to/from a function, which are on the path, must belong to the *same* call statement.[13]

---

[12]Ignore that node 14 is only half shaded for the moment.

[13]or more precisely, parameter-in/-out nodes must form a "matched parenthesis" structure, since calls can be nested.

```
1  secret = 1;
2  public = 2;
3  s = f(secret);
4  x = f(public);
5  p = x;
```

Figure 4.9: Example for context-sensitivity with corresponding SDG. The statement x computes the return value b from the formal input parameter a.

The reason is that a parameter from a specific call site cannot influence the result of a different call site, as all side-effects are represented as parameters. This fundamental idea to obtain context-sensitivity was introduced in [HRB90,RHSR94] and is called HRB slicing. In the example, the path $3 \to 3i \to a \to b \to 4o \to 5$ is not realizable and thus not context-sensitive, as actual parameter $3i$ and return parameter $4o$ do not belong to the same call site.

Interprocedural propagation of security levels is basically identical to intraprocedural propagation, but is based on the HRB backward slice which only includes realizable paths. Equation (4.13) and Theorem 4.3 still hold.[14]

Equations (4.13) and (4.8) can again be interpreted as a dataflow framework. But for reasons of efficiency, we will generate all instances of these equations simultaneously while computing the HRB backward slice. This results in a set of constraints for the $S(x)$, which is solved by an offline fixpoint iteration; the latter being based on the same principles as in dataflow frameworks.

The details of the HRB algorithm are shown in Algorithm 7.[15] Remember that backward slice computation, and thus propagation of security levels is done in two phases:

1. The first phase ignores interprocedural edges from a call site into the called procedure, and thus will only traverse to callees of the slicing criterion (i.e. is only ascending the call graph). Due to summary edges, which model transitive dependence of parameters, all parameters that might influence the outcome of a returned value are traversed, as if the corresponding path(s) through the called procedure were taken.

---

[14]in fact they hold for the naive backward slice as well, because even the naive interprocedural backward slice is correct; it is just too imprecise.

[15]For the time being, replace the test "$v \notin D$" (line 32) by "$true$", as in this section $D = \varnothing$; D will be explained in section 4.7.

Algorithm 7 Algorithm for context-sensitive IFC, based on the precise inter-procedural HRB slicing algorithm

---

1 **procedure** MarkVerticesOfSlice(G, x)
2 **input** G : a system dependence graph
3   x : a slicing criterion node
4 **output** BS : the slice of x (sets of nodes in G)
5   C : the generated set of constraints
6 /* D, R, P are assumed to be global read only data */
7 **begin**
8    $C := \varnothing$
9   /* Phase 1: slice without descending into called procedures */
10   $BS' \leftarrow$ MarkReachingVertices($G, \{x\}, \{\text{parameter-out}\}$)
11   /* Phase 2: slice called procedures
12   without ascending into call sites */
13   $BS \leftarrow$ MarkReachingVertices($G, BS', \{\text{parameter-in}, \text{call}\}$)
14 **end**
15
16 **procedure** MarkReachingVertices($G, V, Kinds$)
17 **input** G : a system dependence graph
18   V : a set of nodes in G
19    $Kinds$: a set of kinds of edges
20 **output** M : a set of nodes in G which are marked by this phase
21   (part of the precise backward slice)
22   C : a set of constraints
23 **begin**
24   $M := V$
25   $WorkList := V$
26   **while** $WorkList \neq \varnothing$ **do**
27   **select** and **remove** node n from $WorkList$
28     $M \cup= n$
29   **foreach** $w \in G$ such that $w \notin M$ and G contains an edge $w \to v$
30   whose kind is not in $Kinds$ **do**
31       $WorkList \cup= w$
32   **if** $v \notin D$ **then**
33         $C \cup= \{\text{"}S(w) \leq S(v)\text{"}\}$ // cf. eq. (4.13) or (4.16)
34   **if** $v \in dom(R)$ **then**
35           $C \cup= \{\text{"}S(v) \leq R(v)\text{"}\}$ // cf. eq. (4.8) or (4.16)
36   **if** $w \in dom(P)$ **then**
37           $C \cup= \{\text{"}P(w) \leq S(w)\text{"}\}$ // cf. eq. (4.13) or (4.17)
38   **else**
39         $C \cup= \{\text{"}P(v) \leq S(v)\text{"}\}$ // cf. eq. (4.19)
40         $C \cup= \{\text{"}S(w) \leq R(v)\text{"}\}$ // cf. eq. (4.20)
41   **fi**
42   **od**
43   **od**
44   **return** M
45 **end**

---

2. In the second phase, starting from the edges omitted in the first phase, the algorithms traverses all edges except call and parameter-in edges (i.e. is only descending the call graph.) As summary edges were traversed in the first phase, there is no need to re-ascend. Again, summary edges are used to account for transitive dependences of parameters.

For propagation of security levels, Algorithm 7 generates constraints involving S, P, and R. These constraints are derived from equations (4.7) and (4.8). We will show later that a solution to these constraints enforces confidentiality.

The summary edges have an essential effect, because they ensure that security levels are propagated (based on the generated constraints) as if they were propagated through the called procedure. In the first phase, no security level is propagated into called procedures and in the second phase, no computed security level is propagated from the called procedure to the call site. Due to summary edges, no security level is "lost" at ignored edges, i.e. they ensure that the security level is propagated along transitive dependences for this calling context, but it cannot change the computed security level at another call site.

We will now argue that Algorithm 7 generates correct and sufficient constraints.

Definition 4.2. *Let a program's SDG be given. The program maintains confidentiality, if for every $a \in dom(R)$ and its HRB backward slice $BS(a)$, equations (4.7) and (4.8) are satisfied.*

Again we postpone the proof that this definition implies noninterference (equation (4.2)), but point out that the definition – as Definition 4.1 – is solidly based on SDG correctness properties and fundamental definitions for confidentiality.

The latter are expressed in equations (4.7) and (4.8). Restricting these equations to the (context-sensitive) backward slices of all points $\in dom(R)$ avoids spurious flow, and is sufficient as these slices contain all nodes affecting equation (4.8). Thus Theorem 4.3 is still valid in the interprocedural case, and the proof remains the same.[16] Thus the PDG-based confidentiality check also works on SDGs: for any $a \in dom(R)$, compute the HRB backward slice $BS(a)$ and check whether all $y \in dom(P) \cap BS(a)$ have $P(y) \leq R(x)$. Remember that this check is valid for any correct backward slice – but the more precise the slice, the less false alarm it generates.

Let us now argue that Algorithm 7 is correct.

Theorem 4.4. *For every $a \in dom(R)$, Algorithm 7 (where $D = \varnothing$) generates a set of constraints which are correct and complete, and thus enforce confidentiality according to Definition 4.2.*

Proof. We may assume that the HRB algorithm itself computes a correct (and precise) backward slice $BS(a)$ for any $a \in dom(R)$.

1. For any $w, v \in BS(a)$ where $w \to v$, the algorithm generates a constraint $S(w) \leq S(v)$, which is necessary according to equation (4.13) and sufficient as edges outside $BS(a)$ cannot influence a.

---

[16]In fact we need a version of theorem 4.2 working on SDGs and backward slices.

Constraints	Minimal Fixpoint
$S(1) \leq S(3i)$	$S(1) = Low/High$
$S(2) \leq S(4i)$	$S(2) = Low$
$S(3) \leq S(3i) \wedge S(3) \leq S(3o) \wedge S(3) \leq S(f)$	$S(3) = Low/High$
$S(3i) \leq S(3o) \wedge S(3i) \leq S(a)$	$S(3i) = Low/High$
$S(3o) \leq \top$	$S(3o) = High$
$S(4) \leq S(4i) \wedge S(4) \leq S(4o) \wedge S(4) \leq S(f)$	$S(4) = Low$
$S(4i) \leq S(4o) \wedge S(4i) \leq S(a)$	$S(4i) = Low$
$S(4o) \leq S(5)$	$S(4o) = Low$
$S(f) \leq S(a) \wedge S(f) \leq S(b)$	$s(f) = Low$
$S(a) \leq S(x)$	$S(a) = Low$
$S(x) \leq S(b)$	$S(x) = Low$
$S(b) \leq S(3o) \wedge S(b) \leq S(4o)$	$S(b) = Low$
$S(5) \leq R(5) \wedge R(5) = Low$	$S(5) = Low$
$P(1) \leq S(1) \wedge P(1) = High$	
$P(2) \leq S(2) \wedge P(2) = Low$	

Figure 4.10: Constraint system for Figure 4.9 generated by Algorithm 7. Parts in gray are only generated for context-insensitive analysis.

2. Furthermore for any $w \in dom(P) \cap BS(a)$, $P(w) \leq S(w)$ is generated which is necessary due to equation (4.13) and sufficient as nodes outside $BS(a)$ cannot influence a. Note that line 36 tests for $w \in dom(P)$ and not $v \in dom(P)$, as otherwise nodes $\in dom(P)$ without predecessors would not generate a P-constraint.

3. Finally, for any $v \in dom(R) \cap BS(a)$, $R(v) \geq S(v)$ is generated which is necessary due to equation (4.8) and sufficient as nodes outside $BS(a)$ cannot influence a. Note that line 34 tests for $v \in dom(R)$ and not $w \in dom(R)$, as otherwise nodes $\in dom(R)$ without successor would not generate a R-constraint.

Thus Algorithm 7 generates exactly the constraints required by (4.8), and constraints exactly equivalent to (4.7). Hence they have the same fixpoint, and fulfill the requirements of Definition 4.2. $\square$

For pragmatic reasons, the fixpoint computation ignores the constraints involving R; these are only incorporated in the SDG-based confidentiality check after a solution for S has been found. The reason is that otherwise illegal flows will show up as an unsolvable constraint system – which is correct, but prevents user-friendly diagnosis. If the R constraints are checked later and one (or more) will fail, chops can be computed for diagnosis as described in section 4.5.3.

For the example above (Figure 4.9), Algorithm 7 computes $BS(5) = \{5, 4o, 4i, 4\}$ in the first phase and adds $\{b, x, a\}$ in the second phase, thus avoiding to add $3i$ or 1 to $BS(5)$. This is context-sensitivity. The corresponding constraints are $S(5) \leq R(5), S(4o) \leq S(5), S(4i) \leq S(4o), S(4) \leq S(4i), S(4) \leq S(4o), S(b) \leq S(4o), S(x) \leq S(b), s(a) \leq S(x)$. Constraints for $BS(3)$ are computed similarly. Figure 4.10 presents the complete list of constraints. It also presents additional constraints which would be added by naive interprocedural slicing (printed in gray). The fixpoint for S (without P constraints) is presented in Figure 4.10 (right column; again results based on naive slicing are shown in gray). The precise solution correctly computes $S(1) = High$, and indeed $P(1) = High \leq S(1)$. The naive solution would compute $S(1) = Low$ and generates a false alarm due to $P(1) \not\leq S(1)$.

4.6.2   Backward Flow Equations

Note that equation (4.13) in fact employs a forward propagation approach: it shows how to compute $S(x)$ if the $S(y)$ for the predecessors y of x are known. The HRB algorithm essentially works just the other way, namely backwards. For reasons of implementation efficiency, previous work has presented flow equations that follow this backward propagation approach.

In this section, we will show how to transform equations (4.13) and (4.8) into an equivalent form which mirrors this backward propagation, while Theorem 4.3 still holds. This will allow a more efficient implementation in connection with the HRB algorithm. The equivalent backward form is based on the following observation: equation (4.5) demands that for every $x \in N$ and $y \in pred(x)$, $S(x) \geq S(y)$ and thus $S(x) \geq \bigsqcup_{y \in pred(x)} S(y)$. The same set of constraints can be expressed as follows: for every $x \in N$ and $y \in succ(x)$, $S(x) \leq S(y)$ (equation (4.11)), and as a consequence,

$$S(x) \leq R'(x) \sqcap \bigsqcap_{y \in succ(x)} S(y) \tag{4.16}$$

In analogy, for equation (4.8) ($a \in \mathrm{dom}(R)$, $S(a) \leq R(a)$), one gets:

$$\forall a \in \mathrm{dom}(P) : P(a) \leq S(a) \tag{4.17}$$

Theorem 4.5. *For the same PDG resp. (intraprocedural) slice, the collected instances of equations* (4.11) *and* (4.8) *generate the same set of constraints as the collected instances of equations* (4.16) *and* (4.17)*.*

Proof.   The individual constraints in Algorithm 7 are equivalent due to the duality $a \leq b \Leftrightarrow a \sqcup b = b \Leftrightarrow a \sqcap b = a$, which has been exploited in the construction of equations (4.16) and (4.17). In forward propagation, we are using a two-phase algorithm that initially ignores constraints involving R in the fixpoint iteration and subsequently checks the omitted constraints with the computed fixpoint of S. In backward propagation, the fixpoint for S is determined without constraints involving P constraints, which again are checked in a second phase. Therefore it is obvious that the fixpoint for S in forward propagation differs from the fixpoint in backward propagation, however, both methods check that the whole set of constraints generated on all paths between all nodes in $dom(P)$ and all nodes in $dom(R)$ is satisfied and are thus equivalent. □

Computing a minimal fixpoint for $S(x)$ from constraints involving S and R and subsequent checking constraints involving P (backward propagation) is therefore equivalent to computing S's fixpoint from S and P with subsequent checking of R-constraints (forward propagation).

4.7 Declassification

IFC as described so far is too simplistic because in some situations one might accept that information with a higher security level flows to a "lower" channel. For instance, information may be published after statistical anonymization, secret data may be transferred over the Internet using encryption, and in electronic commerce one needs to release secret data after its purchase. *Declassification* allows to lower the security level of incoming information as a means to relax the security policy. The password checking method presented earlier is another example: as password tables are encrypted, it does not matter that information from the password table flows to the visible method result, and hence a declassification to *public* at node 14 (where the illegal flow was discovered, see section 4.5) is appropriate – a password-based authentication mechanism necessarily reveals some information about the secret password.[17]

When allowing such exceptions to the basic security policy, one major concern is that exceptions might introduce unforeseen information release. Several approaches for a semantics of declassification were proposed, each focusing on certain aspects of "secure" declassification. The current state of the art describes four dimensions to classify declassification approaches according to *where, who, when* and *what* can be declassified [SS05]. Apart from that, some basic principles are presented that can serve as "sanity checks" for semantic security policies allowing declassifications. These principles are 1. semantic consistency, which is basically invariance under semantics-preserving transformations; 2. conservativity, i.e. without declassification, security reduces to noninterference; 3. monotonicity of release, which states that adding declassification should not render a secure program insecure; 4. non-occlusion which requires that declassification operations cannot mask other covert information release.

4.7.1 Declassification in SDGs

We model declassification by specifying certain SDG nodes to be declassification nodes. Let $D \subseteq N$ be the set of declassification nodes. A declassification node $x \in D$ must have a required and a provided security level:

$$x \in D \implies \big(x \in dom(P) \cap dom(R)\big) \wedge \big(R(x) \geq P(x)\big) \qquad (4.18)$$

Information reaching x with a maximal security level $R(x)$ is lowered (declassified) down to $P(x)$ (note that $R(x) \not\geq P(x)$ does not make any sense,

---

[17]We all know that password crackers can exploit this approach in case weak passwords are used, hence just adding a declassification seems too naive. Additional techniques to protect the table are needed.

as declassification should lower a level, not heighten it). Now a path from node y to a with $P(y) > R(a)$ is *not* a violation, if there is a declassification node $x \in D$ on the path with $P(y) \leq R(x)$ and $P(x) \leq R(a)$ (assuming that there is no other declassification node on that path). The actual security level $S(x)$ will be between $P(x)$ and $R(x)$. In the password example, $D = \{14\}, R(14) = secret, P(14) = public$; and the illegal flow described earlier disappears.

According to Sabelfeld and Sands [SS05], this policy for expressing intentional information release is describing *where* in the system information is released: The set D of declassification nodes correspond to code locations— moreover, in the implemented system the user has to specify the code locations, which are mapped to declassification nodes by the system.

In terms of the propagation equations, a declassification simply changes the computation of S. Equation (4.11) must be extended as follows:

$$S(x) \geq \begin{cases} P(r) & \text{if } x \in D \\ P'(x) \sqcup \bigsqcup_{y \in pred(x)} S(y) & \text{otherwise} \end{cases} \qquad (4.19)$$

Thus the incoming security levels are ignored and replaced by the declassification security level.

Of course, equation (4.8) is still valid for non-declassification nodes, but for $x \in D$ it must be modified as $S(x)$ is the declassified value:

$$\forall x \in dom(R) \setminus D : R(x) \geq S(x) \ \wedge \ \forall x \in D : R(x) \geq \bigsqcup_{y \in pred(x)} S(y) \qquad (4.20)$$

which expresses that normal flow of S is interrupted at $x \in D$.

The following definition resembles Definition 4.2, but incorporates the modified flow equations:

Definition 4.3. *Let a program's SDG be given. The program maintains confidentiality, if for all $a \in dom(R)$ equations (4.19) and (4.20) are satisfied.*

Theorem 4.6. *For every $a \in dom(R)$, Algorithm 7 (where $D \neq \varnothing$) generates a set of constraints which are correct and complete, and thus enforce confidentiality according to Definition 4.3.*

Proof. We have already argued (proof for Theorem 4.4) that for non-declassification nodes the generated constraints correspond exactly to equations (4.8) and (4.7), and thus to the non-declassification cases in equations (4.19) and (4.20). For declassification nodes $d \in D$, Algorithm 7 does no longer generate constraints $S(w) \leq S(d)$, which is indeed required by (4.19), case $x \in D$. Instead it generates $R(d) \geq S(w)$ for $w \in pred(d)$, which is equivalent to the constraints required in (4.20), case $x \in D$. Furthermore, it generates $S(d) \geq P(d)$ which is exactly required by (4.19), case $x \in D$.

Thus Algorithm 7 generates exactly the constraints required by (4.19) and (4.20). Hence they have the same fixpoint, and fulfill the requirements of Definition 4.3. □

In case $D = \varnothing$, Algorithm 7 by theorem 4.4 checks noninterference without declassification. Thus we obtain for free the

Corollary 4.7 (Conservativity of Declassification). *Algorithm 7 is conservative, that is, without declassification it reduces to standard noninterference.*

Let us finally point out a few special situations. It is explicitly allowed to have two or more declassification on one specific path, e.g. $x \rightarrow^* d_1 \rightarrow^* d_2 \rightarrow^* y$. But this only makes sense if $P(d_1) \leq R(d_2)$, as otherwise no legal flow is possible on the path, and $P(d_2) \leq P(d_1)$, as otherwise the second declassification is redundant.

In case there are several declassifications on disjoint paths from x to y, for example $x \rightarrow^* d_1 \rightarrow^* y$, $x \rightarrow^* d_2 \rightarrow^* y$, $x \rightarrow^* d_3 \rightarrow^* y$, ..., it is possible to approximate all these declassifications conservatively by introducing a new declassification d where $R(d) = \bigcap_i R(d_i)$ and $P(d) = \bigsqcup_i P(d_i)$. Any flow which is legal through d is also legal through (one of) the d_i, hence the approximation will not introduce new (illegal) flows. This observation seems unmotivated, but will be the source for an more precise interprocedural IFC, as described in section 4.8.

4.7.2 Monotonicity of Release

Another useful property is *monotonicity of release*, which states that introduction of an additional declassification should not make previously secure programs insecure (i.e. generate additional illegal flow). Formally, this can be defined as follows:

Definition 4.4. *Let a program satisfy confidentiality according to Definition 4.3 and let $d \in N$ where $d \notin D \cup dom(R) \cup dom(P)$. Replace d by $d' \in D$ where d' has the same connecting edges as d, but d' is annotated with R and P. Recompute the actual security levels according to (4.19), yielding $S'(x)$ for $x \in N$. Declassification d' respects monotonicity of release, if equation (4.20) still holds for all $S'(x)$.*

The following theorem states that if the annotations comply with some basic sanity checks, then monotonicity of release can be guaranteed:

Theorem 4.8. *If $R(d') \geq \bigsqcup_{y \in pred(d')} S(y)$, and $P(d') \leq \bigsqcup_{y \in pred(d')} S(y)$, then for $x \in N$, $S'(x) \leq S(x)$.*

The first premise avoids that previously legal flow (where $R'(d') = \top$ as $d' \notin dom(R)$) is now blocked by a too low or arbitrary $R(d')$. Note that $P(d') \leq R(d')$ is required anyway in equation (4.18). The above premise is more precise and avoids that a declassification generates new illegal flows as the outgoing declassification level is too high, or the incoming limit too low. In practice, both requirements are easy to check and do not restrict sensible declassification.

Proof. In the original SDG, $\bigsqcup_{y \in pred(d')} S(y) \leq S(d') \leq \bigcap_{y \in succ(d')} S(y)$, hence in the new PDG $S'(d') = P(d') \leq S(d') = \bigsqcup_{y \in pred(d')} S(y)$ by assumption and equation 4.19. Furthermore, $S'(d) \leq S(d') \leq \bigcap_{y \in succ(d')} S(y) \leq S(y)$ for all $y \in succ(d')$. Hence $S(y) \geq \bigcap_{z \in pred(y)} S(y) \geq S'(y) = S'(d') \sqcup \bigsqcup_{z \neq d' \in pred(y)} S(z)$. The same argument works for the successors of y. By induction[18] $S'(x) \leq S(x)$ follows for all x. $\square$

---

[18]technically, a well-known fixpoint induction

```
1 int foo(int x) {
2   y = ... x ... // compute y from x
3   return y; /*D:confidential -> public*/
4 }
5
6 int check() {
7   int secret = ... /*P:secret*/
8   int high = ...   /*P:confidential*/
9   int x1, x2;
10  x1 = foo(secret);
11  x2 = foo(high);
12  return x2; /*R:public*/
13 }
```

Figure 4.11: Example for declassification

Corollary 4.9. *Under the assumptions of theorem 4.8, declassification d' respects monotonicity of release.*

Proof. For the original SDG, (4.8) and (4.19) are valid for S. In the new PDG, (4.19) is by construction valid for S', and (4.8) is valid for S' since by the theorem $S'(x) \leq S(x)$. □

4.7.3 Confidentiality check with declassification

The original SDG-based confidentiality criterion no longer works with declassification, as information flow with declassification is no longer transitive and slicing is based on transitive information flow. Thus a $P(x)$ in $BS(a)$ where $P(x) \not\leq R(a)$ is not necessarily an illegal flow, as $P(x)$ can be declassified under way. Instead, the criterion must be modified as follows:

Confidentiality Check With Declassification. For every $a \in dom(R) \setminus D$, compute $S(x)$ for all $x \in BS(a)$ by Algorithm 7, and check the following property:

$$\forall x \in dom(P) \cap BS(a) : P(x) \leq S(x) \qquad (4.21)$$

Theorem 4.6 guarantees that the constraints generated by Algorithm 7 and thus the S values (being their minimal fixpoint) are correct. Hence the criterion is satisfied iff Definition 4.3 is satisfied. If the criterion is not satisfied, equation (4.19) is violated and an illegal flow has been detected. As described in section 4.6.1, the S values are computed first, and the criterion (4.21) is checked in a second phase; this allows to generate diagnostics by computing chops.

Let us return to the example in Figures 4.3 and 4.8 and assume $R(14) = public$. As described in section 4.5.3, the analysis reveals an illegal flow $3 \to^* 14$. We thus introduce a declassification: $14 \in D$, $R(14) = secret$, $P(14) = public$ (represented as two colors). Now $S(14) = secret \leq R(14)$, so the confidentiality check will no longer reveal an illegal flow. This may be desirable depending on the security policy, since only a small amount of information leaks from password checking.

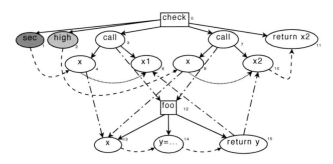

Figure 4.12: System Dependence Graph for Figure 4.11

As another example consider Figure 4.11. In line 3 a declassification D : *confidential* $\rightarrow$ *public* is present. Hence $3 \in D$, $R(3) = $ *confidential* and $P(3) = $ *public*. It seems that a *secret* value can flow from line 10 to line 3, hence in line 3 an illegal flow seems possible $(R(3) \not\succeq S(3))$ because in line 3 we can declassify from *confidential* to *public* but not from *secret* to *public*. But in fact the return value in line 3 is only copied to x1 at line 10, and x1 is dead (never used afterwards and never output). Thus intuitively, the program seems secure.

The SDG for this program is shown in Figure 4.12. By Algorithm 7 x1 is not in the context-sensitive backward slice for line 12, and thus the SDG-based confidentiality criterion will *not* generate a false alarm, but determine that confidentiality is guaranteed. This example demonstrates once more how context-sensitive backward slices improve precision.

4.8 Improving Interprocedural Declassification

Algorithm 7 is correct, but in the presence of declassifications, its precision still needs to be improved. The reason is that Algorithm 7 essentially ignores the effect of declassifications in called procedures: summary edges represent a transitive information flow between pairs of parameters, whereas declassification is intransitive. Using them for computation of the actual security level $S(x)$ implies that every piece of information flowing into a procedure with a given provided security level l will be treated as if it flowed back out with the same level. If there is declassification on the path between the corresponding formal parameters, this approach is overly conservative and leads to many false alarms.

As an example, consider Figure 4.12 again: The required security level for node 11 is *Low* as specified. Algorithm 7 computes $S(2) = S(8) = S(10) = S(11) = $ *Low* due to the summary edge. This will result in a false alarm because the declassification at node 15 is ignored.

4.8.1 Summary Declassification Nodes

In order to respect declassifications in called procedures, and achieve maximal precision, an extension of the notion of a summary edge is needed. The funda-

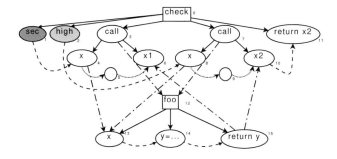

Figure 4.13: SDG for Figure 4.11 with summary declassification nodes

mental idea is to insert a new "summary" declassification node into the summary edge, which represents the effect of declassifications on paths in the procedure body.

Thus the summary edge $x \to y$, representing all paths from the corresponding formal-in node x' to the formal-out node y', is split in two edges, with a declassification node $d \in D$ in between. This new declassification node d represents the declassification effects on all paths from x' to y'.

The constraints on $R(d)$ and $P(d)$ are chosen such that any legal flow through the procedure body is also a legal flow through $x \to d \to y$. In particular, if there is a declassification free path from x' to y', there must not be a summary declassification node, as information flow might be transitive in that case. It is not trivial to determine $R(d)$ and $P(d)$ such that precision is maximized and correctness is maintained, as we will see later. However, once these values have been fixed, Algorithm 7 proceeds as usual.

Figure 4.13 shows the SDG with summary declassification nodes for the example in Figure 4.12. The actual-in nodes 4 and 8 are connected to their corresponding formal-in node 13 with parameter-in edges. The formal-out node 15 is connected to corresponding actual-out nodes 6 and 10 with parameter-out edges. The call nodes 3 and 7 are connected to the called procedure at its entry node 12 with a call edge. The actual-in nodes 4 and 8 are connected via summary edges and summary declassification nodes 5 and 9 to the actual-out nodes 6 and 10. This Figure contains only one declassification at node 15 ($R(15) = confidential$, $P(15) = public$), so for the path between node 13 and 15 the summary declassification nodes 5 and 9 will be set to $R(5) = R(9) = confidential$ and $P(5) = P(9) = \bot$. (The algorithm for this will be presented in the next section.)

Exploiting the summary declassification nodes, algorithm 7 will a) determine that node 1 is not in the backward slice of node 11 and thus cannot influence node 11, and b) $confidential = P(8) \leq S(8) \leq S(8) \leq R(9) = confidential$ and $\bot = P(9) \leq S(9) \leq S(10) \leq R(11) = public$, thus no security violation is found in check. In the second slicing phase, there is no violation either: $S(13) \leq S(14) \leq R(15) = confidential$ and $public = P(15) \leq S(10) \leq R(11) =$

public. Note that the constraint $P(15) \leq S(10)$ is checked in the second phase, such that the trivial constraint $P(9) = \bot$ is sufficient for asserting security, and $R(5) = R(9) = $ *confidential* is exactly the maximal possible value of $S(13)$. This observation leads to the following algorithm for computing P and R for summary declassification nodes.

4.8.2 Computation of $R(d)$ for Summary Declassification Nodes

---

Algorithm 8 Computation of $R(d)$ for Summary Declassification (backward propagation)

---

1 **procedure** SummaryDeclassification(G, L, R)
2 **input** G: a system dependence graph
3   L: a security lattice
4   R: the required annotations
5 **output**: the set of summary declassification nodes (included in G)
6 **begin**
7    $pathEdges = \varnothing$ // *set of transitive dependences already seen*
8   **foreach** formal$-$out node o in G **do**
9      $pathEdges \cup = (o, o, \neg(o \in D), \top)$
10   **od**
11   $workList := pathEdges$
12   **while** $workList$ not empty **do**
13   remove (x, y, f, l) **from** workList
14   **if** x is an formal$-$in node **then**
15   addSummaries(x, y, f, l)
16   **else**
17   **foreach** edge $w \to x \in G$ **do**
18   addToPathEdges(extendPathEdge$((x, y, f, l), w))$
19   **od**
20   **fi**
21   **od**
22 **end**
23
24 **procedure** addToPathEdges(x, y, f, l)
25 **input** (x, y, f, l): a path edge tuple
26 **begin**
27   **if** $(x, y, f', l') \in pathEdges$ where $f' \neq f$ or $l' \neq l$ **then**
28   remove (x, y, f', l') **from** $pathEdges$
29   **fi**
30   **if** $(x, y, f, l) \notin pathEdges$ **then**
31     $pathEdges \cup = (x, y, f, l)$
32     $workList \cup = (x, y, f, l)$
33   **fi**
34 **end**

As summary declassification nodes represent the effect of declassifications on paths in the procedure body, and these can in turn call procedures (even recursively), a simple transitive closure between formal parameters does not yield a correct solution for summary declassification nodes [HRB90, RHSR94].

Algorithm 9 Auxiliary procedures for Summary Declassification Nodes

---

35 **procedure** extendPathEdge($(x, y, f, l), w$)
36 **input**: (x, y, f, l): a path edge tuple
37   w the extension node
38 **output**: a path edge extended by w
39 **begin**
40   **if** $pathEdges$ contains a tuple (w, y, f', l') **then**
41   retrieve (w, y, f', l') **from** $pathEdges$
42   **else**
43     $l' = \top$, $f' = false$
44   **fi**
45   **if** $x \in D$ **then**
46     $l' = l' \sqcap R(x)$
47   **else**
48     $l' = l' \sqcap l$
49   **fi**
50   $f' = f' \vee (w \notin D \wedge f)$
51   **return** (w, y, f', l')
52 **end**
53
54 **procedure** addSummaries(x, y, pf, l)
55 **input**: (x, y, f, l): a path edge tuple
56 **begin**
57   **foreach** actual parameter pair (v, w) corresponding to (x, y)
58   **if** f **then**
59   add summary edge $v \rightarrow_{sum} w$ to G
60       $n := v$
61   **else**
62   add summary declassification node d and edges $v \rightarrow_{sum} d$
63   and $d \rightarrow_{sum} w$ where $R(d) = l$ and $P(d) = \bot$
64   **fi**
65   **foreach** $(w, z, f', l') \in pathEdges$ **do**
66   addToPathEdges(extendPathEdge($(w, z, f', l'), d$))
67   **od**
68   **od**
69 **end**

Instead, a specialized algorithm for summary edges must be leveraged where the computation of the security levels for summary declassification nodes can be integrated. The result can be seen in Algorithms 8 and 9, which incorporate a backward IFC propagation into the algorithm described by Reps et al. [RHSR94] as presented in Algorithm 2 on page 39.

As an example, consider Figure 4.11 again. Here, Algorithm 8 starts with adding node 15 as $(15, 15, false, \top)$ into *pathEdge*. Note that the third element of this tuple is *false*, because 15 is a declassification node. When this tuple is removed from the *workList*, all predecessors of 15 are processed, in particular node 14. For this node, extendPathEdge will not find a previous tuple in *pathEdges* and thus initializes l' and f' to the neutral elements for $\sqcap$, resp. $\vee$. As node 15 is in D, $l' = l' \sqcap R(15) = R(15)$ and $f' = f' \vee false = false$, which yields a pathEdge tuple $(14, 14, false, confidential)$. For its predecessor 13, we get a pathEdge tuple $(13, 13, false, confidential)$ and no other path leads to 13. Since 13 is a formal-in node, addSummaries will add a summary declassification node d where $R(d) = confidential$ and $P(d) = \bot$ between the corresponding actual parameters 4 and 6, and 8 and 10, exactly as we defined these nodes in the previous section.

Theorem 4.10. *IFC with Algorithm 7 and summary declassification nodes determined according to Algorithms 8 and 9 is sound and precise.*

Proof We want to show that Algorithms 8 and 9 results in a superset of the constraints generated for all interprocedurally realizable paths. This guarantees soundness. To demonstrate precision, we show that the additional constraints are trivially satisfied by choosing $P(d) = \bot$ for all summary declassification nodes d, and thus do not change the computed fixpoint. As these algorithms are straightforward extensions of the algorithm presented in [HRB90,RHSR94], we can assume that these algorithms traverse all interprocedurally realizable paths between formal-in and formal-out edges, including recursive calls. For soundness, we need to show two subgoals:

1. If there is an interprocedurally realizable path between a formal-in and a formal-out parameter of the same call-site that does not contain a declassification node, then the algorithm will only generate a traditional summary edge, but no summary declassification node. Due to transitivity of information flow on that path, the summary information must conservatively obey transitivity as well. Algorithm 9 adheres to this requirement using the flag f in line 59. An induction over the length of the pathEdge will show this property:

   If the length of the pathEdge is 0 $(x = y)$, line 9 asserts that if $x \in D$ then the flag f is *false*, else *true*. So let's assume f correctly represents the fact if the pathEdge (x, y, f, l) contains no declassifications. Then line 50 asserts that f' in the extended pathEdge (w, y, f', l') is *true*(i.e. there is no declassification on the path $w \to y$), if $w \notin D \wedge f$ holds. Note that if there have been other paths between w and y previously explored (the condition in line 40 holds), we will only remember if there is *any* path without declassification due to the disjunction in line 50.

2. Otherwise, if all paths between a formal-in and a formal-out parameter of the same call-site contain a declassification, we need to show that for each interprocedurally realizable path, the HRB algorithm with summary declassification nodes computes a superset of the constraints generated for that path. As a consequence of not traversing parameter-in edges, the constraint $S(\text{act-in}) \leq S(\text{form-in})$ is not directly generated by Algorithm 7, and thus must be imposed by the summary declassification node d. As the value of $R(d)$ is determined by computing $S(\text{form-in})$ with the same constraints as in Algorithm 7, we only need to show that using $S(\text{form-out}) = \top$ we get the same result as with the constraint $S(\text{form-out}) \leq S(\text{act-out})$, which is generated by the HRB algorithm. But this follows from the independence of $S(\text{form-in})$ and $S(\text{form-out})$, as each path in-between contains a declassification node which induces no constraint of the form $S(w) \leq S(v)$ for an edge $w \to v$ but only $S(w) \leq R(v)$. □

4.8.3 Beyond PDGs

While SDG precision improves steadily due to ongoing research, precision can also be improved by non-SDG means, as developed in program analysis.

As an example, consider the fragment

"if (h > h) then l = 0"

Naive slicing as well as security type systems will assume a transitive dependence from h to l, even though the if body is dead code. Thus, semantic consistency as postulated in [SS05] is violated. This is not in discrepancy with Theorem 4.1, but comes from analysis imprecision.

Fortunately, SDGs today come in a package with other analyses originally developed for code optimization, such as interprocedural constant propagation, static single assignment form, symbolic evaluation, and dead code elimination. These powerful analyses are performed before SDG construction starts, and will eliminate a lot of spurious flow. The easiest way to exploit such analyses is by constructing the SDG from bytecode or intermediate code. For the above example, any optimizing compiler will delete the whole statement from machine code or bytecode, as it is dead code. Note that the bytecode must be considered the ultimate definition of the program's meaning, and remaining flows in the bytecode – after all the sophisticated optimizations – must be taken all the more seriously.

In addition, we propose an even stronger mechanism on top of SDGs, called *path conditions* (see chapter 5). Path conditions are necessary and precise conditions for flow $x \to^* y$, and reveal detailed circumstances of a flow in terms of conditions on program variables. If a constraint solver can solve a path condition for the program's input variables, feeding such a solution to the program makes the illegal flow visible directly; this useful feature is called a *witness*. As an example, consider the fragment

```
1 a[i+3] = x;
2 if (i>10)
3     y = a[2*j-42];
```

Here, a necessary condition for a flow $x \rightarrow^* y$ is $\exists i, j.(i > 10) \wedge (i+3 = 2j-42) \equiv$ *false*, proving that flow is impossible even though the PDG indicates otherwise.

4.9 Related Work

4.9.1 SDGs and IFC

Several papers have been written about SDGs and slicers for Java, but to our knowledge only the Indus slicer [JRH05] is—besides ours—fully implemented and can handle full Java. Indus is customizable, embedded into Eclipse, and has a very nice GUI, but is less precise than our slicer. In particular, it does not fully support context-sensitivity but only k-limiting of contexts, and it allows time traveling for concurrent programs.

The work described in this paper improves our previous algorithm [HKS06], which was not able to handle declassification in called procedures precisely. However, that work also describes the generation and use of path conditions for Java PDGs (i.e. necessary conditions for an information flow between two nodes), which can uncover the precise circumstances under which a security violation can occur.

While a close connection between IFC and dataflow analysis had been noticed very early [BC85], Abadi et al. [ABHR99] were the first to connect slicing and noninterference, but only for type system based slicing of a variant of λ-calculus. It is amazing that our Theorem 4.3 from Section 4.3 (which holds for imperative languages and their PDGs) was not discovered earlier. Only Anderson et al. [ART03] presented an example in which chopping can be used to show illegal information flow between components which were supposedly independent. They do not employ a security lattice, though.

Yokomori et al. [YOT+02] were probably the first to propose and implement an IFC analysis based on program slicing for a procedural language. It checks for traditional noninterference, and supports the minimal lattice *Low* < *High* only. Their analysis is flow-sensitive, but not context-sensitive nor object-sensitive.

Hammer et al. combined static and dynamic PDG analysis for detection of illegal information flow [HGK06]. It allows the a-posteriori analysis of programs showing unexpected behavior and the computation of an exact witness for reconstruction of the illegal information flow.

4.9.2 Security type systems

Volpano and Smith [VS97] presented the first security type system for IFC. They extended traditional type systems in order to check for pure noninterference in simple while-languages with procedure calls. The procedures can be polymorphic with respect to security classes allowing context-sensitive analysis. They proof noninterference in case the system reports no typing errors. An extension to multi-threaded languages is given in [SV98].

Myers [ML00] defines Jif, an extension of the Java language with a type system for information flow. The JIF compiler [MCN+] implements this language. We already discussed in Section 4.3 that type systems are less precise, but are more efficient. JIF supports generic classes and the decentralized label model [ML00]; labels and principals are first class objects. Note that our PDG-based approach can be generalized to utilize decentralized labels.

Barthe and Rezk [BR05] present a security type system for strict noninterference without declassification, handling classes and objects. NullPointer-Exception is the only exception type allowed. Only values annotated with *Low* may throw exceptions. Constructors are ignored, instead objects are initialized with default values. A proof showing the noninterference property of the type system is given.

Strecker [Str03] formulated a non-deterministic type system including the noninterference proof in Isabelle [NPW02]. It handles major concepts of Micro-Java such as classes, fields and method calls, but omits arrays and exceptions.

Mantel and Reinhard [MR07] defined the first type system for a multi-threaded while language that controls the *what* and the *where* dimension of declassification simultaneously. The type system is based on a definition for the *where* dimension that supersedes their previous definition of intransitive noninterference [MS04], and two variants of a definition for the *what* dimension similar to selective dependency [Coh78]. However, they do not show whether their approach is practically viable.

4.9.3 Verification and IFC

Amtoft et al. [ABB06] present an interprocedural flow-sensitive Hoare-like logic for information flow control in a rudimentary object-oriented language. Casts, type tests, visibility modifiers other than public, and exception handling are not yet considered. Only structured control flow is allowed.

The Pacap case study [BCM+00] verifies secure interaction of multiple Java-Card applets on one smart card. They employ model checking to ensure a sufficient condition for their security policy, which is based on a lattice similar to noninterference without declassification. Implicit exceptions are modeled, but such unstructured control flow may lead to *label creep* (cf. [SM03, Sect. II E]).

Genaim [GS05] defines an abstract interpretation of the CFG looking for information leaks. It can handle all bytecode instructions of single-threaded Java and conservatively handles implicit exceptions of bytecode instructions. The analysis is flow- and context-sensitive but does not differentiate fields of different objects. Instead, they propose an object-insensitive solution folding all fields of a given class. In our experience [HS04] object-insensitivity yields too many spurious dependences. The same is true for the approximation of the call graph by CHA. In this setting, both will result in many false alarms.

An area uncovered by our system is security policies, defining under which circumstances declassification is allowed. Li and Zdancewic [LZ05] define a framework for downgrading policies for a core language with conditionals and fixed-points, yielding a formalized security guarantee with a program equivalence proof.

4.9.4 Static analysis for security

Static analysis is often used for source code security analysis [CM04]. For example, information flow control is closely related to tainted variable analysis. There are even approaches like the one from Pistoia et al. [PFKS05] that use slicing for taint analysis or the one from Livshits and Lam [LL03, LL05] that uses IPSSA, a representation very similar to dependence graphs. However, these analyses only use a trivial security level (tainted/untainted) with a trivial declassification (untaint) and could greatly benefit from our approach. Scholz et al. [SZC08] present a static analysis that tracks user input on a data structure similar to a dependence graph. Like our analysis, it is defined as a dataflow analysis framework and reduce the constraint system using properties of SSA form. Again, this analysis is targeted to bug tracking and taint analysis.

Pistoia et al. [PCFY07] survey recent methods for static analysis for software security problems. They focus on stack- and role-based access control, information flow and API conformance. A unified access-control and integrity checker for information-based access control, an extension of Java's stack-based access control mechanism has been presented in [PBN07]. They show that an implicit integrity policy can be extracted from the access control policy, and that the access control enforces that integrity policy.

Another approach is to use path conditions (as sketched in section 4.8.3) in order to obtain more semantically convincing characterizations and context constraints for sound declassification. Our approach to declassification does currently not offer per-se checks of semantic properties as stipulated by [SS05], but will rely on path conditions to provide precise necessary conditions for a declassification to take place. This approach falls into the category "how" declassification may occur, which has not yet been extensively researched.

For multithreaded programs, PDGs need not only check for classical noninterference, but eventually for possibilistic or probabilistic noninterference. Details of this novel technique will be presented by Giffhorn and Lochbihler [GL].

Chapter 5

Path Conditions

5.1 Introduction

The previous chapter presented our precise approach for information flow control. But no matter how precise the information flow analysis is, it will always answer a binary question only — whether illegal flow between two program points is possible, or whether this is definitely not the case. It may even be able to track down the source point making trouble, but still lack to provide insight into the specific conditions of the security violation. In particular, information flow control mechanisms do not provide "counter examples", e.g. in the form of input values that make the security violation visible.

This chapter will present two approaches that do exactly that, based on the concept of a static path condition [Sne96, RS02, SRK06], which is a precise condition that needs to be satisfiable for information flow between two given program points to be possible. Such a condition can be fed into a constraint solver system which either finds the formula unsatisfiable, which means that the given information flow is definitely impossible and was a false positive in the original analysis, or it may eventually simplify the condition to input variable bindings that trigger that information flow. This chapter extends this notion in two dimensions: First, this concept of a static path condition is extended to the object-oriented features of Java, which impose additional difficulties due to the dynamic nature of type tests of instanceof, dynamic dispatch and exceptions. However, our new approach relies solely on static program analysis and thus allows generating precise conditions for illicit information flow, that say *why* this flow takes place, together with a set of input values that allow reproduction of that illicit flow.

Second, a dynamic variant of path conditions is presented that combines traditional static path conditions with dynamic analyses like dynamic slicing and information collected by program instrumentation. Dynamic slicing yields significantly smaller sets of statements than static slicing, therefore the dynamic path conditions allow a precise post-mortem analysis of a failed program run and might even be leveraged for analyzing how illicit information flow occurred, after prevention by a dynamic information flow control mechanism.

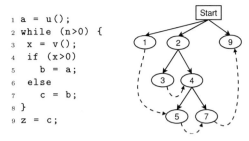

```
1 a = u();
2 while (n>0) {
3   x = v();
4   if (x>0)
5     b = a;
6   else
7     c = b;
8 }
9 z = c;
```

Figure 5.1: A small program and its dependence graph

Both extensions have been implemented in a prototype tool based on the Valsoft infrastructure [Rob05]. Previous results from this effort have been described in [HGK06, HSS08].

5.2 Foundations of Path Conditions

Program dependence graphs (PDG) as presented in chapter 2 are a standard tool to model information flow through a program. Program statements or conditions are represented by the nodes, the edges represent data and control dependences between statements or conditions. A path $x \rightarrow^* y$ means that information can flow from x to y; if there is no path, it is guaranteed that there is no information flow. In particular, all statements (possibly) influencing y (the so-called *backward slice*) are easily computed as $BS(y) = \{x \mid x \rightarrow^* y\}$.

For the small program and its dependence graph in Figure 5.1, there is a path from statement 1 to statement 9, indicating that input variable a may influence output variable z. Since there is no path $1 \rightarrow^* 4$, there is definitely no influence from a to x.

A *chop* for a *chopping criterion* (x, y) is the set of nodes that are part of an influence of the (source) node x on the (target) node y. This is the set of nodes that lie on a path from x to y in the PDG: $CH(x, y) = \{z \mid x \rightarrow^* z \rightarrow^* y\}$. For convenience, we will also use $CH(x, y)$ for the set of paths between x and y.

5.2.1 Intraprocedural Path Conditions

In order to make program slicing more precise, Snelting introduced *path conditions* [Sne96], which are necessary conditions for information flow between two nodes. The formulae for the generation of path conditions are quite complex (for details, see [SRK06]), and only the most fundamental formulae will be given here:

$$PC(x, y) = \bigvee_{\text{Path } P = x \rightarrow^* y} \bigwedge_{z \in P} E(z) \quad \text{where}$$

$$E(z) = \bigvee_{P \text{ Control Path } Start \rightarrow^{cd*} z} \bigwedge_{\nu \rightarrow^{cd} \mu \in P} c(\nu \rightarrow \mu) \quad (5.1)$$

$PC(x, y)$ is a necessary condition for flow from x to y, and $E(z)$ is a necessary condition for the execution of z. A control path is a path that consists of control dependence edges only. Thus, $E(x)$ is computed along all control paths from the *Start* node of the function to x based on the conditions $c(\nu \rightarrow \mu)$ associated with dependence edge $\nu \rightarrow \mu$. For control dependences, $c(\nu \rightarrow \mu)$ is typically a condition from a while- or if-statement. Program variables in a path condition are (implicitly) existentially quantified, as they are necessary conditions for potential information flow.

Because the paths between the criterion nodes are based on the computed chops, we will be interested in the set of paths $P_1, P_2, \cdots \in CH(x, y)$ and a slightly relaxed notation for path conditions is used:

$$PC(x, y) = \bigvee_{P \in CH(x,y)} \bigwedge_{z \in P} E(z)$$

In [SRK06] Snelting et al. argue why this formula is correct and precise, and why it improves slicing considerably. They also show that cycles in $CH(x, y)$ can safely be eliminated for computation of $PC(x, y)$, such that the formula is always finite. For the example in Figure 5.1, the following execution and path conditions are computed:

$$c(2 \rightarrow 3) \equiv c(2 \rightarrow 4) \equiv (n > 0), \quad c(4 \rightarrow 5) \equiv (x > 0),$$
$$c(4 \rightarrow 7) \equiv (x \leq 0),$$
$$E(1) \equiv true, \quad E(3) \equiv (n > 0), \quad E(5) \equiv (n > 0) \wedge (x > 0),$$
$$PC(1, 5) \equiv E(1) \wedge E(5) \equiv (n > 0) \wedge (x > 0)$$

In the presence of data structures like arrays or pointers, additional constraints will be generated. For data dependences, $\Phi(\nu \rightarrow \mu)$ is a condition constraining information flow through data types. As an example we consider arrays (a full presentation can be found in [SRK06]): A data dependence $\nu \rightarrow \mu$ between an array element definition $a[E_1] = \ldots$ and a usage $\ldots = a[E_2]$ generates $\Phi(\nu \rightarrow \mu) \equiv E_1 = E_2$; all other data dependences will generate $\Phi(\nu \rightarrow \mu) \equiv true$. The equation to compute a path condition now becomes:

$$PC(x, y) = \bigvee_{P \in CH(x,y)} \left(\bigwedge_{z \in P} E(z) \wedge \bigwedge_{u \rightarrow v \in P} \Phi(u \rightarrow v) \right) \tag{5.2}$$

For clarification consider the following program fragments and their path conditions:

```
1    a[i+3] = x;
2    if (i>10)
3        y = a[2*j-42];
```

$$PC(1, 3) \equiv (i > 10) \wedge (i + 3 = 2j - 42)$$

which, apart from the execution condition, contains a term that requires the two index expressions to be equal, and

```
1 x = a;                        1 x₁ = a;
2 while (x < 7) {               2 while (x₂=Φ(x₁,x₃),x₂<7){
3   x = y + x;                  3   x₃ = y + x₂;
4   if (x == 8)                 4   if (x₃ == 8)
5     p(x);                     5     p(x₃);
6 }                             6 }
```

Figure 5.2: Multiple variable assignments

```
1   a[i+3] = x;
2   if ((i>10)&&(j<5))
3     y = a[2*j-42];
```

$$PC(1,3) \equiv (i > 10) \wedge (j < 5) \wedge (i + 3 = 2j - 42)$$
$$\equiv \text{false}$$

which is not satisfiable, as the index expression term and the execution conditions contradict.

These examples indicate that path conditions give precise conditions for information flow, and can sometimes determine that such flow is impossible even though there is a path in the graph. Note that in practice path conditions tend to be large and a constraint solver is used to simplify them.

Multiple Variable Assignments

Computing path conditions based on the original program text may render the condition unsatisfiable even if the influence is possible. As an example, consider the code in Figure 5.2 (left) and the (primitive) path condition

$$PC(1,5) \equiv (x < 7) \wedge (x = 8)$$

between a in line 1 and x in line 5. This condition is unsatisfiable, although there is definitely a way how line 1 can influence line 5. The problem is that the program contains multiple assignments to the variable x that this path condition cannot distinguish. For static path conditions this problem is solved by using a variant of SSA-form [CFR+91] of the program. That way, different variable definitions are distinguished and eventually brought together using the ϕ operator, thus replacing multiple variable assignments with single assignments. Figure 5.2 (right) shows the SSA form of the original program (left).

The SSA form makes our path condition solvable by distinguishing between different definitions of the variable x:

$$PC(1,5) \equiv (x_2 < 7) \wedge (x_3 = 8)$$

Transforming a program into SSA form, however, modifies the code representation and is thus not desirable for dependence graphs in ValSoft which are close to the source code structure. In order to maintain the code structure, an assignment form similar to the SSA form is used: Index numbers represent the node numbers in the dependence graph, allowing a precise distinction between different variable occurrences. Path conditions as

$$(e\_puf[idx] == " + ")$$

are thus written as

$$(e\_puf_{99}[idx_{98}] ==_{97} " + "_{101})$$

The ϕ operator does not occur in the code structure itself, but is only used for computing path conditions.

Weak and Strong Path Conditions

For a given chop between two statements x, y, one can usually define more than one path condition. Still, every single instance is a necessary condition for information flow along the chop. To argue about quality, a partial order[1] $\leq$ is defined for the pair (x, y)

$$PC'(x, y) \leq PC(x, y) \qquad \text{iff} \qquad PC(x, y) \Rightarrow PC'(x, y)$$

In such a case $PC(x, y)$ is called *stronger* than $PC'(x, y)$. Stronger path conditions are usually easier to solve by the constraint solver and thus more favorable.

Note that the precision of the underlying chop affects the strength of the path condition: if two chops exist where one is more precise than the other $CH(x, y) \subset CH'(x, y)$, then every path $P \in CH(x, y)$ in the smaller chop is also a path in the larger chop. Thus, the smaller chop generates a stronger path condition, since the disjunction in the path condition runs over fewer paths:

$$\bigvee_{P \in CH(x,y)} \bigwedge_{z \in P} E(z) \Rightarrow \bigvee_{P \in CH'(x,y)} \bigwedge_{z \in P} E(z)$$

This fact forms the theoretic basis for Section 5.4.2, as the dynamic chop is usually smaller than the static chop.

Adding another conjunctive term R to the path condition is a different way to strengthen it. In Section 5.4.3 logical formula will be generated from dynamic trace data and conjunctively combined with the original path condition, yielding a stronger (or equal) path condition:

$$PC(x, y) \wedge R \geq PC(x, y)$$

5.2.2 Interprocedural Path Conditions

In analogy to interprocedural slicing and chopping, interprocedural path conditions need to be restricted to *realizable* [Kri05] paths. Intuitively, this means that a path in the system dependence graph (SDG) [HRB90] — i.e. several PDGs connected by interprocedural edges according to the call graph — that enters a procedure through a certain invocation site must not leave it at a different invocation site. As an illustration, consider Figure 5.3. Here, there are only

---

[1]In fact, path conditions form only a preorder. Modulo equivalence one obtains a partial order [SRK06, Ram94].

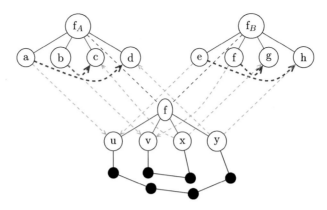

Figure 5.3: Abstract structure of multiple invocations of method f

two realizable paths at call site A (left), namely from parameter a to d and from b to c. These transitive dependences, stemming from dependences in method f, are represented in the SDG as summary edges (dashed in Figure 5.3). The path from a to h is invalid, as parameters from one invocation cannot influence another invocation.

In the following, we will focus on path conditions where start and end node are in the same method (same-level), and will concentrate on object-oriented constructs. The general case, where start and end node of the path condition lie in different methods, can be constructed from concatenating several same-level conditions. However, this is not specific to Java and has been addressed in previous work [SRK06].

Path conditions factor out common subpaths with virtual decomposition [SRK06]; common subpaths between formal parameters connected by a summary edge have been found good candidates for such decomposition. Virtual decomposition ignores call and parameter-passing edges but includes summary edges instead. A specific Φ condition (which is conjunctively added to the execution condition) represents the condition for information flow along a summary edge [SRK06]. This condition is induced by the path condition between the corresponding formal parameters combined with conditions that represent parameter binding. In Figure 5.3 the condition between a and d would be:

$$\Phi(a \to d) \equiv u = a \wedge PC(u,y) \wedge d = y$$

Thus $PC(u,y)$ can be reused at other call sites with a different parameter binding.

Details of path condition generation are not presented here, but the reader should be aware that making path conditions work for full C and realistic programs required years of theoretical and practical work [Sne96, RS02, Rob05, SRK06]. The major steps include that programs must be transformed into single assignment form first (see above); and while PDG cycles can be ignored, due to the high number of cycle-free PDG paths in realistic programs, interval analysis for irreducible graphs must be exploited to obtain a hierarchy of nested sub-PDGs; BDDs are needed to minimize the size of path conditions. Today, the implementation ValSoft can handle C programs up to approx. 10000 LOC and generate path conditions in a few seconds or minutes.

5.3 Static Path Conditions for Java

In this section, we present the first path condition generator for Java which relies solely on static program analysis. Naturally, the main problem in generalizing path conditions from procedural languages like C to Java was the treatment of object-oriented features such as dynamic dispatch and dynamic type checks.

5.3.1 Overview

Path conditions are generated according to all possible dependence paths from the source to the target point and a constraint solver reduces these conditions to input values that trigger information flow between these two points. Such input values have been named "witnesses" in [SRK06], and may be quite helpful e.g. in law suits concerning security violations. However, [SRK06] only defines path conditions for procedural languages. A naive integration of object-oriented constructs in path conditions suffers from these conditions containing dynamic type checks, which constraint solvers cannot simplify statically. Thus witnesses cannot be generated, rendering these path conditions only a first step towards realistic applications.

This section presents a detailed study of object-oriented language constructs based on Java's language specification, as well as solutions for their integration into a path condition that contains only program variables and values. We start discussing dynamic type checks à la `instanceof` and extend the solutions found there to dynamic dispatch and exception handling. All these constructs are based on dynamic type checks. These checks can either be approximated conservatively, or — using program slicing — be transformed into a subcondition that no longer involves the program's types but ranges over program variables. Thus we present the first approach to generate realistic path conditions for Java. These conditions give more practical information than the conditions for dynamic dispatch presented in [HKS06], and allow constraint solvers to find input values that satisfy these conditions.

5.3.2 Dynamic Type Tests

In this section, we explore the precise semantics of the `instanceof` operator in order to utilize it in path conditions. Informally, the result of the expression `e instanceof T` is true iff the value of the expression e is not `null` and e has a runtime type that is below the type constant T in the type hierarchy [GJSB05]. A compile time error occurs, when no path exists in the type hierarchy from T to the static type of e. The language thus allows e to have a static type which is equal to or below T in the hierarchy, even though in that case, unless e is null, the expression will always evaluate to *true*. All this is well known, but path conditions require a precise formalization of the instanceof semantics.

Precise semantics for instanceof

Java's reference types are identical to the defined classes (and interfaces) in a program, so the terms type and class (interface) are used interchangeably. We write $A <: B$ if A is a subclass of B. A type hierarchy is the transitive closure of the subclass ($<:$) relation. Let $\mathfrak{C}$ be the set of class types, $\mathfrak{J}$ the set of interface types, $\mathfrak{R} = \mathfrak{C} \cup \mathfrak{J}$ the set of reference types, $\mathfrak{P}$ the set of primitive types and $\mathfrak{A}$ the set of array types. Further let $\mathfrak{S} = \{\text{java.io.Serializable}, \text{Cloneable}, \text{Object}\}$. The notation $e : \tau$ denotes that e has dynamic/runtime type τ, and $e :: \tau$ denotes static typing, respectively.

The type hierarchy induces concrete sets of types that satisfy the instanceof operator: Let Γ_τ denote the set of types in the hierarchy that evaluate to *true* in the instanceof τ expression, i.e.

$$e \text{ instanceof } \tau \equiv e : \rho \wedge \rho \in \Gamma_\tau \tag{5.3}$$

For brevity, we assume a special null-type with $\Gamma_{\text{null}} = \varnothing$. Then the definition of instanceof in the JLS [GJSB05] requires:
If $\tau \in \mathfrak{R}$ then

$$\rho \in \Gamma_\tau \quad \text{iff} \quad (\rho \in \mathfrak{C} \wedge \rho <: \tau) \vee (\rho \in \mathfrak{A} \wedge \tau \in \mathfrak{S}) \tag{5.4}$$

else if $\tau \in \mathfrak{A}$ then

$$\rho \in \Gamma_\tau \quad \text{iff} \quad \rho = \rho'[\,] \wedge \tau = \tau'[\,] \wedge \rho' \in \Gamma_{\tau'} \tag{5.5}$$

else if $\tau \in \mathfrak{P}$ then

$$\rho \in \Gamma_\tau \quad \text{iff} \quad \rho = \tau \tag{5.6}$$

The last term of equation (5.5) corresponds to Java's covariant array anomaly, that may result in type safety problems when storing into arrays. When the complete type hierarchy is given at analysis time, Γ_τ can easily be computed from the type hierarchy with e.g. class hierarchy analysis (CHA) [DGC95] or more refined analyses like rapid type analysis (RTA) [BS96] and the XTA algorithm [TP00]. A few special cases of Γ_τ are of high importance:

$$\Gamma_{Object} = \mathfrak{C} \cup \mathfrak{A}, \text{ which is infinite in principle}^2 \text{ due to } \mathfrak{A} \tag{5.7}$$

$$\Gamma_{Cloneable} = \{X \mid X <: Cloneable\} \cup \bigcup_{c \in \mathfrak{R} \cup \mathfrak{A} \cup \mathfrak{P}} c[\,] \tag{5.8}$$

$$\Gamma_{\tau[\,]} = \bigcup_{c \in \Gamma_\tau} c[\,] \tag{5.9}$$

The last equation hereby describes how to resolve an array type ($\tau[\,]$) based on the Γ_τ of its base type.

---

[2]In Java, the number of array dimensions is bounded by 255 [LY99].

```
1  // pre: B extends A
2  public class InstanceOfExample {
3    static boolean pred = true;
4    public static void main(String[] args) {
5      A a = pred ? new A() : new B();
6      System.out.println(instanceOf(a));
7    }
8    public static int instanceOf(A sel) {
9      int result = 0;
10     if (sel instanceof B)
11       result = 42;
12     return result;
13   }
14 }
```

Figure 5.4: An example for the instanceof operator

5.3.3 Path Conditions for instanceof

The Γ_τ constructed in the previous section are necessary to describe the generation of precise path conditions for instanceof. Note that these path conditions still contain dynamic type tests of the form $expr : \rho$; these will be removed by transformation in the next section.

Algorithm 10 Path condition for instanceof

Input: An expression $expr$ instanceof τ
Output: Corresponding path condition with dynamic type tests.

1: **if** $\tau = Object \vee (\tau \in \mathfrak{S} \wedge expr :: \tau'[]) \vee (\tau = \tau'[] \wedge \tau' \in \mathfrak{P})$ **then**
2:    **return** $expr \neq null$
3: **else**
4:    **return** $expr \neq null \wedge (\bigvee_{\gamma_i \in \Gamma_\tau} expr : \gamma_i)$
5: **end if**

Algorithm 10 presents how path conditions for instanceof expressions are computed; the algorithm is based on the precise instanceof semantics above. The differences between equations (5.4)–(5.6) and the algorithm stem from optimizations which are done at compile time, see the JLS [GJSB05]. For example, $\Gamma_{int[]} = \{int[]\}$, therefore the type test is done at compile time and no further runtime constraint is required but the test for null.

Obviously, the more refined Γ_τ is determined, the more precise the condition for the instanceof expression becomes. As points-to analysis is usually a prerequisite for precise slicing, points-to results can be leveraged to increase precision of Γ_τ. If the number of possible runtime types thereby reduces to less than or equal to 1, the path condition can immediately be reduced to $true$ (if the remaining type is an instance of τ, provided that the expression can never be null) or $false$. As usual, determining Γ_τ requires whole-program analysis either without reflection, or using conservative approximations (e.g. [LWL05]).

For the example program in Figure 5.4, the initial path condition between the parameter in line 8 and the return value in line 12 is

$$PC(\texttt{sel}_8, \texttt{result}_{12}) \equiv sel \text{ instanceof } B$$

as no other path between these program points exists in the PDG. Since B is no special type, Algorithm 1 replaces this condition by

$$PC(\texttt{sel}_8, \texttt{result}_{12}) \equiv sel \neq null \wedge sel : B$$

Exploiting backward slices in type tests

Path conditions for `instanceof`, as described so far, are of limited practical value, as they may contain type tests with no link to variable values (e.g. $sel : B$), and thus cannot serve as a witness. This section presents a novel technique to transform such conditions into a form containing only program variables and values, which thus can be used to generate witnesses. The fundamental idea is to *replace variables in runtime type checks by their backward slice.*

The conditions in the last section contained terms of the form $\bigvee_{i \in \Gamma_\tau}(e : \gamma_i)$ for some type τ, that are essentially runtime checks. Program slicing offers a means to replace these conditions with terms that only reference program variables. The term $e : \gamma_i$ depends on the last definition of e and will evaluate to *true* only if e had been assigned an instance of γ_i. The program dependence graph allows to resolve places from which γ_i-allocations reach a given statement. This value flow is contained in the so-called backward data slice [BGS97], or more precisely, the statements in a thin slice [SFB07]. In a backward data slice, only data dependences and parameter edges are traversed, but control dependences are not. This variant yields only those statements whose value may have an influence on the slicing criterion. The thin slice is even more restrictive, in that it only computes value flow, i.e. those statements that define a value that is used at the criterion node, which is exactly what we are interested in.

The following steps are to be taken to generate this refined path condition:

1. Determine the basic path condition p according to Algorithm 10 in section 5.3.2

2. Compute the backward data slice or thin slice for the parameter e of the `e instanceof` τ operator

3. For each type in p extract the allocation sites of that type from the slice

4. Concatenate the path conditions from the program's start node to each of these allocation sites and from there to the `instanceof` expression with *logical or*

5. Replace the dynamic type checks in the basic path condition with the term generated in the last step.

Formally, with $J_i := \{a_{i,j} \in BS_{thin}(e) \mid a_{i,j}$ is an allocation site of type $\gamma_i\}$ we obtain the fundamental equation

$$e : \gamma_i \Rightarrow \bigvee_{j=1}^{|J_i|} \Big(PC(\texttt{Start}, a_{i,j}) \wedge PC(a_{i,j}, e) \Big) \qquad (5.10)$$

Informally, when e has runtime type γ_i, the program must have passed an allocation site of that type, and this is only possible at one of the allocation sites that reach expression e. Interprocedural reaching definitions are modeled in the thin slice. $PC(\texttt{Start}, a_{i,j})$ in equation (5.10) is necessary to reach allocation site $a_{i,j}$ (included in the thin slice) from the program's beginning, and $PC(a_{i,j}, e)$ is required to get from there to expression e. Note that taking one of these paths (i.e. $PC(\texttt{Start}, a_{i,j}) \wedge PC(a_{i,j}, e)$ holds) does not guarantee that e has dynamic type $a_{i,j}$ as slicing may be conservative, so equation (5.10) is only an implication.

This equation has the additional advantage that the number of terms becomes finite due to the finite number of allocation sites, as opposed to the theoretically infinite sets $\Gamma_{\tau[]}$. If the program representation contains all default initializations of variables explicitly, tests for $\texttt{null}$ can be omitted if the backward data slice does not contain such a value.

Considering the example in Figure 5.4 again, the condition from Algorithm 10 ($sel \neq null \wedge sel : B$) needs to be refined using equation (5.10). The test for $\texttt{null}$ is redundant, as all program paths define $\texttt{sel}$ with a non-$\texttt{null}$ value. The backward data slice of $\texttt{sel}$ yields both allocations in line 5, where only the second has appropriate type. Hence equation (5.10) collapses to

$$PC(\texttt{sel}_8, \texttt{result}_{12}) \equiv sel : B \equiv \big((pred = true) \wedge !pred \wedge true \big) \equiv false \quad (5.11)$$

Thus the parameter $\texttt{sel}$ cannot influence the outcome of this method, even though the program slice says so.

5.3.4 Dynamic Dispatch

Dynamic dispatch has great influence on path conditions: In contrast to statically bound methods, a virtual method call might have multiple possible target methods, one of which is executed at runtime according to the type of the target object. As an example, Figure 5.5 shows a method invocation site for a target object of static type $\texttt{A}$, which could dispatch either to $\texttt{A.f()}$ or $\texttt{B.f()}$. The invocation site holds two parameter nodes $\texttt{a}$ and $\texttt{b}$ where two summary edges (dashed) model the transitive flow that is possible between the formal parameters in the possible target methods.

A naive path condition

Since it is statically unknown which target method is executed, one might obtain the following naive path condition for dynamic dispatch of method $\texttt{f}$, which simply disjuncts all possible cases:

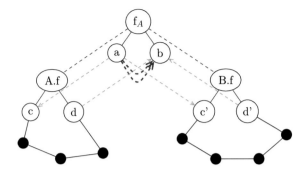

Figure 5.5: Virtual method call with two possible targets and summary edges

$$PC_{\mathtt{f}}(x,y) \equiv \bigvee_{i=1}^{n} PC_{\gamma_i.\mathtt{f}}(x,y) \qquad (5.12)$$

where x and y are in general two actual parameters of the call (connected by a summary node), $PC_{\gamma_i.\mathtt{f}}(x,y)$ is the condition of the invocation target for type γ_i between the formal parameter nodes corresponding to x and y. Note that not all subclasses must redefine $\mathtt{f}$, so $\gamma_i.\mathtt{f}$ might in fact reference a definition of $\mathtt{f}$ in a superclass of γ_i. For example, if C <: B <: A and only C and A (re)define $\mathtt{f}$, then B.f is actually A.f.

For Figure 5.5, equation (5.12) yields

$$PC(a,b) \equiv \big((c = a) \wedge PC_A(c,d) \wedge (b = d)\big) \\ \vee \big((c' = a) \wedge PC_B(c',d') \wedge (b = d')\big)$$

For the example program in Figure 5.6, the path condition between x and y on line 11 would be:

$$PC(x,y) \equiv PC_A(x,y) \vee PC_B(x,y) \vee PC_C(x,y) \\ \equiv x < 1 \vee x < 2 \vee x < 3 \equiv x < 3 \quad (*)$$

where PC_A, PC_B, PC_C are the standard path conditions for the three (re)definitions of f between the formal parameter nodes corresponding to x and y.

While this path condition is correct (it is a necessary condition for information flow) and easy to build, it is too imprecise since the program semantics disallows more than one target method. We will therefore develop an approach to handle dynamic dispatch similar to the `instanceof` expression in the last section.

Exploiting slices again

Previous work [HKS06] already presented a first step towards interprocedural path conditions, precisely expressing the semantics of dynamic dispatch. The

```
1  class A {
2    int result = 42;
3    int f(int x) {
4      if (x < 1)
5        result = x;
6      return result;
7    }
8    public static void main(String[] args) {
9      A o = new B();
10     int x = 2;
11     int y = o.f(x);
12 }}
13 class B extends A{
14   int f(int x) {
15     if (x < 2)
16       result = x;
17     return result;
18 }}
19 class C extends A {
20   int f(int x) {
21     if (x < 3)
22       result = x;
23     return result;
24 }}
```

Figure 5.6: Example program for dynamic binding

basic terms essentially become *implications* on the target object's runtime type.[3] For the example program in Figure 5.6, the path condition between x and y on line 11 would be:

$$PC(x,y) \equiv (o : A \Rightarrow PC_A(x,y)) \wedge (o : B \Rightarrow PC_B(x,y))$$
$$\wedge (o : C \Rightarrow PC_C(x,y)) \quad (**)$$

In general, for a dynamically dispatched call y = o.f(x), the JLS [GJSB05] induces the following fundamental condition:

$$PC_\mathbf{f}(x,y) \equiv \bigwedge_{i=1}^{n} (o : \gamma_i \Rightarrow PC_{\gamma_i.\mathbf{f}}(x,y)) \quad (5.13)$$

An alternative formulation of this condition is:

$$PC_\mathbf{f}(x,y) \equiv \bigvee_{i=1}^{n} (o : \gamma_i \wedge PC_{\gamma_i.\mathbf{f}}(x,y)) \quad (5.14)$$

Theorem 5.1. *Let $o \neq$ null. Then*

$$\bigwedge_{i=1}^{n} (o : \gamma_i \Rightarrow PC_{\gamma_i.\mathbf{f}}(x,y)) \equiv \bigvee_{i=1}^{n} (o : \gamma_i \wedge PC_{\gamma_i.\mathbf{f}}(x,y))$$

---

[3] [HKS06] used 'instanceof' in the example, which might be misleading due to Java's **instanceof** operator. The formulae in this work present the exact semantics.

Proof. 1. "$\Rightarrow$": Let $\bigwedge_{i=1}^{n}(o : \gamma_i \Rightarrow PC_{\gamma_i.\mathtt{f}}(x, y))$. As exactly one of the potential target methods of dynamic dispatch will be executed, we know $\exists! \, k. \, o : \gamma_k$ (where γ_k is the run-time type of o). Thus from the premise we conclude $PC_{\gamma_k.\mathtt{f}}(x, y)$. Hence $o : \gamma_k \wedge PC_{\gamma_k.\mathtt{f}}(x, y),^4$ therefore $\bigvee_{i=1}^{n}(o : \gamma_i \wedge PC_{\gamma_i.\mathtt{f}}(x, y))$.

2. "$\Leftarrow$": Let $\bigvee_{i=1}^{n}(o : \gamma_i \wedge PC_{\gamma_i.\mathtt{f}}(x, y))$. As above we know that $\exists! \, k. \, o : \gamma_k$. Then also $\exists! \, k. \, o : \gamma_k \wedge PC_{\gamma_k.\mathtt{f}}(x, y)$ holds. Now let $i \in 1..n$. If $i \neq k$, then $\neg(o : \gamma_i)$, thus the implication $o : \gamma_i \Rightarrow PC_{\gamma_i.f}(x, y)$ holds trivially. If $i = k$, by assumption $PC_{\gamma_i.\mathtt{f}}(x, y)$ holds and hence the implication $o : \gamma_i \Rightarrow PC_{\gamma_i.\mathtt{f}}(x, y).^5$ Thus $\bigwedge_{i=1}^{n}(o : \gamma_i \Rightarrow PC_{\gamma_i.\mathtt{f}}(x, y))$. □

The proof for theorem 5.1 relies on the fact that not more than one of the disjunctions can be satisfied at the same time, and holds provided $o \neq$ null. In case $o =$ null, formula (5.14) is more precise than (5.13), as it correctly evaluates to false: a flow of information through the method body is impossible, since an exception is thrown. Equation (5.14) is therefore *stronger* [SRK06] (i.e. more favorable) than (5.13) and especially than equation (5.12), as we add conjunctive terms in equation (5.14).

However, both path conditions are of limited practical value, as they again contain dynamic type tests and thus cannot serve as a witness. But again equation (5.10) is applicable to this condition, so the dynamic type tests can be transformed to a complex path condition with no explicit type tests. In general, we obtain the equation

$$PC_{\mathtt{f}}(x, y) \equiv \bigvee_{i=1}^{n}\left(\left(\bigvee_{j=1}^{|J_i|} PC(\mathtt{Start}, a_{i,j}) \wedge PC(a_{i,j}, o)\right) \wedge PC_{\gamma_i.\mathtt{f}}(x, y)\right) \quad (5.15)$$

Note that the condition of equation (5.15) is slightly weaker (but still conservative) than equation (5.14), as equation (5.10) is no equivalence but an implication. For Figure 5.6, we obtain:

$$PC(x, y) \equiv (false \wedge PC_{\mathtt{A}}(x, y)) \vee (true \wedge PC_{\mathtt{B}}(x, y)) \vee (false \wedge PC_{\mathtt{C}}(x, y))$$
$$\equiv x < 2 \quad (***)$$

as the backward data slice contains only the allocation in line 9, so this condition is more precise than the basic formula (5.12). Note that ($**$) was already more precise than ($*$), while ($***$) now collapses to a simple condition without type tests "$x < 2$", which is more precise than the "$x < 3$" in ($*$).

5.3.5 Exceptions

In principle any subtype of `Throwable` can be caught in Java, even subtypes of `Error`. The latter indicate a VM failure from which recovery is typically not possible, so catching `Errors` or `Throwable` is discouraged and not discussed in this paper.

---

[4]Note that in general $((A \Rightarrow B) \wedge A) \Rightarrow (A \wedge B)$
[5]Note that in general $(A \wedge B) \Rightarrow (A \Rightarrow B)$.

```
1  public static void main(String[] args) {
2    System.out.println(exceptionMethod(1));
3  }
4  public static int exceptionMethod(int i) {
5    try {
6      return 5/i;
7    } catch (ArithmeticException e) {
8      return 0;
9    } catch (RuntimeException e) {
10     return Integer.MAX_VALUE;
11 }}
```

Figure 5.7: Example for exception handling

As finally blocks are always executed, they can be incorporated into the CFG as usual and do not impose new challenges for path conditions. However, catch blocks can alter the control and data flow and must therefore be treated accordingly. It is possible to have multiple catch blocks for the same try block. In this case, the appropriate handler is determined according to the exception's class. The (textually) first catch block a thrown exception matches handles that exception, matching is done according to the instanceof relation [LY99].

In order to generate appropriate path conditions for this well-known exception behavior pattern, we model multiple catch as follows: Multiple catch blocks can be translated to a typeswitch construct which is branched to when an exception is raised. This modeling results in control dependences labeled with type boundaries, for which execution conditions based on instanceof expressions can be leveraged in a straightforward manner. If multiple blocks would match, it is conservative to have multiple conditions evaluate to $true$. However, to represent Java's semantics precisely and to achieve maximum precision, we need to ensure that types that are caught in previous catch blocks may not evaluate to true.

Formally, let $E = < e_1, \ldots, e_k >$ be the sequence of exception handlers associated with a try block with type boundaries e_i. Then the control condition for the typeswitch branch involves a dynamic type test of the form $e : \rho \wedge \rho \in \Gamma_{e_i}$. Using the adjusted definition of $\Gamma'_{e_i} = \Gamma_{e_i} \setminus (\bigcup_{j=1}^{i-1} \Gamma_{e_j})$ represents the exact semantics of exception handling and thus will report more precise results when applied to Algorithm 10 and equation (5.10).

As an example consider Figure 5.7, where the path condition between parameter i and the second catch block is to be computed. The original path condition yields:

$$i = 0 \wedge exc_1 \in \Gamma_{\texttt{RuntimeExc}}$$
$$\equiv i = 0 \wedge (exc_1 : \texttt{RuntimeExc} \vee exc_1 : \texttt{ArithmethicExc})$$
$$\equiv i = 0 \wedge (i = 0 \vee false) \equiv i = 0$$

as no other exception but ArithmeticException can be thrown in exceptionMethod, while Algorithm 10 with the refined Γ' will result in the condition

139

$$i = 0 \land exc_1 \in \Gamma'_{\texttt{RuntimeExc}} \equiv i = 0 \land exc_1 : \texttt{RuntimeExc} \equiv i = 0 \land false \equiv false$$

showing that this `catch` block is actually dead code.

Interprocedural Exceptions

Java supports two types of exceptions: Unchecked and checked exceptions. The former are any subtype of `RuntimeException` with the main purpose of signaling a problem of bytecode interpretation. Most bytecode instructions involved with object references and array access may for example throw `NullpointerExceptions` or `ArrayIndexOutOfBoundsExceptions`. Nearly every method in Java might throw an exception, and this needs special attention when modeling interprocedural exception handling. For each invocation site, our SDG contains two return value nodes (one for the usual return value and one for an uncaught exception), and two successors: one if method invocation terminated normally and the other for abrupt termination due to an uncaught exception [CPS+99]. Those two successors are control dependent on the call site. However, the predicate of the call site is not the result of the call but induced by the semantics of our model. In our SDG it corresponds to the term $exc \neq null$, where exc is the variable that stores the uncaught exception. Therefore, the control dependences can be viewed as summarizing the conditions which lead or do not lead to abrupt termination.[6] In a conservative approximation, these conditions can be set to $true$, assuming that both cases are feasible.

A more precise modeling retraces the conditions for abrupt termination to occur. This corresponds to generating the subconditions between the invocation node and the return value node for normal termination, and the exception node for abrupt termination, respectively. Considering Figure 5.7 again, the `print` statement is only executed, if `exceptionMethod` terminates normally. As we have already seen, all exceptions in `exceptionMethod` are caught, so the print statement is always executed, the PC for normal termination of `exceptionMethod` reduces to $true$.

5.3.6 Concurrency

Another important language feature of Java, namely concurrency, has been addressed in previous work already. Two approaches have been proposed in [SRK06] to generate conditions in the presence of concurrency: Interference dependence (inter-thread data dependence) can either be treated like usual data dependence. However, since interference is not transitive, this will result in overly conservative conditions. Alternatively, only possible program executions, so-called *threaded witness*threaded witnesses, are considered valid paths for path condition computation, which requires more expensive slicing and chopping algorithms. An evaluation of precise concurrent slicing algorithms can be found in Giffhorn and Hammer's work [GH09].

---

[6]This is equivalent to manually checking for error codes in C

140

5.3.7   Path Conditions for Information Flow Control

When we discover an interference at a statement s where the required security level $R(s)$ is not larger than the actual (computed) security level $S(s)$, we can investigate the source of this interference. We distinguish between *immediate* and *transitive* interference. The immediate interference exists between s and its predecessors which lead to the computed security level $S(s)$. Usually, only a subset of the predecessors is responsible for the interference—it is the minimal subset $N \subseteq pred(s)$ that lead to $S(s)$: $S(s) = \bigsqcup_{y \in N} S(y)$.

Path conditions give the condition PI of the immediate interference and we can compute it through

$$PI = \bigwedge_{y \in N} PC(y, s).$$

Often, we are more interested in the *transitive* interference, i.e. the interference between a statement s with a required security level of l and a statement x with a provided security level p, where there is a path $x \rightarrow^* s$ which "transmits" p to s. To investigate the transitive interference, we use the correspondence between slicing and noninterference. The first step is to compute the backwards slice $BS(s)$ that contains all statements that may influence s. From $BS(s)$ we extract all statements with a provided security level as the possible set of information sources:

$$T = \{x \in BS(s) \mid x \in \mathrm{dom}\ P\}$$

The computed security level cannot be smaller as (or not comparable to) any provided security level at its sources: $\forall x \in T : P(x) \leq S(s)$. Again, we need the minimal subset T' of T that computes $S(s)$: $S(s) = \bigsqcup_{y \in T'} S(y)$. Path conditions give the condition PT of the transitive interference and we can compute it through

$$PT = \bigwedge_{y \in T'} PC(y, s)$$

Note that there may exist multiple minimal subsets N and T' and we might want to examine all of them.

5.4   Dynamic Path Conditions in Dependence Graphs

The previous sections developed analyses that statically enforce a certain security policy. Ensuring that security breaches are impossible at compile time is favorable to registering a violation at runtime, where at least the information is leaked, that some illicit event has happened. Still, static checks can only assert the validity of the specified properties. For unforeseen incidents security-sensitive modules usually contain some sort of "flight recorder". It allows the a posteriori reconstruction of problems leading to a—possibly fatal—error.

This section presents a new approach leveraging data recorded during program execution—the program *trace*—for the a posteriori detection and isolation of problem causes. The trace is used to improve precision in two ways, which may as well be combined: First, a dynamic slicing algorithm identifies all statements that actually influenced the fatal statement during program execution.

The dynamic slice is generally much smaller than the static slice and thus, a smaller set of statements has to be examined. If a statement in the slice is suspicious, a path condition can be computed between the suspicious and the fatal statement. Path condition generation is based on a chop between the suspicious and the fatal statement. The dynamic chop between these statements is, again, generally much smaller than the static chop (chops contain the statements that participate in an influence from a source to a target statement). Thus, a dynamic chop contains a smaller number of paths between the two statements, leading to a less conservative path condition. Second, the observed values of program variables are transformed into additional logical constraints, which, conjunctively combined, improves the precision of path conditions.

This dynamic path condition allows the precise reconstruction of the scenario that lead to the fatal error (*post-mortem analysis*). If the dynamic path condition is unsatisfiable, there was definitely no influence between the given statements even though the dynamic chop indicated otherwise. But if the path condition is satisfiable, it serves as a "witness" for the illegal information flow: A constraint solver will resolve the path condition to input values which triggered the illegal flow. These input values can be given to the program again and the influence becomes visible once more. In case of safety violations, these input values thus serve as witnesses for the illegal behavior.

5.4.1 Program Tracing

Trace data, also known as a runtime protocol of variable bindings and their def-use locations, plays a role for dynamic slicing (cf. Section 5.4.2) and for refinement of path conditions (cf. Section 5.4.3).

To collect trace data one has to execute the program in a controlled environment, which motivated the employment of a standard debugger like the gdb. We implemented a debugger driver that abstracts away from the actual debugger in use, offering the tracer a standard interface for controlled execution.

The used tracing approach is based on a static dependence graph. Any information that the tracer (and the debugger) needs for controlled execution, like where to set break points and used/defined variables, are extracted from a fine-grained system dependence graph (SDG). Fine-grained means that statement nodes are expanded to an *Abstract Syntax Tree* (*AST*) [Kri03a]. This fine-grained structure forms a prerequisite for building path conditions in general. It also allows detailed tracing of variable bindings, where variables that need to be recorded before statement execution (variables used for the computation) are distinguished from the variable(s) defined by the statement, which is recorded after execution. Thus every statement is mapped to a set of variables and their role (Definition, Use). The control dependence information is extracted from the SDG.

In the tracing phase, the program is executed statement by statement, where for every statement the attached variables are traced, either before or after the execution of the statement. For procedure calls the tracer maps the actual parameters to the formal parameters. This implies a Use and Definition role at the same time, which are traced before the execution of the method call. Note

1	**LINE** 11	1	**LINE** 11
2	USE Z	2	USE Z
3	DEF X	3	DEF X
4	**LINE** 12	4	**LINE** 12
5	USE X	5	USE X
6	**LINE** 13	6	**LINE** 13
7	USE Y	7	USE Y
8	DEF X	8	
9	**LINE** 14	9	**LINE** 14
10	USE X	10	USE X

Figure 5.8: Incorrect dependence by gap in protocol

that a trace 'inlines' the called procedures and thus, is automatically context-sensitive.

Third Party Code

A problem well known in static program analysis arises for dynamic analyses as well: Libraries (especially provided by a third party) usually do not provide source code nor the debugging information needed to collect tracing data. I.e. any side-effect produced by a library call does not generate the tracing information to produce correct dynamic dependences. When the debugging information is extracted from the static SDG that problem arises already during construction of the SDG. But even if one did not depend on a static dependence graph would one face the same problem.

A possible solution has been employed by static analysis designers for some years now: One writes stubs for those library methods and conservatively adds the summary dependences at the invocation point.

Incomplete Traces

Besides the problem of third party code, other reasons exist, why a trace could be incomplete: Either the tracer looses information, maybe on purpose for restricted memory, or because of limitations of the tracing approach. But it depends on the purpose whether the detail of the traced data suffices to gain sound results. As mentioned at the beginning of this section, our goals are dynamic slicing resp. chopping (cf. Section 5.4.2) and the refinement of path conditions with dynamic variable data (cf. Section 5.4.3).

Dynamic slicing does not depend on the actual values of variables but on the def-use relations of variables. Missing entries in the trace will most probably lead to false dependences and thus incorrect dynamic slices. As an example consider Figure 5.8. While in the left protocol line 10 depends on the definition in line 8, this entry has been missed in the protocol on the right. The dynamic slice will determine a dependence to line 3 then, which is incorrect.

With gdb controlling the program execution and the fine-grained variable tracing, one cannot guarantee the correctness of the program trace in all cases: First one has to assert that one line of source code has not more than one statement. Code like x = a + x; x++; will not result in a detailed protocol since the debugger works only line-based and will thus report only one definition and one use of x instead of two, respectively. Tools like GNU indent produce code that circumvents these problems.

Multiple assignments to the same variable in one statement like x = a + x++ are undefined in ANSI-C and will thus be ignored. Under certain circumstances, however, our technique will produce fragmentary traces in special cases: a statement with two method calls like x = f(a) + g(b) may yield an incorrect value for b as the debugger cannot stop between the method calls to allow accurate parameter tracing. A solution to this problem is the combination of static slicing and dynamic slicing similar to [ZG04]. Another solution would be to transform the source program to a program that has at most one assignment or one function call per statement.

5.4.2 Dynamic Slicing

Dynamic program slicing was introduced by Korel and Laski [KL88]. Dynamic slicing builds a *dynamic dependence graph* (*DDG*) computed from the real dependences arising during program execution. Therefore, a dynamic dependence graph usually is considerably smaller than a static dependence graph, which has to relay on conservative approximations not to relinquish soundness.

For illustration consider Figure 5.1 again. If the execution trace is 1,2,3,4,7,9 then the static backward slice of node 9 is the whole graph. The dynamic slice of 9 does, in contrast, not contain the statements 1 and 5 as those did not contribute to the value of z in the given run.

Once a program trace has been collected, dynamic slicing typically falls to two tasks: In the *preprocessing* phase a dynamic dependence graph is generated by processing the collected data. In the *slicing* phase this graph is traversed to build the dynamic slice for the given slicing criteria.

A naive approach to dynamic slicing would mark all statements encountered during program execution, reduce the static dependence graph to the corresponding nodes, and do static slicing on that graph. This approach is, however, imprecise which can be illustrated on Figure 5.1: With the execution trace 1,2,3,4,7,2,3,4,5,9 the naive algorithm would mark all nodes visited, yielding a dynamic slice that contains the whole graph. Node 5 had no effect on node 7, though, as the definition of b took place after the use. So, nodes 1 and 5 should not be in the dynamic slice.

As a remedy, Agrawal [AH90] proposed not to work on the static dependence graph but on the tracing protocol, which shows a linear program with all loops unrolled. From that data the dynamic dependence graph needs to be computed. Its nodes usually represent basic blocks rather than single statements, which build the nodes of the static variant. Dependences point from a variable use to its last definition. It may be a bit confusing that dynamic edges are reversed compared to static edges. Dynamic (backward) slicing thus follows all edges starting from the slicing criterion:

$$dBS(y) = \{x \mid y \rightarrow^* x\}$$

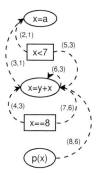

Figure 5.9: Dynamic data dependence graph for figure 5.2. Control dependence edges are omitted for readability

Since the length of the runtime protocol is in principle unbounded, the space requirement of the context-sensitive dynamic dependence graph for long program runs explodes. Therefore several ways to compact this graph were proposed.

Agrawal [AH90] noted that the number of statements in a program is bounded and hence, the number of different slices must be bounded, too. He found that nodes with the same transitive dynamic dependences could be merged. This graph was called *dynamic dependence graph!reduced* (*RDDG*)Reduced Dynamic Dependence Graph. While this representation is quite compact and gives a program slice in $O(1)$ (the transitive dependences are stored in every node), different instances of the same node (e.g. in a loop) cannot be distinguished. So the reduced size of the graph results in a loss of precision.

Context-sensitivity is a property that is not granted with such an approach. As a consequence of the linearity of the trace, however, dynamic slicing can be done in a context-sensitive manner, if labels are added to the edges [ZGZ03, ZGZ05]. The labels contain additional information to disambiguate the distinct execution instances of the statements that the edge links. Zhang et al. call this dynamic graph the *dynamic data dependence graph*. As an example consider Figure 5.2 together with the execution trace 1,2,3,4,2,3,4,5. The graph contains edge labels that capture the execution time of the involved statements. The check whether x<7 on line 2 is executed at time 2 and depends on the value of x computed in line 1 at time 1. Thus the edge contains these timestamps: $(2,1)$. The node corresponding to line 3 (we will use the terms node/statement/line interchangeably for this example) is dependent on the execution of statement 1 in the first instance of the while-loop, represented by an edge marked $(3,1)$; in the second it is dependent on the last instance of itself: the loop edge is marked with the execution times $(6,3)$.

The dynamic program slice is computed in the dynamic data dependence graph using the following formula (let $x \rightarrow_l y$ denote the edge from x to y with the timestamp label $l = (t_1, t_2)$):

$$dBS_{cs}(y,t) = \{x \mid \exists \text{ Path } p : (y = x_0 \rightarrow_{l_0} \cdots \rightarrow_{l_{n-1}} x_n = x) :$$
$$l_0 = (t, t_0) \wedge$$
$$\forall 0 < i < n-1 : l_i = (t_{i-1}, t_i) \wedge l_{i+1} = (t_i, t_{i+1})\}$$

In our example, the dynamic slice of the first execution of line 2 (with timestamp 2) is line 2 itself and line 1. Line 3 is not included, as the edge with timestamp 5 is not followed. Starting from line 2 with timestamp 5, however, we will have to include line 3 and come back to line 1. This small example already illustrates the power of edge labels.

Similar to the dynamic program slice, it is possible to define a dynamic program chop in the dynamic data dependence graph:

$$dCH_{cs}(x,y,t_x,t_y) = \{x_i \mid \exists \text{ Path } p : (y = x_0 \rightarrow_{l_0} \cdots \rightarrow_{l_{n-1}} x_n = x) :$$
$$l_0 = (t_y, t_0) \wedge l_{n-1} = (t_{n-2}, t_x) \wedge$$
$$\forall 0 < i < n-1 : l_i = (t_{i-1}, t_i) \wedge l_{i+1} = (t_i, t_{i+1})\}$$

A dynamic chop contains all nodes that are part of a path from x to y in the dynamic data dependence graph that starts at y with timestamp t_y and ends at x with timestamp t_x.

The dynamic data dependence graph is not restricted in space, though, and the graph can only be built if the runtime protocol is entirely processed which may take too much time for long-running applications. Zhang et al. [ZGZ03, ZGZ05] thus proposed—apart from this *full preprocessing* algorithm (FP)—two variants that do not build the graph beforehand: *no preprocessing* (NP) and *limited preprocessing* (LP). The NP algorithm entirely forbears from constructing the dependence graph and, when slicing, runs back the linear trace to find the most recent definition of the given variable. Hence, NP has a worst case complexity of $O(N^2)$ which is unacceptable for large slices or for many slicing criteria. Even with the use of caching by marking statements already in the slice not to be followed again, this complexity cannot be lowered. The best compromise between the FP and NP algorithms is, according to the authors, the LP algorithm, which introduces summary information at a given offset between two such entries in the tracing protocol. Still, the complexity cannot be reduced by an order of magnitude but only by a constant factor.

We implemented all the mentioned algorithms for dynamic slicing and evaluated them on our test suite (cf. Section 7.4.2). Our experiments approve the results of Zhang et al. [ZGZ03, ZGZ05]. On average over 100 slicing criteria for `agrep`, the cached LP algorithm was, with about 20 seconds and 4.7 MB memory, faster than NP with about 21 sec and FP with 26 sec, consuming insignificantly more memory than the NP algorithm, which used 4.4 MB ram, and better than FP needing 6.4 MB.

5.4.3 Dynamic Path Conditions

Refinement by Dynamic Chopping

When constructing a path condition from a statement to another, all paths between those two statements are determined with a chop in the static dependence graph. As mentioned in Section 5.2.1, the accuracy of the path condition for the executed program can be increased if a dynamic chop is used instead. The dynamic dependence graph usually contains only the dependence edges that actually took place and thus the dynamic chop will yield a much smaller number of paths between those two statements.

As an example, consider Figure 5.1 again. If the execution trace is 1,2,3,4,7,9 then the dynamic chop between 2 and 9 is 2,3,4,7,9. Statement 5 is never executed in this setting and thus can be removed from the dynamic chop. A static chop would conservatively have to add it. With the dynamic chop one omits the paths 2,3,4,5,7,9 and 2,4,5,7,9 in the path condition between 2 and 9.

Although our path condition generator reuses partial information and thus half the number of paths does not yield a 50% shorter path condition, this small example already shows the impact of this refinement.

Refinement by Traced Values

In order to strengthen a given path condition PC with runtime information, the trace is analyzed to retrieve the variable assignments. As the analyzed program went through a series of assignment states during runtime, all of them have to be captured in a restrictive clause R. This clause, in turn, can be used to make path conditions stronger.

First, the intersection V of variables used in the path condition PC and the trace T is determined:

$$V = \{v \mid v \in var(T) \cap var(PC)\}$$

For each variable v the values it carried during the trace are extracted, let $\beta(v)$ be the set of values w_i that variable v has contained:

$$\beta(v) = (v = w_1) \vee (v = w_2) \vee \ldots$$

Now the restrictive clause R can be described as the conjunction of all variable value sets:

$$R = \bigwedge_{v_i \in V} \beta(v_i)$$

In order to make the path condition PC stronger, the results from Section 5.2.1 are used and both clauses are conjunctively combined

$$PC' = PC \wedge R$$

yielding the stronger and thus more precise path condition PC'.

Because of the SSA-like form, variables only match if their index numbers are the same, so that multiple assignments are handled. This makes it mandatory

```
 1 LINE  1
 2 USE  a_2  2
 3 DEF  x_1  2
 4 LINE  2
 5 USE  x_3  2
 6 LINE  3
 7 USE  y_5  2
 8 USE  x_6  2
 9 DEF  x_4  4
10 LINE  4
11 USE  x_7  4
12 LINE  2
13 USE  x_3  4
14 LINE  3
15 USE  y_5  2
16 USE  x_6  4
17 DEF  x_4  6
18 LINE  4
19 USE  x_7  6
20 LINE  2
21 USE  x_3  6
22 LINE  3
23 USE  y_5  2
24 USE  x_6  6
25 DEF  x_4  8
26 LINE  4
27 USE  x_7  8
28 LINE  5
29 USE  x_8  8
30 LINE  2
31 USE  x_3  8
```

Figure 5.10: A simple program trace for Figure 5.2

for the program trace to list variables along with their respective node numbers as in Figure 5.10 which shows a simple trace for a run of the program from Figure 5.2.

Note that the node numbers are different to the SSA-numbers from Figure 5.2 and thus, the path condition for a flow from line 1 to line 5 is $PC(1,5) = (x_3 < 7) \wedge (x_7 = 8)$. For this path condition the trace yields the variable assignments

$$R = (x_3 = 2 \vee x_3 = 4 \vee x_3 = 6 \vee x_3 = 8) \wedge (x_7 = 4 \vee x_7 = 6 \vee x_7 = 8)$$

Again, both clauses are conjunctively combined to $PC' = PC \wedge R$ yielding the stronger and thus more precise path condition PC':

$$PC' = (x_3 = 2 \vee x_3 = 4 \vee x_3 = 6) \wedge (x_7 = 8)$$

Correctness of Dynamic Path Conditions

Sometimes only fragments of a trace are available due to a "defective recorder" or intentionally to save memory. While fragmented traces are generally useless for dynamic slicing (see Section 5.4.1), they still hold valuable information for strengthening path conditions.

However, incomplete tracing information is prone to lead to wrong path conditions. For example, consider the simple path condition $(x > 1)$ for a program where the trace yields the restrictive clause

$$(x = 0 \lor x = 1)$$

while the variable assignment states actually were

$$(x = 0 \lor x = 1 \lor x = 2)$$

The restricted path condition

$$PC' = (x > 1) \land (x = 0 \lor x = 1) \equiv false$$

would be in contradiction to the actual program state $(x = 2)$ and thus definitely rules out data dependence where it may actually be possible.

To avoid unsound path conditions, it is conservatively assumed that there is an additional *unknown* value $\bot$ for each variable representing the assignments which occurred but were not traced due to some reason. This measure yields a correct conservatively restricted path condition being as precise as the fragmentation of the trace allows. For our example, the resulting path condition is

$$(x > 1) \land (x = 0 \lor x = 1 \lor x = \bot)$$
$$\equiv (x > 1 \land x = \bot) \equiv x > 1$$

Only if the completeness of the trace (at least for certain variables, see Section 5.4.1) can be guaranteed, one may abandon this conservative measure (for those variables).

It may seem that using this trick one doesn't gain any additional information of dynamic variable data. To show the advantage of variable traces containing unknown values, consider the path condition PC(1,5) of Figure 5.1. With a fragmented variable trace forming the conservative restrictive clause $(x = 5 \lor x = \bot) \land (n = 3 \lor n = \bot)$ the improved path condition from 1 to 5 will be:

$$PC(1,5) \equiv (n > 0 \land x > 0) \land (x = 5 \lor x = \bot) \land (n = 3 \lor n = \bot)$$

It is immediately clear that the traced variable values $x = 5$ and $n = 3$ may trigger an influence from line 1 to line 5.

This tiny example shows that while conservative restrictive clauses cannot be used to evaluate a clause of the path condition to *false*, they may reveal input values that triggered an illegal information flow.

5.4.4 Related Work

Symbolic execution is a technique that executes a program with symbols instead of concrete values for the parameters. During execution, a predicate Φ (initially *true*) is built that constrains the values. When a branch is taken, the predicate is updated to reflect the condition for that branch. As it represents the conditions for taking the current path through the CFG, it is often called *path condition* as well, however as it only represents the condition for taking a specific path, it is more like an execution condition in our work. Today's systems for symbolic execution are mainly based on theorem provers or model checking. Theorem prover based systems like in ESC/Java [FLL+02] require manual annotations to generate verification conditions, while our path conditions analyze a given chop fully automatically. Other systems rely on model checkers e.g. [DRH07] which are semi-automatic but need to cope with state explosion. Most symbolic execution systems perform a per-method analysis only, while our approach automatically generates precise interprocedural path conditions.

Recent work by Jhala has been focusing on path slicing [JM05]. It takes as input one particular path in the CFG and eliminates all the operations that are irrelevant towards the reachability of the target location. The result is a condition for the reachability of the target location, its infeasibility is sufficient for the infeasibility of the path. The technique does not work on the PDG but on the CFG only. It has shown effective for elimination of counterexamples provided by the model checker Blast. For our application this approach does not seem beneficial as it needs to check every single path on its own, while path conditions produce a necessary condition for all paths between two statements and share common subterms.

Parametric program slicing [FRT95] allows specification of constraints over the program's input. A term rewriting system extracts a program slice satisfying these constraints. Conditioned program slicing [CCL98] is a similar technique that slices based on a first order logic formula on the input variables. The conditioned slice is based on deleting statements while preserving the program's behavior. Both approaches differ from path conditions in that they do not determine input values but take them as input. In contrast, path conditions provide a logic formula that must be satisfied for an information flow to be feasible. Constraint solvers reduce this condition to input values that satisfy the formula.

Boolean path conditions as presented in this work and in [Sne96, RS02, Rob05, SRK06] cannot express temporal properties. For example, they cannot express that it is necessary for a specific flow that a loop condition holds and *later* it does no longer, such that the loop terminates. Boolean conditions become conservative when analyzing loops and conditions that involve loop variables. A recent approach by Lochbihler and Snelting [LS09] extends path conditions with temporal logic to circumvent these imprecisions. Witnesses are created by model checking instead of constraint solvers.

Dynamic Analyses Correctly and efficiently collecting trace data is a non-trivial task. Several solutions have been proposed in literature:

Venkatesh [Ven95] implemented a low-level approach for tracing C programs. His prototype implementation called SLICE instruments the source code to write a program trace during execution. With this experience, the authors recommend object-code instrumentation for future implementations together with several reasons. Nonetheless, this implementation is faster than tracing with a traditional debugger.

Zhang et al. [ZGZ03] follow a different low-level approach to create a program trace: The program source is compiled with the Trimaran system, a compiler for the Explicitly Parallel Instruction Computing (EPIC). An interpreter takes the generated object code and creates the program trace during execution. Since C programs are normally not interpreted, this approach is valid mostly for theoretical evaluations.

All low-level approaches usually do not slow down program execution as much as a debugger does. However, as our work is based on the static dependence graph which must be mappable to source, these approaches did not suit our needs.

Dynamic program slicing has been a topic in active research for several years now. Various approaches, either for dynamic slicing on its own, or combined with static elements have been proposed. To mention all of them would be out of scope of this work.

Chen et al. [CX01b] describe a dynamic slicing algorithm that is based on a static PDG providing the information where to set break points for the debugger. The static dependence graph is confined to the nodes and edges that have been visited to build the dynamic dependence graph. Slicing is done following all edges in that graph.

Tip [Tip95] embarks on a different strategy: He uses the abstract syntax tree (AST) instead of a dependence graph and interprets the program. The approach is language independent but only available for the custom-built language "L".

Zhang et al. recently proposed another way to reduce the vast amount of data that is stored in the program trace. They compute the dynamic slices during program execution and store them in binary decision diagrams (BDDs) [ZG04].

Wang et al. [WR04] presented a dynamic slicing technique for Java that compresses the program trace on-the-fly and obtains two to three orders of magnitude compression with little overhead. A lossless compression algorithm finds a high repetition pattern in the sequence of (memory and control) addresses captured by the tracer separately. They also propose a dynamic slicing algorithm which operates directly on the compressed data and can thus save the uncompressing time. Such an algorithm may not only be suitable for languages with extensive pointer usage. We expect the repetition pattern for our variable trace to yield a similar compression rate. Since the slicing algorithm runs on the compressed data with no dynamic dependence graph used, multiple slicing requests require traversing the trace multiple times at a significant time overhead.

Chapter 6

Implementation

All the analyses described in this thesis have been implemented. Figure 6.1 shows the architecture of the Valsoft/Joana system. This set of tools comprises several techniques for precise analysis of security properties. Other applications for the base techniques like slicing have been proposed in literature (see [BG96, dL01, HH01, BH04, Kri05, MM07]) but are beyond the scope of this thesis. The components of this diagram are described in more detail in the following sections.

6.1 Frontends

Currently, SDGs can be constructed for both C and Java code. For C, we extended the commercial slicer system CodeSurfer [ART03] with a plugin that creates files compatible with our graph format. This approach complements the Valsoft SDG generator created previously in our group [Kri03a]. Adding a commercial product to our tool suite allows cross-checking of results; one would naturally assume the commercial product more mature, if differences appear. However, CodeSurfer may admittedly become unsound for very large programs [And08]. The challenge in converting CodeSurfer dependence graphs arises as slicing forms a base technology for path conditions. Path conditions require a fine-grained SDG structure similar to an abstract syntax tree, but CodeSurfer supports only coarse-grained SDGs. Yet, CodeSurfer grants access to a control flow graph, such that postprocessing of its dependence graph together with the CFG yields the desired information.

For Java, this thesis defines a precise representation of bytecode programs (see chapter 2), and our generator reflects this design. It is based on the Harpoon/Flex compiler frontend from MIT.[1] This framework offers an SSA-based intermediate representation of bytecode, and inserts explicit checks at all instructions possibly throwing exceptions, such that control flow due to implicit and explicit exceptions is conservatively modeled. From there, our tool generates fine-grained (for path conditions) and coarse-grained (for all other analyses) system dependence graphs. First, a pointer analysis determines the call graph and points-to relations, after that the dependence graph for each method is

---

[1]This library has been abandoned by now, and is currently being replaced by a generator based on WALA (`wala.sourceforge.net`)

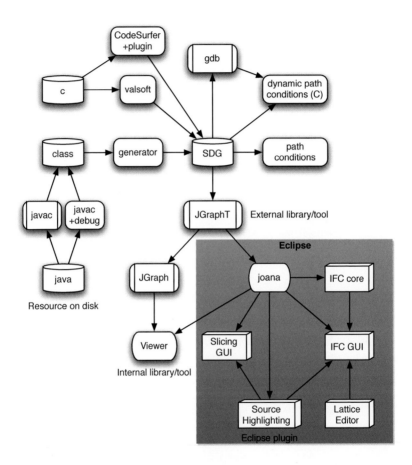

Figure 6.1: Valsoft/Joana architecture

created and interprocedural side-effects are incorporated. Finally data dependences due to these side-effects are inserted and optionally summary edges are computed. Interference dependences (see chapter 3) are added as requested.

6.1.1   Stubs

The Harpoon frontend accepted full bytecode for Java up to version 1.4. We found that the changes in executable bytecode for Java 1.5 were so marginal, that a small patch to that library now allows to parse bytecode up to version 1.6. However, the library is another issue. It is well known that as of JDK 1.4.2, even the simplest "Hello world" program loads 248 library classes! And for later versions the library is even bigger and more classes are loaded. Yet, many of these classes do not contribute to the transitive dependences of the analyzed program. For example, it does not matter *how* a special locale determines the upper and lower case version for a given character. What matters is that the resulting character depends on the input parameter. Such a transitive dependence can be modeled via *method stubs*. A stub is a placeholder method that models the necessary semantics of the original method such that all possible dependences are included into the dependence graph. Type systems use a quite similar technique to represent the effects of library calls, e.g. in Jif, library methods need to be annotated in accordance to their semantics.[2] Providing these annotations is equally error-prone as writing stubs for libraries (e.g. Askarov [AS05] reports a false annotation discovered in his experiments). Still, in principle all analyses need to model library methods to avoid excessive analysis cost.

For our analyses, we created stubs for native methods and important library methods for two versions of Java:

- First, we created stubs for all native methods of JavaCard 2.2. JavaCard is an implementation for very restrictive execution environments like smartcards. Therefore, JavaCard contains only the sequential parts of Java and the library has been pruned. With the stubs for native methods and the ability to analyze the bytecode of the library, our experiments in chapter 7 include all effects of user and library code.

- Second, we provided stubs for the essential parts of the standard library. In particular, the effects of java.lang are included in our stubs except for very problematic constructs like dynamic class loading. Such constructs are well beyond the scope of this thesis, solutions can be found e.g. in Livshits et al. [LWL05]. At certain points we cut parts of the call graph, when dependences can be included without loading a myriad of other library classes (see the Locale example above). Still, these stubs induce conservative approximations of the original dependences and remove excessive analysis burden.

---

[2]A second reason for the need for Jif's annotation mechanism is that it lacks the ability to analyze bytecode, therefore the standard library cannot be analyzed.

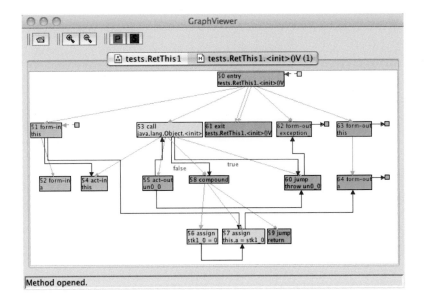

Figure 6.2: The graph viewer with an example PDG

6.2 Analyses based on SDGs

The generated dependence graphs are stored on disk, from where they are parsed with an ANTLR[3] grammar, and stored in the open source graph library JGraphT.[4] When we decided to use that library, the author first contributed Java 1.5's generics to that library, resulting in type-safe graphs (specifically no explicit downcasts for node and edge types) for our custom algorithms. The Joana library is based on JGraphT and provides a long list of algorithms for slicing, chopping, and related analyses. In particular, all analyses presented and implemented in the original Valsoft [Kri03a] have been integrated. This core library therefore forms the basis for nearly all other libraries and Eclipse plugins presented in the sequel.

6.3 Graph Viewer

The Valsoft infrastructure [Kri03a] already contained a visualization component for dependence graphs. However, a crucial library of that program had been provided by a company in binary form only, such that graphs with new features like interference dependence could not be parsed and displayed with that software. Therefore we decided to re-implement the viewer based on the JGraph[5] library,

---

[3]http://www.antlr.org/
[4]http://jgrapht.sourceforge.net
[5]http://www.jgraph.com/

as an adapter for JGraphT existed. Furthermore, JGraph contains some free layout algorithms, which we extended by a new layouter using the Brandes/Köpf algorithm [BK01] in a Sugiyama setting. This layouter corresponds well to the structure of our PDGs.

Figure 6.2 shows an example PDG in the graph viewer. Note that interprocedural edges are visualized by edges from/to tiny rectangles. These rectangles represent nodes in another method, which is opened when the tiny rectangle is double-clicked. Note that a spanning tree of the control dependences yields the layers for the Sugiyama layout (shown as orange edges). The horizontal position in these layers is determined according to node numbers. Thus the program order in basic blocks is preserved from left to right. The data dependences are inserted between the layers as blue broken edges in a Manhattan layout.

6.4 Path Conditions

For both static and dynamic path conditions presented in chapter 5, a prototype implementation has been integrated into the original framework [Rob05].

We have implemented a prototype path condition generator for Java based on the existing implementation for C and the dependence graph generator for Java presented in chapter 2, and demonstrate the feasibility of our extensions with preliminary case studies. For the implementation, we concentrated on the new concepts and automatically benefited from all constructs that share a common representation with C. For the prototype, the fine-grained Java SDG was adapted to interface with the C path condition generator. Thus the procedural Java constructs are tackled by the existing path condition machinery. For the object-oriented constructs, we concentrated on dynamic dispatch — the most characteristic feature of object oriented programming — according to equation (5.15). At the time of this writing, the precise conditions for `instanceof` and exceptions are not yet integrated and are approximated conservatively; the same is true for some other Java constructs. The precise formulae for these constructs will be integrated in the near future. Still, all conditions presented in the evaluation (chapter 7) have been generated by the current prototype.

The dynamic path conditions have also been integrated into the existing implementation. To collect the dynamic trace data, the standard debugger `gdb` was leveraged. A debugger driver abstracts away from the actual debugger in use, so we might as well replace `gdb` by another debugger. The tracer thus offers a standard interface for controlling the execution. The breakpoints and other data needed for control of the debugger is extracted from the fine-grained SDG. In the tracing phase, the program is executed statement by statement, and all required information is traced. From that trace, a dynamic slice is built that is generally more precise than the static slice.

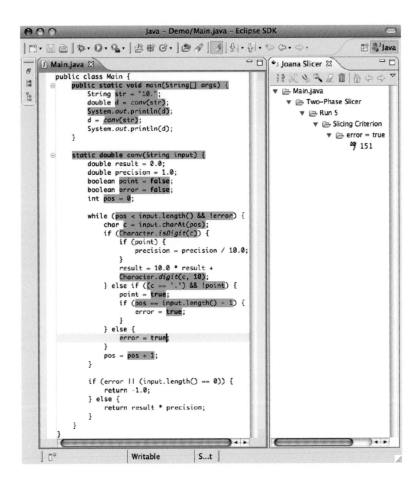

Figure 6.3: The slicing plugin with an example program.

6.5 Eclipse Plugins

As a GUI for the Joana library, several Eclipse[6] plugins have been created [GH08]. The first GUI provides access to all slicing and chopping algorithms of the Joana library. The computed slices and chops are highlighted in the source code. Highlighting requires a mapping between bytecode instructions and source locations. Fortunately, most class files contain rudimentary debug information, which the compiler inserts into class files. In most cases, this debug information can serve as a mapping which corresponds to the intuition. But note that this information was not meant for highlighting but debugging purposes only, so for some cases the highlighted regions may deviate from the expected parts of the programs. In our plugin structure, the SDG generation and highlighting are outsourced to the Source Highlighting plugin, which allows access from both plugins that require this service, namely the slicing and IFC GUI (described later).

The example in Figure 6.3 shows a simple conversion method, that calculates the double value of a string parameter. The slice from the second `error = true` statement (depicted in light blue) is shown in darker blue. Note that for this example, the precise source positions from our custom extension of `javac` have been taken. Otherwise, the whole line would be highlighted once a node of that line is contained in the slice. The slice points out that only part of the conversion method influences the error checking code of the slicing criterion: The `result` and `precision` variables have no influence on that statement but constitute a separate result of that method. In fact, the method returns the special value -1 if an error occurs, in all other cases it returns the computed value.

For detailed manual inspection of SDGs, the SDGView presents the SDG nodes in a tree view with predecessors, successors, and parents, as an alternative to the graphical SDG viewer. Therefore, this view allows manual reconstruction of how one statement influences another. As an example consider Figure 6.4, which shows the entries for node 55 depicted in Figure 6.2. For navigating quickly through the SDG, the root node can be specified, and the standard home, forward and backward buttons provide the well-known functionality.

6.5.1 Plugins for Information Flow Control

We have implemented SDG-based IFC, including declassification, as described in chapter 4. The prototype is an Eclipse plugin, which allows interactive definition of security lattices, automatic generation of SDGs, annotation of security levels to SDG nodes via source annotation and automatic security checks. At the time of this writing, the Java slicer and security levels are fully operational.

We implemented the lattice editor based on the GEF graph editing framework of Eclipse. The lattice elements are represented as bit vectors [GMR94,AKBLN89] to support fast infimum/supremum operators when checking for illegal information flow. It is worth noting that the algorithm of Ganguly et al. computes incorrect results without adding synthetic nodes into edges that span more than one level (where levels are defined in terms of the longest path between

---

[6]http://eclipse.org

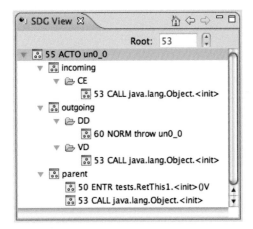

Figure 6.4: The SDGView for node 55 in Figure 6.2

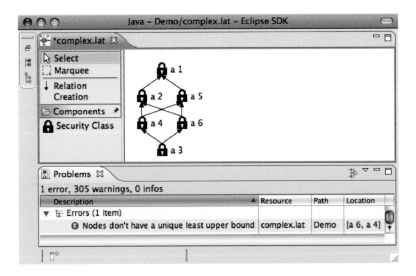

Figure 6.5: The lattice editor in Eclipse with illegal graph

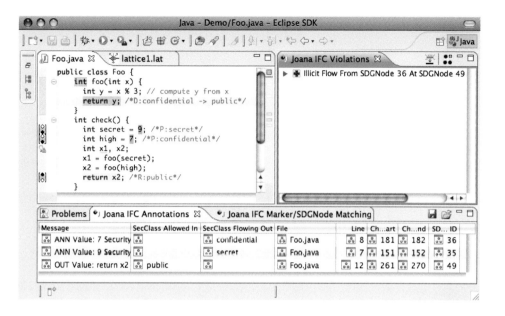

Figure 6.6: Example of Figure 4.11 without declassification in our Eclipse plugin

two nodes). The authors were not very specific concerning this restriction. Fortunately, these synthetic nodes can safely be removed from the lattice after conversion to a bit vector. Our editor attempts to convert the given graph to such a lattice. If this fails, the user is notified that the graph does not represent a valid lattice. Otherwise the lattice can be saved on disk for annotations. Figure 6.5 shows an example of a non-trivial graph. But the lattice conversion fails for this graph, as the elements "a 4" and "a 6" do not have a unique upper bound: Both "a 2" and "a 5" are upper bounds for these elements, which violates a crucial property of lattices. The problem view at the bottom displays a detailed message to the user that describes the violation. If one of the relation edges between those four elements were removed, a valid lattice would be generated, which can be leveraged for annotating the source code.

The IFC algorithm was implemented in a two-stage version: As the first step, the summary declassification nodes are computed. If the dependence graph already contained summary edges, these need to be removed first. Still, generating summary edges during SDG generation was not in vain: As summary declassification nodes can only arise between nodes that used to be connected by a summary edge, we can omit building the transitive closure of dependences for all nodes that are not target of a summary edge. Algorithm 8 of chapter 4 is therefore only initialized with these actual-out nodes. Note that this optimization does not improve the worst case complexity of the algorithm, but it reduces analysis time in practice (see section 7.3.5). As a second step, the IFC constraints are propagated through the backward slice of each output channel according to Algorithm 7 of chapter 4. Our implementation does not generate these constraints explicitly, but performs a fixed point analysis as presented in section 4.5.2.

Figure 6.6 shows the example program of Figure 4.11 but without declassification in the `foo` method. The Eclipse plugin features a full-fledged view for annotations and security violations. User annotations are shown in the Joana IFC Annotations view at the bottom of the figure. The message shows the kind of annotation (ANN stands for provided security level, OUT for required security level, and RED for declassification with both). Next to the message, the R and P annotations are shown. The rest of the entries describe the annotated source position and the ID of the SDG node. Another View, called "Joana IFC Marker/SDGNode Matching" allows precise matching of the selected source to its respective SDG node according to the debug information provided in the class file. The last view, depicted on the right in Figure 6.6 lists all violations found by the last IFC checking. For the example program, a run of the IFC algorithm determines a security violation between nodes 36 ($P(36) = secret$) and 49 ($R(49) = public$) because of the missing declassification in `foo`. When this declassification from *confidential* to *public* is introduced, no illicit flow is detected.

Chapter 7

Evaluation

The previous chapters defined several precise analyses which can be leveraged
for security purposes. This chapter now presents empirical evidence of their
practicability, scalability, and precision. First, we will evaluate the precision
of our new side-effect analysis for program slicing (see chapter 2) Second, we
assess the effectiveness of our improved algorithm that determines interference
dependence (see chapter 3), and contrast it to previous definitions, which did
not take points-to information into account.

Next, we evaluate our slicing-based definition of information flow control
(see chapter 4). To analyze practicability, we thoroughly present Jif, the only
implementation of an information flow type system, and compare it to our system. The gain in precision is examined by a case study with an example Jif
program, which we converted back to standard Java. A detailed evaluation of
our IFC algorithm on a set of benchmark programs illustrates its scalability.

Finally, we present case studies for path conditions (see chapter 5). Both
static path conditions for Java with its object-oriented language constructs, and
dynamic path conditions for C are presented. These studies illustrate that both
extensions provide precise results for realistic programs.

7.1   Slicing Java Programs

Our initial presentation of the Java slicer [HS04] aimed at an evaluation of
the imprecision between an approximate modeling of parameter objects and our
precise object trees. However, we could not learn from Liang and Harrold [LH98]
how sound k-limiting works. So we fell back to comparing our sound model
with unsound k-limiting, i.e. we measured the effect of omitting the dependences
induced by deeper levels all-together. As a matter of fact, we found that unsound
k-limiting may miss up to 90% of the nodes in the correct slice. While this
evaluation showed that deeper nested levels have great impact on slicing of
Java programs, this comparison was not what we originally had in mind. But
even after several years we could not find a sound approximation for the missed
dependences of k-limiting.

However, the Indus/Kaveri slicer [JRH05] propagates an alternative approach to data dependence computation: They essentially add data dependences

163

Nr	Name	LOC	Nodes	Edges	Time	Summary
1	Dijkstra	618	2281	4999	4	1
2	Enigma	922	2132	4740	5	1
3	Lindenmayer	490	2601	195552	5	10
4	Network Flow	960	1759	3440	6	1
5	Plane-Sweep	1188	14129	386507	24	13
6	Semithue	909	19976	595362	24	33
7	TSP	1383	6102	15430	15	2
8	Union Find	1542	13169	990069	36	103
9	JC Wallet	252	18858	68259	8	9
10	JC Purse	9835	135271	1002589	145	742
11	mp	4750	271745	2405312	141	247

Table 7.1: Data for benchmark programs

between all definition statements to all matching use statements of a given field and ignore method boundaries for that purpose. It should be straightforward to prove such a model correct for context-insensitive slicing. Therefore, this thesis shows the effectiveness of our object trees in comparison to method-spanning data dependences.

Note that data dependences that cross method boundaries violate a precondition for two-phase slicing, for context-sensitive slicing in such a model one needs extra context recovery at method boundaries each time a slice is computed. We did not include such a complex[1] analysis. Instead, we compare our context-sensitive slicer to the context-insensitive slicer using our SDG and to the context-insensitive slicer for the relaxed notion of dependences graph described above.

Table 7.1 shows the benchmark programs for this experiment. We evaluated a benchmark of 8 student programs with an average size of 1kLoc, and two medium-sized JavaCard applets. The student programs use very few API calls, and for nearly all we designed stubs (see section 6.1.1) as to not miss essential dependences. One JavaCard applet is called "Wallet",[2] the "Purse" applet is from the "Pacap" case study [BCM+00]. Both applet SDGs contain all the JavaCard API PDGs, native methods have been added as stubs.

For every program, the LOC and SDG size (nodes and edges) is given. The time to construct these SDGs has been split into two numbers: the column 'time' displays the time for building the SDG and the intermediate representation and pointer analysis. The next column shows the time to insert the summary edges. This number is given separately, as summary edge computation has cubic complexity.

Figure 7.1 shows the average slice slices as a percentage of the graph size, which is 100%. For the slice and graph sizes, only true instruction nodes were counted in order to make the comparison independent from additional parameter nodes. For each of these instruction nodes, a backward slice was computed

---

[1]Krinke [Kri02] shows that explicitly context-sensitive slicing is very expensive.

[2]http://www.javaworld.com/javaworld/jw-07-1999/jw-07-javacard.html

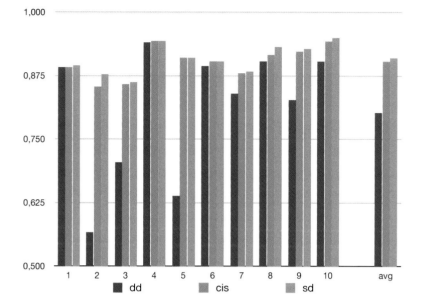

Figure 7.1: Evaluation of context-sensitive slicing with object trees

for three variants of graph and slicing algorithm. The first variant (dd) takes
the SDG presented in chapter 2 together with context-sensitive two-phase slicing; the second (cis) uses the same graph but applies context-insensitive slicing
(i.e. the transitive closure of dependences); and the third variant applies context-
insensitive slicing to an interprocedural program dependence graph, where data
dependences for fields may span method boundaries. Remember that we could
not apply context-sensitive slicing on this graph as it is not compatible to an
SDG. The results show that context-sensitive slices are on average 13% smaller
than context-insensitive slices. The differences between the context-insensitive
variants are, as expected, negligible: On average, slicing the graph with object
trees resulted marginally smaller slices (the difference is about one basis point)
than with method-spanning data dependences.

7.2 Evaluating Interference Dependence

Apart from usual data dependences our SDG contains interference dependence
caused by memory access in different threads. To compare the effectiveness of
our algorithm of chapter 3, which computes a safe approximation of interference
dependence, we measured the number of interference edges and compared this
number with the one reported in Ranganath and Hatcliff [RH04] and type-based
approaches as used in [HCD+99]. Table 7.2 shows the result of our analysis: We
examined the same programs as in [RH04], i.e. a suite of benchmarks from the

JavaGrande Forum.[3] These programs consist of a range of programs, from very small to medium-sized. Especially the smaller programs allow manual inspection to verify which interferences are spurious and which real. This does not only allow relative comparisons but also how far we are from the (undecidable) minimal number. The left hand side of the table shows the result from [RH04], the columns showing, from left to right, the number of interference edges when only taking typing information into account, when using the specialized escape analysis developed in that paper, and when using entity information, respectively. The next columns display our results for these benchmarks: They display the number of interference dependences, from left to right, using type information only, with thread numbers and aliasing as presented in chapter 3, and after pruning spurious interference dependences with a simple happens-before analysis [GH09]. The last column shows the number of interference dependences as determined by manual inspection (where possible).

The first three benchmarks in Table 7.2 are micro-benchmarks with the only purpose to test and evaluate a virtual machine implementation's synchronization constructs. Therefore, the absolute number of interference dependences in these examples is relatively low, one benchmark ForkJoin does not even expose a single one. Nevertheless, both Ranganath and our analysis report a considerable number of dependences. Manual inspection of our results yields that we have spurious reports mainly due to cases where a field is defined in a constructor of a thread object that is subsequently started. When these two operations are embedded in a loop, our happens-before analysis, developed for precise slicing of concurrent programs [GH09], will merge both statements for being in the same strongly connected component. Thus the constructor appears to happen in parallel to the started thread. However, the constructor only handles data that is local to its object. Therefore, these dependences are already modeled as fork-in dependences (which are equivalent to parameter dependences) at the statement starting the thread such that adding interference dependence here is redundant. Currently, our analysis does not feature a thread-locality analysis that detects these false positives.

Still, our analysis based on thread numbers and a simple happens-before analysis results in significantly less interference edges than Ranganath's escape analysis. This is not surprising, as aliasing is more precise than escape analysis.

The next four benchmarks, are essentially SIMD[4] programs, i.e. several instances of a thread class operate on independent portions of data. But some of the benchmarks require communication of intermediate results, so the number of interference dependence reflects mainly the communication effort. A manual inspection of these programs reveals that LUFact's and SOR's contribute 139 and 85 interference dependences, respectively. It is surprising, that Ranganath report only 24 and 23 dependences here, maybe they did not report the number of dependences due to array access, which is the main source of interference in these benchmarks. Including array access, our analysis reports 212 and 115 de-

---

[3] http://www.javagrande.org/
[4] Single Instruction, Multiple Data

pendences, respectively. The difference to the real number again results mainly to constructors before thread creation.

`Crypt`, `Series` and `SparseMatmult` do not communicate extensively. Thus their real number of interferences is nearly zero, and our analysis only reports 95, 8 and 12 dependences, respectively. With a context-sensitive pointer analysis, 64 dependences can be pruned for `Crypt`, resulting in a total of 31 interferences, which again excels Ranganath's reports.

Comparing our results with Ranganath's, aliasing clearly excels over escape analysis results as a base for interference computation. An interesting result is that context-insensitive alias analysis may perform worse than a rather cheap but context-sensitive escape analysis as presented in [RH04]. So context-sensitivity seems more mandatory than aliasing analysis. However, context-sensitive aliasing information gives a significant gain in precision over escape information only. Benchmarks with array access are clearly not modeled in [RH04], so a fair comparison for these is impossible.

Table 7.2: Evaluation of interference dependence in comparison to [RH04]

	Result from [RH04]			Our results			
	type	escape	entity	type	thread#	+ HB	real
Barrier	117	29	29	56	37	17	7
ForkJoin	1929	155	16	17	12	11	0
Sync	122	36	36	44	32	26	6
Crypt	1228	180	58	1023	325	95/31	0
LUFact	3624	181	24	1358	291	276	139
SOR	2318	162	23	541	144	115	85
Series	2138	157	8	105	22	8	0
SparseMatmult	3833	183	14	236	22	11	1
MolDyn	8026	373	209	8794	5340	5288	?
MonteCarlo	5245	309	11	516	263	126	?
RayTracer	1330	171	166	1059	412	221	?

7.3 Information Flow Control

This section presents empirical studies about precision, scalability, and practicability of our new information flow analysis developed in chapter 4. It starts with an elaboration on the current state of the art in language-based information flow control. The language Jif is the only implementation of a Java-like language with built-in information flow control. We will show that the applicability diminishes significantly, as the language design is centered around the information flow control type system. Traditional Java programs therefore need significant refactoring for compliance with Jif's constraints (see e.g. [AS05]). The later parts of this section concentrate on empirical evaluations of accuracy and scalability.

7.3.1 JIF

The only implementation of a type system for a non-trivial imperative language is Jif [MCN⁺], originally called Jflow. It provides a Java-like language extended by *labeled types*, comprising an ordinary Java type like String, and a security label which is part of the program's security policy. Each security label restricts the information that may flow into the annotated variable. The labels implicitly form a complete lattice in the decentralized label model [ML00]. This model allows multiple principals that form some sort of access control on the information they own. They can allow other principals to read that data, declassify data and transfer authority to other principals and code. In version 3, Jif's decentralized label model was augmented with integrity checking.

The major advantages of security type systems can be found in Jif as well: Type checking is cheap and compositional. It is therefore possible to check each class in isolation and compose an application of the pieces later without the need to analyze the program as a whole. In principle, compositionality applies to libraries as well. However, due to the sheer size of Java's standard classes and the lack of publicly available source code, Jif does not provide security annotation but for the most central classes. And even for these, there is no semantic guarantee (see the paragraph on libraries below).

But first, we evaluate the dimensions of analysis precision of Jif's type system.

Flow-insensitivity

Like most type-based approaches, Jif partitions the set of variables and fields into disjoint sets (such as *secure* and *public* data). If information illicitly flows e.g. from the *secure* to the *public* partition, Jif already considers that program insecure, even if the *public* variable is no longer alive after that flow. This can be seen in the program fragment in Figure 4.2 on page 94, which is intuitively secure, as the assignments from the if-block are killed by the subsequent definition. Type systems like Jif will spuriously reject that code because confidential information has an influence on the value in a public variable.

Based on the original definition of noninterference [GM82, GM84] (see section 4.3), however, this program fragment is secure: Classic noninterference states that the two streams of (*public*) output of the program should be indistinguishable even if they differentiate on (*secret*) input. In other words, *secure* input is not allowed to flow to *public* output channels. This definition is reflected in our slicing-based approach, which only checks for *secret* data that might flow to *public* output. But type systems cannot check that precise property since it requires data flow analysis like in our slicing approach.

Context-Insensitivity

Partitioning variables and fields into disjoint sets has the additional disadvantage that the analysis becomes context-insensitive: As a result, data structures or even simple utility methods cannot be reused for different security levels. One would need to write one Vector class or cosine-method for each security level, and this would even be worse for multi-parameter methods. As a remedy, Jif supports various kinds of polymorphism to allow reusable code, similar to Java 5's generics for collections. But like these, the programmer needs to annotate all data structures with type parameters when they are to be used in different security policies. Jif offers defaults to relief that burden, but this can be both a blessing and a curse as these defaults may be inconsistent with the semantics. A recent case study for Jif [AS05] found that a Java library wrapper had insufficient annotation, which may result in undetected security violations. Apart from that, polymorphic classes are subject to certain restrictions (see type discriminants on page 171) which limits their applicability.

Object-Insensitivity

Similar to contexts, different objects might want to store data with different security labels. However, type systems label each field statically with a single security label. Again, some remedy can be achieved by polymorphism, with the same problems as before. Another way to achieve object-sensitivity are runtime-labels, but these require program instrumentation, which induces an additional execution time and space overhead.

Differences to Java

Even though Jif compiles down to standard Java (but requires an additional runtime system provided as a jar library), there are certain differences between Jif and Java. Some of these limitations are standard in any kind of language-based IFC analyses:

Threads Like most languages, Jif does not prevent threads from communicating information via the timing of modification of shared variables or synchronization. Such channels can only be controlled by *possibilistic* [SV98] and *probabilistic* [SS00a, Smi06] IFC. No implementation of a type system for these security policies has been reported. However, our slicing-based IFC can be extended to probabilistic noninterference [GL]. We are currently integrating a checker for this security policy in our system.

Finalizers run in a separate thread in Java and could exploit the shared variable covert channel. Therefore, Jif does not support finalizers. Most static analyses also ignore them, as they are rarely needed in Java and their exact execution time is unknown. Java only guarantees that their execution happens when the garbage collector finds an object no longer reachable from the program's active state. However, there is no guarantee that a finalizer will be run at all. However, some program analyses treat finalizers conservatively, e.g. [LH03].

Timing channels are extremely hard to counter if an adversary has access to a clock independent from the system. These physical side channels are not covered by language-based information flow control except for Agat's type system [Aga00] and Sabelfeld and Sand's strong security [SS00a].

Resource exhaustion like `OutOfMemoryError` or `StackOverflowError` can be used as a information leak. Jif treats these Errors as fatal such that at most one bit of information can leak per program execution. Code that tries to catch such errors can easily be identified with program analysis. Since an error is not meant to be recovered in [GJSB05], it is straightforward to disallow code which catches errors. Thus the JVM terminates upon such a problem.

Termination channels Like timing channels, this type of channel is very hard to suppress. It is usually undecidable how long a program will remain in a certain block of code, or — in the extreme — whether it will terminate at all. Jif does not control these channels. However, for slicing-based IFC there are alternative definitions of control dependence [PC90, RAB⁺07, Amt08] that make all subsequent statements dependent on possibly non-terminating statements. With these definitions, termination leaks will be discovered but the analysis becomes more conservative than with standard control dependence. This may result in more false positives, as termination is undecidable.

Other limitations of the Jif language make conversion of Java classes to Jif difficult:

Final arguments In contrast to Java, method arguments are always implicitly `final` in Jif, allowing them to be used as type parameters for Jif's annotations. This pragmatic design decision does not significantly restrict the programmer, since Java only supports call-by-value parameter passing. But it may require refactoring of legacy Java code to produce legal Jif source.

HashCode The default implementation of `java.lang.Object` can be used to communicate information covertly, thus Jif requires each class to redefine this method. This restriction is overly strong in practice. As `hashCode` is supposed to map different objects to different values [GJSB05], a field-value based implementation may result in poor performance of HashMaps and HashSets.

Static variables can also be exploited as a covert channel based on the the order of their invocation through the class loader. Therefore, Jif inhibits all static variables (but not static methods). Even though static variables can be refactored to normal variables, all realistic programs and especially libraries make use of that concept, in particular for defining constants, which improves code modularization. Since most static variables are only initialized once in their defining classes' static initializer, simple checks can be used to eliminate covert channels without ruling out the whole concept.

Unchecked exceptions In Java, all subclasses of `java.lang.Runtime`-`Exception` do not have to be declared in a method's `throws` clause. These exceptions can also be defined by a Java program but they are mainly used by the virtual machine to trap problems like array-out-of-bounds, null pointers and other common problems that are implicitly checked during bytecode interpretation. These exceptions might be thrown by so many bytecode instructions that requiring their declaration or inclusion in try/catch blocks seemed overly burdensome for the designers of the Java language. But Jif requires exactly that! Slicing-based information flow control can track the exceptions from where they are thrown to a matching catch clause and raises a security policy violation only if such a flow transmits secret information to public channels. Therefore the programmer is not overwhelmed by dealing with usually trivial exceptions.

As an example, consider the password checking example in Figure 4.3 on page 97, taken from [ML00]. Even this trivial code requires two catch-blocks, for NullPointer- and IndexOutOfBoundsExceptions. Both apply the dreaded catch-all-do-nothing anti-pattern, that empirical evidence shows to make bug-detection a lot harder. It is in total contradiction to Dijkstra's principle of the weakest precondition and may produce hard-to-track inherited errors.

Type discrimination on parameters In casts or instanceof expressions, Jif allows no classes that are parametrized with a security label. Like Java's generics, this information is erased during compilation. This seems overly restrictive since parametrized classes are so essential for code reuse [ML00, AS05]. Parameterized expressions could be permitted if the parameters where statically known to be matched, but this is currently not supported.

Libraries Existing libraries are not annotated with security labels and so cannot be flow-checked with Jif. While Jif provides wrapper classes to the most important library classes like collections, many other libraries are not supported even if the source or bytecode is provided. Since Java's popularity is based to a big extent on the availability of a large standard library and numerous custom libraries, such restrictions impede the proliferation of security typed languages.

Regarding the limitations listed above, it becomes evident why language-based information flow control did not gain real impact on security engineering in more than ten years of its existence. Zdancewic states that "despite this large body of literature and considerable, ongoing attention from the research community, information flow based enforcement mechanisms have not been widely (or even narrowly!) used" [Zda04]. Only recently some programs have been written in the Jif language, however, only in the academic field [MCN+]. We argue that for practical use, a realistic language must be analyzable without major restrictions.

7.3.2 Slicing-Based Information Flow Control

The remainder of this section will concentrate on our new form of information flow control based on program slicing as presented in chapter 4. We will compare its features to Jif and also point out directions where a closer integration of other work on information flow control is required.

7.3.3 Flow-, Context- and Object-Sensitivity

Program dependence graphs can be constructed to allow flow-, context- and object-sensitive analysis. For flow-sensitive analysis various derivatives of SSA-form have been presented in literature, and even an SSA-form for heap objects [FKS00] was proposed. Two-phase-slicing of the system dependence graph [HRB90] is context-sensitive, mainly due to summary edges, which subsume transitive dependence between method parameters. For object-sensitive results, the field structure of parameters passed to method calls need to be represented according to the references and modifications in this method and transitively called methods (see chapter 2). A precise analysis of these parameters requires points-to analysis. Several publications on points-to analysis in the last decade have improved the performance and scalability enormously and thus, today flow-, context- and object-sensitive analyses for realistic programs are feasible [MRR02, LH03, LL03, WL04, LH08], which again sustains the precision of dependence graphs.

Another benefit of slicing based information flow control is that once the graph is built, the checker is independent of the actual source language, which facilitates building of reusable checkers. The Valsoft infrastructure contains frontends for C and Java so all these languages can be checked with the same infrastructure when the dependence graph is annotated with security levels.

Noninterference

Theorem 4.1 on page 96 states that for two nodes n, a in the dependence graph if $n \notin BackwardSlice(a) \lor \mathrm{label}(n) \leq \mathrm{label}(a)$ then the noninterference criterion is satisfied between n and a. Thus, if there exists a path $n \rightarrow^* a$ and $\mathrm{label}(n) \nleq \mathrm{label}(a)$ then a (potential) security violation has been found. While the proof is independent of the specific language or slicing criterion, it is clear that a more precise slicer will have a lower false positive rate. Thus flow-, context- and object-sensitive slicing as described earlier allow very precise results that outdo those computed by Jif's type system, without the additional burden of annotating classes and methods with polymorphic security types.

As data and control dependence are formally defined in terms of reaching definitions resp. post-dominance in the control flow graph [FOW87], program slicing is indeed no less formal than type systems, in the contrary, it has been shown that dependence graphs accurately represent the semantics of a program (see section 2.2.2). Even more, a machine-checked proof of the correctness of our information flow control mechanism is in preparation [qui].

Information flow checking in dependence graphs is similar to type systems but not the same: Denning-style security labels are attached to *nodes* in the graph, not to variables. So even if the annotations in line 13 and 14 of Figure 4.6 on page 100 look similar to a type declaration, the semantics is totally different; another definition of the same variables might get a completely different label or none at all. Note that this has nothing to do with dynamic labeling, where labels are created at runtime. Here labels are statically determined, but variables are not partitioned into disjoint sets according to their label. Therefore, we can leverage the original and more general notion of noninterference of Goguen and Meseguer [GM82, GM84].

7.3.4 Case Studies

As an initial micro-benchmark to compare our approach with type-based IFC, let us reconsider the program from Figure 4.6 on page 100. Remember that PDG-based IFC guarantees that there is no flow from the `secure` variable (annotated $P(11) = High$ to the first output statement in line 19. Hence we analyzed the program from Figure 4.6 using Jif [MCN+]. Jif uses a generalization of Denning's lattices, the so-called decentralized label model. It allows to specify sets of security levels (called "labels" based on "principals") for every statement, and to attach a set of operations to any label. This is written e.g. $\{o_1 : r_1, r_2; o_2 : r_2; r_3\}$ and combines access control with IFC. Our approach could in principle be generalized to use the decentralized label model as well.

But note that even decentralized labels can not overcome the imprecision of type-based analysis. As an example, we adapted the first part of Figure 4.6 to Jif syntax and annotated the declaration of o and both instantiations of A with the principal `{pp:}`. The output statement was replaced by an equivalent code that allowed public output. Jif reports that secure data could flow to that public channel and thus raised a false alarm. In fact, no annotation is possible that makes Jif accept the first part of Figure 4.6 without changing the source code.

A JavaCard Applet

As another case study for IFC we chose the JavaCard applet called `Wallet`[5]. It is only 252 lines long but with the necessary API parts and stubs the PDG consists of 18858 nodes and 68259 edges. The time for PDG construction was 8 seconds plus 9 for summary edges.

The Wallet stores a balance that is at the user's disposal. Access to this balance is only granted after supplying the correct PIN. We annotated all statements that update the balance with the provided security level *High* and inserted a declassification to *Low* into the `getBalance` method. The methods `credit` and `debit` may throw an exception if the maximum balance would be exceeded or if there is insufficient credit, resp. In such cases JavaCard applets throw an exception, and the exception is clearly dependent on the result of a condition involving balance. The exception is not meant to be caught but percolates to the JavaCard terminal, so we inserted declassifications for these exceptions as well. Besides this intended information flow, which is only possible upon user request and after verifying the PIN, our analysis proved that no further information flow is possible from the balance to the output of the JavaCard.

---

[5]see Table 7.1 on page 164

Figure 7.2: The lattice for analyzing the battleship example

Note that this JavaCard applet — while operating on a restricted variant of Java — leverages many features of this standard: In particular we analyzed quite a few static variables and included all control flow due to implicit exceptions into our analysis without the need to explicitly declare or catch these. Therefore, this benchmark, again, cannot be certified with Jif.

The Battleship Example

The previous experiments demonstrated that our new approach is more general than Jif, because we can analyze realistic programming languages and accept a larger number of secure programs due to increased precision. The next step in our evaluation will examine a native Jif program to get a direct comparison of practicability between these two systems. As a benchmark program, we chose the battleship example, which comes with every Jif installation and implements a non-GUI version of the popular battleship game. In this game, two players place ships of different lengths on a rectangular board and subsequently "bombard" random cells on the opponents board until one player has hit all the cells covered by adversary ships.

The source code of this program consists of about 500 lines plus the required libraries and stubs. These yield an SDG consisting of 10207 nodes and 77290 edges. For this example we use a standard diamond lattice, where $all \leq player \leq noOne$ and $all \leq other \leq noOne$ but neither $player \leq other$ nor $other \leq player$ (see Figure 7.2). This ensures that secret information of one player may not be seen by the other player and vice versa.

Before this example program could be analyzed by our IFC analysis, it had to be converted back to regular Java syntax. This included removal of all security types in the program, conversion of all syntactic anomalies like parentheses in throws clauses, and replacing all Jif peculiarities like its own runtime system. Most of this process required manual conversion. We annotated the ship placement strategy in the players initialization method with the security level $P(n) = player$. The three declassification statements of the original Jif program are modeled as declassifications from $player$ to all in our system as well. Then we annotated all parameters to `System.out.println` with $R(x) = all$, which corresponds to the original program's variable annotation.

When we checked the program with this security policy, illicit information flow was discovered to all output nodes. Manual inspection found that all these violations were due to implicit information flow from the players initialization

```
1  /**
2   * Initialize the board by placing ships to cover numCovered coords.
3   */
4  void init/*{P:}**/(int/*{}**/numCovered) {
5      // Here what we would do in a full system is make a call to
6      // some non-Jif function, through the runtime interface, to
7      // get the position of the ships to place. That function would
8      // either return something random, or would implement some
9      // strategy. Here, we fake it with some fixed positions for
10     // ships.
11     final Ship/*[{P:}]**/[] myCunningStrategy = {
12         new Ship/*[{P:}]**/(new Coordinate/*[{P:}]**/(1, 1), 1, true),
13         new Ship/*[{P:}]**/(new Coordinate/*[{P:}]**/(1, 3), 2, false),
14         new Ship/*[{P:}]**/(new Coordinate/*[{P:}]**/(2, 2), 3, true),
15         new Ship/*[{P:}]**/(new Coordinate/*[{P:}]**/(3, 4), 4, false),
16         new Ship/*[{P:}]**/(new Coordinate/*[{P:}]**/(5, 6), 5, true),
17         new Ship/*[{P:}]**/(new Coordinate/*[{P:}]**/(5, 7), 6, false),
18     };
19
20     Board/*[{P:}]**/board = this.board;
21     int i = 0;
22     for (int count = numCovered; count > 0 && board != null; ) {
23         try {
24             Ship/*[{P:}]**/newPiece = myCunningStrategy[i++];
25             if (newPiece != null && newPiece.length > count) {
26                 // this ship is too long!
27                 newPiece = new Ship/*[{P:}]**/(newPiece.pos,
28                                                count,
29                                                newPiece.isHorizontal);
30             }
31             board.addShip(newPiece);
32             count -= (newPiece==null?0:newPiece.length);
33         }
34         catch (ArrayIndexOutOfBoundsException ignored) {}
35         catch (IllegalArgumentException ignored) {
36             // two ships overlapped. Just try adding the next ship
37             // instead.
38         }
39     }
40 }
```

Figure 7.3: Initialization method of a Player in Battleship

methods, more precisely, due to possible exceptions thrown in these methods. However, closer inspection found that all of these exceptional control flow paths are in fact impossible.

As an example consider the initialization method in Figure 7.3. If the program checks whether an SSA variable is null, and only executes an instruction involving this variable if it is not (cf. line 25), then no null-pointer exception may ever be thrown at that instruction. However, our intermediate representation currently does not detect that fact, even if two identical checks for null are present in the intermediate representation, one directly succeeding the other. Jif seems to support such local reasoning. But also less trivial examples, where a final variable is defined in the constructor, such that it may never be null in any instance method. With more analysis effort, such cases can be detected, even in the interprocedural case [Hub08]. Jif can only support non-local reasoning with additional user annotations.

Apart from null-pointer problems we found exceptional control flow due to array stores, where Java must ensure that the stored value is an instance of the array components, because of Java's covariant array anomaly. When a variable of an array type $a[\,]$ is assigned an array of a subtype $b[\,]$ where $b \leq a$, then storing an object of type a into that variable throws an `ArrayStoreException` (see lines 11-17 in Figure 7.3). Here Jif seems to have some local reasoning to prune trivial cases. Our intermediate representation does currently not prune such cases, however, with the pointer analysis results we use for data dependences, such impossible flow could easily be removed.

Lastly, for interprocedural analysis, we found that our intermediate representation models exceptional return values for all methods, even if a method is guaranteed to not throw any exception. A more precise modeling of such cases can render the control flow in calling methods more precise and remove spurious implicit flow. Jif requires user annotations for such cases, as all possibly thrown exceptions must either be caught or declared, even `RuntimeExceptions`, which do not have to be declared in usual Java.

Currently, our tool does not offer such analysis, so there are only external means to detect such spurious cases: Either by manual inspection, theorem proving (e.g. pre-/post-conditions), or path conditions. After verifying that such flow is impossible, we can block the corresponding paths in the dependence graphs, and we do that with declassification. In contrast to normal declassifications, where information flow is possible but necessary, this declassification models the guarantee that there is no information flow. As future work, we plan to integrate analyses which prune impossible control flow to reduce the false positive rate and thus the burden of external verification.

After blocking information flow through exceptions in Player's initialization, our IFC algorithm proved the battleship example secure with respect to the described security policy. No further illicit information flow was discovered. During the security analysis, based on only four declassifications, 728 summary declassification nodes were created. This result shows that summary declassification nodes essentially affect analysis precision, as they allow context-sensitive slicing while blocking transitive information flow at method invocation sites. Instead they introduce a declassification that summarizes the declassification effects of the invoked methods. Note that the original Jif program contained about 150 annotations (in Figure 7.3 these are shown as gray comments), most of which are concerned with security typing. Some of these annotations model, however, principals and their authority. This is a feature of the decentralized label model that we currently do not support. Still the number of annotations is at least an order of magnitude higher than with our analysis. For a program that contains only 500 lines of code (including comments), this means that the annotation burden in Jif is considerable.

One of the reasons, why slicing-based IFC needs less annotations than type systems is that side-effects of method calls are explicit in dependence graphs, so no end-label (which models the impact of side-effects on the program counter) is required, neither are return-value or exception labels. Those are computed as summary information representing the dependences of called methods.

Apart from these labels, Jif requires explicit annotations to verify any non-trivial property about exceptional control flow. In particular, many preconditions like non nullness need to be included into the program text instead of its annotations, e.g. explicit tests for null pointers or catch clauses, which are typically followed by empty handlers as in the example shown in Figure 4.6 on page 100. Preconditions are therefore included as runtime tests to enable local reasoning. Such coding style is an ordeal from the software engineering perspective, as it impedes source comprehension and may conceal violated preconditions. What one really wants to have is verification that such cases cannot happen in any execution and thus do not need to be included into the source code.

7.3.5 Scalability

The last sections demonstrated the precision and practicability of our approach. To validate the scalability of our new slicing-based information flow control, we measured execution times on a number of benchmarks with varying numbers of declassification and using lattices based on different characteristics. The benchmark programs are the same as those in Table 7.1 on page 164, except for the the program mp which is the implementation of a mental poker protocol [AS05]. This program displays the following characteristics: Its source code is about 4750 lines long (18801 including all necessary libraries and stubs), the generated SDG contains 271745 nodes and 2405312 edges and takes about 36MB on disk. The time for building the SDG was 141 sec plus 247 sec for the summary edges.

Table 7.3 shows the characteristics of the lattices we used in our evaluations: The first column displays the number of nodes in the lattice, the next column the maximal height of the lattice. The number of impure nodes in the lattice, which is shown in the next column, represents all nodes that have more than one parent in the lattice. The final column displays the number of bits needed in the efficient bitset encoding of Ganguly et al. [GMR94]. This encoding allows near-constant[6] computation of infima (greatest lower bounds), which will turn

---

[6]The infimum computation is in fact constant, but we need hashing to map lattice elements to bitsets.

	nodes	height	impure	bits
Lattice A	5	5	0	6
Lattice B	8	4	1	5
Lattice C	8	6	2	10
Lattice D	12	8	2	14
Lattice E	24	11	7	25
Lattice F	256	9	246	266

Table 7.3: Characteristics of the lattices in the evaluation.

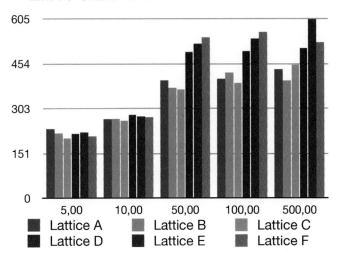

Figure 7.4: Average execution time (y-axis, in seconds) of IFC analysis for the unionfind benchmark with different lattices and varying numbers of declassifications (x-axis)

out to be essential for our evaluation. The lattices for evaluation have been designed such that they cover different characteristics equally: Lattice A is a traditional chain lattice, lattice B is more flat and contains an impure node. Lattice F has been automatically generated by randomly removing edges from a complete subset lattice of 9 elements. Conversion to bitset representation is only possible for the Hasse diagram, i.e. the transitive reduction partial order, which is not guaranteed by random removal of order edges. So we included a reduction phase before bitset conversion. Interestingly, Table 7.3 illustrates that the bitset conversion usually results in a representation with size linear in the number of lattice nodes.

Figure 7.4 shows the average execution time of 100 IFC analyses (y-axis, in seconds) for the unionfind benchmark of Table 7.1 using the lattices of Table 7.3. We chose the unionfind benchmark here, as it had the longest execution time, and the other benchmarks essentially show the same characteristics. For all IFC analyses we annotated the SDGs with 100 random security levels as provided

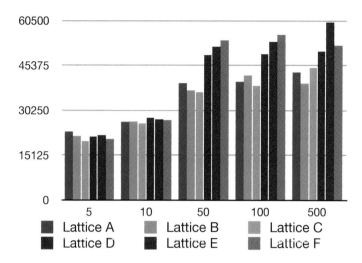

Figure 7.5: Time for summary declassification nodes (in seconds) of unionfind with different lattices and varying numbers of declassifications (x-axis)

and required security level, respectively. Moreover, we created 5 to 500 random declassifications to measure the effect of declassification on IFC checking (shown on the x-axis). The numbers illustrate that our IFC algorithm is quite independent of the lattice structure and size. In particular, we got a sub-linear increase in execution time with respect to the lattice (and bitset) size. Apart from that, the increase with the number of declassifications is also clearly sub-linear, since the number of declassifications increases more than linear in our experiments (see y-axis). Figure 7.5 depicts the execution time for computing summary declassification nodes, which is a prerequisite for precise IFC checking (see section 4.8), therefore they have been acquired once for each combination of program, lattice, and declassifications. They were determined with the same random annotations as the numbers of Figure 7.4. Note that we did only compute summary information between nodes that were originally connected by summary edges. These numbers expose the same sub-linear correlations between time and lattice size or numbers of declassifications, respectively.

Figure 7.6 and 7.7 show the average execution time (y-axis, in seconds) of 100 IFC analyses and the time for summary declassification node computation, respectively, for all benchmark programs using the largest lattice and varying numbers of declassifications. Lines in this graph use the scale depicted on the right, while bars use a different scale, such that we included the numbers into each bar. For most programs, the analyses took less than a minute, only three programs required more time, namely semithue, purse and unionfind. Again, we found the correlation between execution time and numbers of declassifications sub-linear. In fact, the execution time for many benchmarks was lower with 500 declassifications than with 100. These number clearly illustrate the scalability

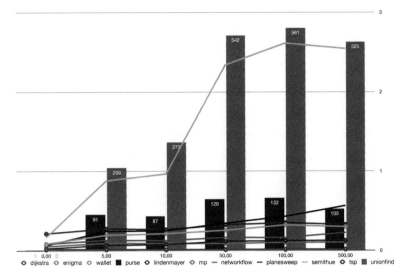

Figure 7.6: Average execution time (y-axis, in seconds) of IFC analysis for all benchmark programs with the largest lattice and varying numbers of declassifications (x-axis). Bars use a different scale.

of our information flow control analysis. There is no clear correlation between the number of nodes in the dependence graph and analysis time.

However, there seems to be a correlation between the number of edges in the SDG and the execution time. Unlike slicing, our IFC analysis is not linear in the number of SDG nodes and edges, but must find a fixed point in the constraint system with respect to the given lattice. Therefore, it may traverse a cycle in the SDG as often as the lattice is high, and when cycles are nested this effect may even get worse. Our current implementation does not circumvent these effects, so one observes that the programs with most edges yield to a substantial increase in analysis time. But note that the largest program, mp, does not belong to the outliers but behaves good-naturedly. One reason might be the different program structure, which can also be seen from original summary edge computation (see Table 7.1), which is considerably lower than for other large programs. This program does — unlike JavaCard applets and our student programs — not have a big loop in the main method which may invoke nearly all functionality. Concluding, we assume that the program's structure plays a bigger role than the pure number of nodes or edges for analysis time.

While future work must evaluate the impact of standard slicing optimizations on this technique for faster fixed point computation, we think that 1 minute execution time, as observed by the majority of our test cases, is definitely reasonable for a security analysis. But even the three outliers require maximally 1.5 hours (including summary declassification analysis), which should be acceptable for a compile-time analysis that usually needs to be done only once.

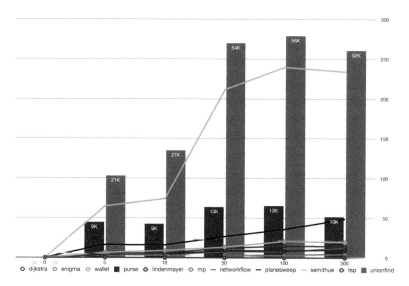

Figure 7.7: Time for summary declassification nodes (y-axis, in seconds) for all benchmark programs with the largest lattice and varying numbers of declassifications (x-axis). Bars use a different scale.

7.3.6 Future Work

While we presented evidence for precision, scalability, and practicability, there is still room for further improvements: In particular, we expect that optimizations for slicing, e.g. as presented by Binkley et al. [BHK07], apply to our information flow analyses as well. These techniques produce up to 71% reduction in runtime and thus significantly improve scalability. Further research must evaluate, which of these techniques are applicable to information flow control.

7.4 Case Studies for Path Conditions

Path conditions are precise necessary conditions for information flow control between two statements. Therefore they can invalidate or specify the exact conditions for information flow as determined by the techniques presented in the last section. Furthermore they provide insight on the circumstances that lead to declassification, which supplies semantic justification for such constructs. This section presents case studies that demonstrate the feasibility and precision of the extensions presented in chapter 5. First, we will focus on static path conditions for Java as described in section 5.3, later dynamic path conditions (see section 5.4) for C will be evaluated. Note that all conditions presented in this section have been generated by the current prototype.

```
 1 public class Weighing {
 2   public static final int NORMAL = 0;
 3   public static final int PAPER_OUT = 1;
 4   public static void main(String[] args) {
 5     char input = args[0].charAt(0);
 6     weigh(PAPER_OUT, 1.0f, input);
 7   }
 8   public static void weigh(int status,
 9       float kal_kg, char input) {
10     float u = 1.0f; // calibration factor
11     float u_kg = 0.0f; // initial value
12     while (true) {
13       u_kg = u * kal_kg;
14       if (status == PAPER_OUT) {
15         if (input == '+') {
16           kal_kg = 1.1f;
17         }
18         if (input == '-') {
19           kal_kg = 0.9f;
20         }
21       }
22       print(u_kg);
23     }
24   }
25   public static void print(float u_kg) {...}
26 }
```

Figure 7.8: Simplified weighing machine controller

```
 1 ( NOT Weighing.print((1.0 * kal_kg))
 2 ++ (input = 43)
 3 ++ (1 = 1) )
 4 OR
 5 ( NOT Weighing.print((1.0 * kal_kg))
 6 ++ (input ≠ 43)
 7 ++ (input = 45)
 8 ++ (1 = 1) )
```

Figure 7.9: Path condition of Figure 7.8 from line 9 (input) to 22

```
 1 public class PCExc {
 2   int secret;
 3   public static void main(String[] args) {
 4     System.out.println(excMethod(1));
 5   }
 6   public static int excMethod(int check) {
 7     try {
 8       PCExc pce = new PCExc();
 9       pce.secret = check;
10       throw pce;
11     } catch (PCExc pce) {
12       return pce.secret;
13     }
14 }}
```

```
 1   exc_0 instanceof PCExc
 2 ++ (exc_0 ≠ null)
```

Figure 7.10: Illicit information flow through an exception and corresponding path condition

7.4.1 Static Path Conditions for Java

Before entering the peculiarities of Java, an example program will demonstrate that shared language constructs of Java and C also share the analysis in path conditions. Therefore as a first case study, we considered the example in Figure 7.8, which is a Java version of a weighing machine controller and does not use dynamic dispatch. The example shows that procedural Java constructs are handled quite similar to the C case. Thus the path condition in Figure 7.9 naturally supports standard Java and finds the illicit paths from the keyboard buffer to the printed weight. The first line says that the print method may not throw an exception, so the while loop may execute another time. (The current implementation does not yet replace interprocedural exception handling with the corresponding summarizing path condition, as presented in section 5.3.5.) The second line says that input must be the ASCII of '+', and the third that status equals PAPER_OUT. Note that values are often substituted for variables when they have been found constant by the SSA-form. The terms after the disjunction represent the analogous case, where the input is '-'.

Now, we can inspect object-oriented constructs: As a second example, we examined the program from Figure 5.4 on page 133 with our prototype which yields

$$PC(\text{sel}_8, \text{result}_{12}) \equiv (\text{new class A}) : B$$

Since A is not a subtype of B, this condition is not satisfiable, and the PDG contains no other dependence between sel and result. Thus the parameter sel cannot influence the return value, even though the program slice says so.

Figure 7.10 demonstrates precise exception handling. The program indirectly transmits a secret value via a caught exception, which is then made public by printing it to the screen. This illicit flow is detected by the path condition,

```
 1 public class A {
 2   public int foo(int x) {
 3     if (x < 17) {
 4       return x;
 5     } else {
 6       return 0;
 7     }
 8   }
 9 }
10 public class B extends A {
11   public int foo(int x) {
12     if (x > 42) {
13       return x;
14     } else {
15       return 0;
16     }
17 }}
18 public class SolvableDynDispatch {
19   int main_decd;
20   int main_inp;
21   public static void main(...) {
22     System.out.println(
23       dynDisp(main_decd, main_inp));
24   }
25   static int dynDisp(int dcd,int in){
26     A dynamic;
27     int result;
28     if (dcd == 1) {
29       dynamic = new A();
30     } else
31       dynamic = new B();
32     result = dynamic.foo(in);
33     return result;
34 }}
```

Figure 7.11: Example for dispatch

which checks information flow between line 6 (check) and the return value in line 12. The first line represents the catch block that only accepts a PCExc, and the second line requires this exception not to be null. Both conditions are always true in this catch block, so the path condition reduces to *true*, illustrating that the illicit flow will always take place.

The last program in Figure 7.11 illustrates exploitation of backward slices for dynamic dispatch of the method call in line 32. The condition computed by our tool between in and result on this line is shown in Figure 7.12. It is determined based on the detailed path condition presented in section 5.3.4. Two cases are possible for the virtual bound method: Either the target object has type A (upper case), or B (lower case). A third case contains conflicting terms and is therefore omitted in Figure 7.12 as it will be removed by automatic constraint solvers. A closer examination of the conditions reveals: Line 1 stems

```
1 ( (17 > x)
2 ++ dynamic = new class A
3 ++ (dcd = 1) )
4 OR
5 ( (x > 42)
6 ++ dynamic = new class B
7 ++ (dcd ≠ 1) )
8 OR ...
```

Figure 7.12: Excerpt of path condition for Figure 7.11

from the condition in A.foo, the next two lines show the subcondition from dynamic binding: line 3 stems from line 28. The term after the disjunction represents the analogue condition for a B object.

This condition can easily be transformed to input values that trigger output of the second input value by a constraint solver, e.g $(dcd, in) = (1, 16)$ creates an A object, and $(0, 43)$ a B object. These inputs can serve as a witness for information flow from the input to the result.

Generating this path condition takes less than a second on a standard PC. Although the implementation of precise conditions for Java features is not finished yet, we expect that generating Java path conditions takes about the same time as traditional ones. Empirical evaluation in previous work has shown that this is possible within a few minutes even for larger programs [SRK06].

7.4.2 Dynamic Path Conditions for C

Five case studies will show the impact of dynamic information on path conditions for actual programs. Table 7.4 lists the programs used for evaluation purposes together with lines of code and the number of nodes and edges in the (static) SDG. The programs ptb_like and mergesort are included in this thesis (Figures 7.13 and 7.19). The remaining programs are taken from the GNU project.

Program	LOC	Nodes in SDG	Edges in SDG
ptb_like	35	134	334
mergesort	59	244	640
cal	678	2388	6149
agrep	3990	22961	81203
patch	7998	30774	246754

Table 7.4: Example programs for case studies

Our first goal was to show the impact of dynamic chopping in contrast to static chopping. Remember from sections 5.2.1 and 5.4.3 that smaller chop sizes result in more precise path conditions. Table 7.5 shows the number of nodes and edges for the static chop followed by these numbers for the dynamic chop. The chopping criterion is given in the format *from: line-column, to: line-column*. For

Program	static		dynamic		criterion
ptb_like	65	173	49	124	9-8, 33-53
mergesort	123	299	97	216	45-14, 21-8
cal	240	648	0	0	228-10, 281-18
	134	315	44	92	367-12, 551-3
agrep	13170	40324	0	0	605-15, 638-7
(sgrep.c)	13138	40144	961	2345	96-14, 121-9
patch	16529	246754	6314	81365	825-23, 935-10

Table 7.5: Evaluation of static vs. dynamic chop sizes

the program `agrep` the criteria refer to the file `sgrep.c`. They were chosen in a way to find statements in the code which involve several variables that possibly influence each other, preferably in loops. The goal was to produce interesting path conditions. For example, the static chop in the program `ptb_like` (listed in Figure 7.13) from line 9 to line 33 (u_kg) contains 65 nodes connected by 173 edges. The dynamic chop, however, 49 nodes and 124 edges. It is clear that the latter subgraph contains a noticeable smaller number of paths than the subgraph induced by the static chop. Sometimes the dynamic chop can rule out a dependence between two statements completely: Consider the first lines of the programs `cal` and `agrep`. One can see that the dynamic chop for these criteria is empty. The following evaluation of using traced variable values to improve precision in dynamic path conditions contains another example of that kind. In all these cases there was definitely no (illegal) information flow between the chopping criteria although the static chop indicated so.

After showing that dynamic chopping can considerably reduce the number of paths and thus yield a more precise path condition, that narrows down the reasons for an (illicit) influence, we will present excerpts of path conditions and augment them with the restriction condition, which is based on trace data (partly using incomplete traces). Again, this information reveals variable values which may have contributed to the necessary condition that triggered an illegal information flow.

The first example `ptb_like`, shown in Figure 7.13, is taken from a weighing machine controller[7]. Such a program represents perfectly the security relevant software we have in mind for this approach: There is a part of the program, the so-called calibration path, that contains all paths from the sensor (`p_ab`) to the value display, in this case the weight stored in u_kg (line 33). For a certificate that the machine is correctly calibrated one needs to assure that there is no way to influence the calculation of the weight, for example from the keyboard. Consider the static path condition between the keyboard buffer `p_cd` in line 9 and the display of `u_kg`, the actual weight, in line 33. The final path condition is shown in Figure 7.14. Note that & represents bitwise logical and. An illegal information flow could only happen, if the keyboard buffer `p_cd` contained one of the special characters '+' or '-'. Since our run uses an keyboard buffer containing only ones, we expect the dynamic path condition to evaluate to *false*.

---

[7]It is actually the original program to the Java version in Figure 7.8

```
 1 #define TRUE 1
 2 #define CTRL2 0
 3 #define PB 0
 4 #define PA 1
 5 void printf();
 6 void main()
 7 {
 8   int p_ab[2] = {0, 1};
 9   int p_cd[2] = {1, 1};
10   char e_puf[8] =
      {'0','0','0','0','0','0','0','0'};
11   int u = 0;
12   int idx = 0;
13   float u_kg = 0.0;
14   float kal_kg = 1.0;
15
16   while(TRUE) {
17     if ((p_ab[CTRL2] & 0x10)==0) {
18       u = ((p_ab[PB] & 0x0f) << 8) +
            (unsigned int)p_ab[PA];
19       u_kg = (float) u * kal_kg;
20     }
21     if ((p_cd[CTRL2] & 0x01) != 0) {
22       for (idx=0;idx<7;idx++) {
23     e_puf[idx] = (char)p_cd[PA];
24     if ((p_cd[CTRL2] & 0x10) != 0) {
25       if (e_puf[idx] == '+')
26         kal_kg *= 1.01; /* illegal */
27       else if (e_puf[idx] == '-')
28         kal_kg *= 0.99; /* illegal */
29     }
30       }
31       e_puf[idx] = '\0';
32     }
33     printf("Article:␣%7.7s\n" +
          "␣␣␣%6.2f␣kg␣␣␣␣",e_puf,u_kg);
34   }
35 }
```

Figure 7.13: ptb_like

```
 1 ( ((p_cd[0] & 0x01) != 0)
 2 ∧ ((p_cd[0] & 0x10) != 0)
 3 ∧ ((p_ab[0] & 0x10) == 0)
 4 ∧ (e_puf[idx] == '+')
 5 ∧ (idx < 7) )
 6 ∨
 7 ( ((p_cd[0] & 0x01) != 0)
 8 ∧ ((p_cd[0] & 0x10) != 0)
 9 ∧ (e_puf[idx] == '-')
10 ∧ ((p_ab[0] & 0x10) == 0)
11 ∧ (e_puf[idx] != '+')
12 ∧ (idx < 7) )
```

Figure 7.14: Static path condition for ptb_like

```
 1 ... ∨
 2 ( e_puf == <unknown>
 3 ∧ idx == 0
 4 ∧ p_cd == {1, 1}
 5 ∧ p_ab == {0, 1}
 6 ∧ ((p_cd[0] & 0x01) != 0)
 7 ∧ ((p_cd[0] & 0x10) != 0)
 8 ∧ (e_puf[idx] == '-')
 9 ∧ ((p_ab[0] & 0x10) == 0)
10 ∧ (e_puf[idx] != '+')
11 ∧ (idx < 7) )
12 ∨ ...
```

Figure 7.15: Excerpt of a dynamic path condition for ptb_like

```
1  ((p_cd[0] & 0x01) != 0)
2 ∧ ((p_cd[0] & 0x10) != 0)
3 ∧ ((p_ab[0] & 0x10) == 0)
4 ∧ (e_puf[idx] == '+')
5 ∧ (idx < 7)
```

Figure 7.16: Dynamic path condition of illegal flow in ptb_like

Using a dynamic chop immediately reveals this fact: the static path condition describes a path that was not taken during runtime, the precise *dynamic* path condition yields *false*. The dynamic path condition based on the *static* chop, in contrast, consists of ten conjunctive blocks, one of which is shown in Figure 7.15. Dynamic trace data is shown in bold, e_puf has not been traced (incomplete trace). As one can see, the particular predicates

$$p\_cd \; -- \; \{1, \; 1\}$$

and

$$((p\_cd[0] \; \& \; 0x10) \neq 0)$$

contradict each other, so that the given block evaluates to *false*. The same goes with the other blocks and we get the expected result *false*. The path condition cannot be fulfilled; the necessary path was not taken. This result proves that the keyboard buffer had no influence on the output presented to the consumer.

In another scenario, the input p_cd = {0xff, '+'} (instead of line 9) has been traced. Upon entering '+' on the keyboard, the displayed value is too high. With the dynamic path condition the detection of the illicit influence is done automatically: Figure 7.16 shows the path condition for the adapted program based on the dynamic rather than the static chop. With the traced input one can exactly determine why the illicit information flow took place. Together with the definition of e_puf[idx] in line 23, adding the restrictive condition yields:

```
1  (p_cd[0]  == 0xff)
2 ∧ (p_ab[0]  == 0)
3 ∧ (p_cd[1]  == '+')
4 ∧ (idx < 7)
```

This path condition already shows why there was an illegal information flow during program execution giving detailed information why the program produced incorrect output (the weight on the machine): The display was influenced by some debug flags and the input of '+' during the 7 rounds of the for-loop. The programmers simply had forgotten to remove the debugging code from the final version. This information can act as a witness to reproduce the illicit behavior. In this small example one can easily see that the calibration factor u_kg is increased in line 26 by such an input. For larger examples a human would most probably not detect illegal statements so easily.

As another example, consider the program mergesort from Figure 7.19. Figure 7.17 shows the statically computed path condition between 999 in line 45

```
1   (left < right)
2 ∧ (idx1 <= ((left + right) / 2))
3 ∧ (data[idx1] >= data[idx2])
4 ∧ (idx2 <= right)
```

Figure 7.17: Static path condition for mergesort

```
1    right == 4
2 ∧  left == 4
3 ∧  data == 1
4 ∧  idx2 == 5
5 ∧  ((left + right) / 2) == 3
6 ∧  idx1 == 3
7 ∧ (left < right)
8 ∧ (idx1 <= ((left + right) / 2))
9 ∧ (data[idx1] >= data[idx2])
10 ∧ (idx2 <= right)
```

Figure 7.18: Excerpt of a dynamic path condition for mergesort

and temp in line 21. This time, using a dynamic chop does not help strengthening the path condition as the dynamic chop is identical to the static chop regarding the paths relevant to the path condition. The dynamic path condition, however, yields 40 conjunctive blocks, one of which is shown in Figure 7.18. Dynamic trace data is again shown in bold. Due to contradictions within the particular blocks, the condition can be fully evaluated to *false*: there was no program state traced which would have fulfilled the static path condition.

As our examples show, dynamic path conditions are usually a good deal bigger than their statically computed counterparts, but also more precise as they hold more information. Each dynamic path condition is tied to a particular program run, though. If a dynamic path condition evaluates to *false* this does not necessarily hold for each program execution, especially if user input is involved. But dynamic path conditions are a precise means for finding witnesses for illegal program behavior.

Omission errors

Dynamic slices can only show *that* some influence took place or not. Sometimes one would like to know *why* an expected influence did *not* happen during program execution. In literature [AHKL93, GABF99, WR04] several approaches were proposed to enrich the dynamic slice with the "culpable" control predicates, i.e. those predicates that triggered a branch to an execution path on which the expected potential data dependence did not come into effect. But adding only the predicates to the slice does not reveal what actually went wrong. Our approach returns the exact conditions for a data flow to happen. The static path condition augmented with the restrictive clause can be fed into a constraint solver to detect the contradictions between the variable trace and the values

```
 1 int data[100];
 2 int temp[100];
 3
 4 void move (int *from, int fst, int lst,
 5             int *to, int idx) {
 6   while (fst <= lst)
 7     to[idx++] = from[fst++];
 8 }
 9
10 void merge (int fst, int mid, int lst) {
11   int idx, idx1, idx2;
12
13   idx = 0;
14   idx1 = fst;
15   idx2 = mid + 1;
16
17   while ((idx1 <= mid) && (idx2 <= lst)) {
18     if (data[idx1] < data[idx2])
19       temp[idx++] = data[idx1++];
20     else
21       temp[idx++] = data[idx2++];
22   }
23
24   if (idx1 > mid)
25     move (data, idx2, lst, temp, idx);
26   else
27     move (data, idx1, mid, temp, idx);
28
29   move (temp, 0, lst - fst, data, fst);
30 }
31
32 void mergesort (int left, int right) {
33   int m;
34   m = (left + right) / 2;
35   if (left < right) {
36     mergesort (left, m);
37     mergesort (m + 1, right);
38     merge (left, m, right);
39   }
40 }
41
42 int main () {
43   int i;
44
45   data[0] = 999;
46   data[1] = 1;
47   data[2] = 23;
48   data[3] = 55;
49   data[4] = 44;
50
51   mergesort (0, 4);
52
53   for (i = 0; i < 5; ++i) {
54     printf ("%d⎵", data[i]);
55   }
56   printf ("\n");
57
58   return 0;
59 }
```

Figure 7.19: mergesort

expected by the predicates. In Figure 7.18, the subclauses 1 and 2 contravene the sub-clause 7. That is the reason why the path(s) yielding that conjunctive block have not been executed. As pointed out in the description of `mergesort`, the dynamic chop is identical to the static chop. Adding only the control predicates as proposed by previous solutions would just reveal the conditions shown in Figure 7.17. The user would have to find those conditions in the slice and interpret them to find the information he or she was really looking for: the condition in Figure 7.18. The dynamic path conditions thus helps localizing flaws in the program by detecting contradictions between expected and actual execution paths.

Chapter 8

Conclusion

This thesis presented several algorithms for precise analysis of programs in realistic programming languages like Java or C. It extends program dependence graphs to all features of Java bytecode, most prominently method parameters with nested field structures. In contrast to other slicers for Java, our system generates a system dependence graph, for which the standard two-phase context-sensitive slicing algorithms can be leveraged.

For multi-threaded Java, we defined a precise approximation of interference dependence (with respect to the presented undecidability results), which arises when a shared variable is defined in one thread and used in another thread. Based on the new Java memory model, our definition leverages points-to information, which improves precision compared to previous definitions based on type or escape information.

When the binary information, whether one statement might influence another given statement is not sufficient, path conditions yield the detailed circumstances of the influence and can even eliminate false positives. This thesis found that for object-oriented constructs one needs to include detailed information on variable types to gain conditions suitable for automatic constraint solvers. The described techniques extend the traditional path conditions, and allow precise conditions for all object-oriented features. Furthermore, dynamic trace data allows a 'flight recorder' principle and improves the precision of path conditions for a specific program execution.

The main contribution of this work is a novel approach for information flow control based on system dependence graph as defined in this thesis. The flow-sensitivity, context-sensitivity, and object-sensitivity of our slicer extends naturally to information flow control and thus excels over the predominant approach for information flow control, namely security type systems.

The evaluation section showed that our new algorithm for information flow control dramatically reduced annotation burden compared to type systems, due to its elevated precision. Furthermore, empirical evaluation showed the scalability of this approach. While it is clearly more expensive than security type systems, the evaluation demonstrates that security kernels are certified in reasonable time. As this certification process is only needed once at compile time, even an analysis that takes hours is acceptable when it guarantees security for the whole lifetime of a software artifact. As a consequence, this thesis makes recent developments in program analysis applicable to realistic programming languages. The presented system implements the first information flow control analysis for a realistic language, namely Java bytecode.

Appendix A

Appendix

The following tables show the details of the execution times depicted in section 7.3.5 for comparison purposes.

Table A.1: Execution time (in sec) of summary declassification node computation with different numbers of declassifications

program	lattice	0	5	10	50	100	500
dijkstra	A	0	0	0	0	0	0
enigma	A	0	0	0	0	0	0
wallet	A	0	7	8	11	15	12
purse	A	0	8552	8368	8378	14386	15622
lindenmayer	A	0	5	5	6	7	9
mp	A	0	3	3	3	3	5
networkflow	A	0	4	4	8	7	10
planesweep	A	0	16	16	24	26	40
semithue	A	0	57	60	138	156	180
tsp	A	0	6	6	10	11	10
unionfind	A	0	23147	26417	39514	40017	43183
dijkstra	B	0	0	0	0	0	0
enigma	B	0	0	0	0	0	0
wallet	B	0	8	8	9	17	15
purse	B	0	8951	8491	13352	13327	9679
lindenmayer	B	0	5	5	6	6	9
mp	B	0	4	3	3	3	5
networkflow	B	0	4	4	7	7	10
planesweep	B	0	16	16	26	32	39
semithue	B	0	58	65	160	162	164
tsp	B	0	6	6	10	11	11
unionfind	B	0	21659	26523	37051	42094	39401
dijkstra	C	0	0	0	0	0	0
enigma	C	0	0	0	0	0	0
wallet	C	0	8	8	9	17	18
purse	C	0	9015	7874	8111	12921	12899

program	lattice	0	5	10	50	100	500
lindenmayer	C	0	5	5	7	6	11
mp	C	0	3	3	3	3	5
networkflow	C	0	4	5	7	7	14
planesweep	C	0	15	13	22	26	39
semithue	C	0	61	72	157	199	192
tsp	C	0	5	5	10	12	11
unionfind	C	0	19950	25905	36508	38639	44684
dijkstra	D	0	0	0	0	0	0
enigma	D	0	0	0	0	0	0
wallet	D	0	8	9	14	18	21
purse	D	0	8398	7701	11548	11913	14634
lindenmayer	D	0	5	6	8	7	13
mp	D	0	3	3	3	4	5
networkflow	D	0	4	4	9	8	14
planesweep	D	0	13	13	19	27	39
semithue	D	0	67	67	196	192	220
tsp	D	0	5	6	11	12	12
unionfind	D	0	21499	27810	49010	49312	50244
dijkstra	E	0	0	0	0	0	0
enigma	E	0	0	0	0	0	0
wallet	E	0	8	8	12	12	22
purse	E	0	8758	8734	9037	13682	21963
lindenmayer	E	0	5	6	7	8	13
mp	E	0	3	3	3	3	4
networkflow	E	0	4	4	8	8	13
planesweep	E	0	14	14	20	30	43
semithue	E	0	71	81	222	215	246
tsp	E	0	6	5	13	12	14
unionfind	E	0	21951	27321	51800	53477	60051
dijkstra	F	0	0	0	0	0	0
enigma	F	0	0	0	0	0	0
wallet	F	0	7	9	14	21	20
purse	F	0	8984	8565	12820	13117	10368
lindenmayer	F	0	4	5	9	9	10
mp	F	0	4	3	3	4	5
networkflow	F	0	4	4	8	8	13
planesweep	F	0	16	16	27	36	49
semithue	F	0	65	74	212	240	234
tsp	F	0	6	6	12	15	15
unionfind	F	0	20658	27037	53967	55846	52176

Table A.2: Average execution time (in sec) of 100 IFC analyses with different numbers of declassifications

program	lattice	0	5	10	50	100	500
dijkstra	A	0.02	0.02	0.01	0.01	0.01	0.01
enigma	A	0.01	0.01	0.01	0.01	0.01	0.01
wallet	A	0.09	0.2	0.19	0.24	0.27	0.22
purse	A	0.91	86.44	84.79	84.97	144.97	157.4
lindenmayer	A	0.03	0.07	0.08	0.09	0.09	0.12
mp	A	0.05	0.09	0.09	0.09	0.1	0.1
networkflow	A	0.08	0.13	0.12	0.17	0.15	0.19
planesweep	A	0.07	0.25	0.25	0.32	0.34	0.47
semithue	A	0.16	0.76	0.84	1.63	1.79	2.02
tsp	A	0.17	0.24	0.27	0.32	0.31	0.28
unionfind	A	1.44	233.63	266.46	397.64	402.54	434.48
dijkstra	B	0.02	0.02	0.01	0.01	0.01	0.02
enigma	B	0.01	0.01	0.01	0.01	0.01	0.01
wallet	B	0.1	0.19	0.18	0.2	0.27	0.25
purse	B	0.93	90.55	85.94	134.57	134.45	97.83
lindenmayer	B	0.03	0.08	0.08	0.08	0.08	0.12
mp	B	0.06	0.1	0.09	0.09	0.09	0.1
networkflow	B	0.09	0.14	0.13	0.17	0.16	0.2
planesweep	B	0.07	0.24	0.24	0.34	0.4	0.47
semithue	B	0.16	0.77	0.86	1.79	1.81	1.83
tsp	B	0.18	0.25	0.25	0.32	0.29	0.29
unionfind	B	1.38	218.83	267.43	372.61	423.26	396.63
dijkstra	C	0.01	0.02	0.01	0.01	0.02	0.02
enigma	C	0.01	0.01	0.01	0.01	0.01	0.01
wallet	C	0.1	0.18	0.18	0.22	0.29	0.29
purse	C	1.04	91.13	79.72	82.2	130.24	130.13
lindenmayer	C	0.03	0.08	0.08	0.09	0.09	0.14
mp	C	0.06	0.09	0.09	0.08	0.09	0.11
networkflow	C	0.09	0.15	0.14	0.17	0.17	0.25
planesweep	C	0.06	0.23	0.21	0.3	0.35	0.46
semithue	C	0.16	0.83	0.93	1.79	2.2	2.14
tsp	C	0.19	0.25	0.25	0.29	0.32	0.29
unionfind	C	1.52	201.9	261.38	367.28	388.54	449.57
dijkstra	D	0.02	0.02	0.02	0.02	0.02	0.02
enigma	D	0.01	0.01	0.01	0.01	0.01	0.01
wallet	D	0.11	0.2	0.2	0.27	0.31	0.32
purse	D	0.84	84.92	77.95	116.39	120.06	147.32
lindenmayer	D	0.03	0.08	0.09	0.11	0.1	0.15
mp	D	0.05	0.08	0.08	0.09	0.09	0.1
networkflow	D	0.1	0.15	0.14	0.19	0.17	0.24
planesweep	D	0.07	0.21	0.21	0.26	0.35	0.46
semithue	D	0.19	0.9	0.9	2.19	2.15	2.42
tsp	D	0.21	0.27	0.3	0.37	0.33	0.32

program	lattice	0	5	10	50	100	500
unionfind	D	1.35	217.15	280.77	492.6	495.55	505.41
dijkstra	E	0.02	0.02	0.01	0.01	0.02	0.02
enigma	E	0.01	0.01	0.01	0.01	0.01	0.01
wallet	E	0.1	0.18	0.17	0.23	0.23	0.32
purse	E	0.93	88.59	88.38	91.42	137.88	220.73
lindenmayer	E	0.03	0.08	0.09	0.1	0.11	0.16
mp	E	0.06	0.09	0.1	0.09	0.1	0.1
networkflow	E	0.1	0.15	0.15	0.18	0.18	0.24
planesweep	E	0.07	0.23	0.23	0.29	0.38	0.52
semithue	E	0.19	0.95	1.04	2.45	2.39	2.7
tsp	E	0.19	0.28	0.28	0.35	0.37	0.34
unionfind	E	1.47	221.85	275.65	520.44	537.56	603.67
dijkstra	F	0.02	0.02	0.01	0.01	0.02	0.02
enigma	F	0.01	0.01	0.01	0.01	0.01	0.01
wallet	F	0.09	0.2	0.22	0.26	0.32	0.3
purse	F	0.98	91.86	66.129	37.132	29.104	65.
lindenmayer	F	0.03	0.07	0.08	0.12	0.12	0.13
mp	F	0.06	0.09	0.09	0.09	0.1	0.1
networkflow	F	0.09	0.13	0.13	0.17	0.16	0.23
planesweep	F	0.07	0.25	0.25	0.35	0.43	0.56
semithue	F	0.17	0.88	0.97	2.34	2.61	2.54
tsp	F	0.22	0.28	0.27	0.33	0.35	0.33
unionfind	F	1.55	208.88	272.9	542.11	560.84	525.3

Bibliography

[ABB06]   Torben Amtoft, Sruthi Bandhakavi, and Anindya Banerjee. A logic
            for information flow in object-oriented programs. In *POPL '06:
            Conference record of the 33rd ACM SIGPLAN-SIGACT sympo-
            sium on Principles of programming languages*, pages 91–102, New
            York, NY, USA, 2006. ACM.

[ABHR99]   Martín Abadi, Anindya Banerjee, Nevin Heintze, and Jon G.
            Riecke. A core calculus of dependency. In *POPL '99: Proceedings
            of the 26th ACM SIGPLAN-SIGACT symposium on Principles of
            programming languages*, pages 147–160, New York, NY, USA, 1999.
            ACM.

[ADS93]   Hiralal Agrawal, Richard A. Demillo, and Eugene H. Spafford. De-
            bugging with dynamic slicing and backtracking. *Softw. Pract. Ex-
            per.*, 23(6):589–616, 1993.

[Aga00]   Johan Agat. Transforming out timing leaks. In *POPL '00: Proceed-
            ings of the 27th ACM SIGPLAN-SIGACT symposium on Princi-
            ples of programming languages*, pages 40–53, New York, NY, USA,
            2000. ACM.

[Agr94]   Hiralal Agrawal. On slicing programs with jump statements. In
            *PLDI '94: Proceedings of the ACM SIGPLAN 1994 conference on
            Programming language design and implementation*, pages 302–312,
            New York, NY, USA, 1994. ACM.

[AH90]   Hiralal Agrawal and Joseph R. Horgan. Dynamic program slicing.
            In *PLDI '90: Proceedings of the ACM SIGPLAN 1990 conference
            on Programming language design and implementation*, pages 246–
            256, New York, NY, USA, 1990. ACM.

[AH03]   Matthew Allen and Susan Horwitz. Slicing Java programs that
            throw and catch exceptions. In *PEPM '03: Proceedings of the 2003
            ACM SIGPLAN workshop on Partial evaluation and semantics-
            based program manipulation*, pages 44–54, New York, NY, USA,
            2003. ACM.

[AHKL93]   Hiralal Agrawal, Joseph R. Horgan, Edward W. Krauser, and Saul
            London. Incremental regression testing. In *ICSM '93: Proceed-*

           ings of the Conference on Software Maintenance, pages 348–357, Washington, DC, USA, September 1993. IEEE Computer Society.

[AKBLN89] Hassan Aït-Kaci, Robert Boyer, Patrick Lincoln, and Roger Nasr. Efficient implementation of lattice operations. *ACM Trans. Program. Lang. Syst.*, 11(1):115–146, 1989.

[Amt08]   Torben Amtoft. Slicing for modern program structures: a theory for eliminating irrelevant loops. *Inf. Process. Lett.*, 106(2):45–51, 2008.

[And94]   Lars Ole Andersen. *Program Analysis and Specialization for the C Programming Language*. PhD thesis, DIKU, University of Copenhagen, May 1994. (DIKU report 94/19) Available at ftp.diku.dk/pub/diku/semantics/papers/D-203.dvi.Z.

[And08]   Paul Anderson. 90% perspiration: Engineering static analysis techniques for industrial applications. In *Proc. IEEE International Working Conference on Source Code Analysis and Manipulation*, pages 3–12, Los Alamitos, CA, USA, September 2008. IEEE Computer Society.

[ART03]   Paul Anderson, Thomas Reps, and Tim Teitelbaum. Design and implementation of a fine-grained software inspection tool. *IEEE Transactions on Software Engineering*, 29(8), August 2003.

[AS05]   Aslan Askarov and Andrei Sabelfeld. Security-typed languages for implementation of cryptographic protocols: A case study. In *Proc. European Symp. on Research in Computer Security (ESORICS'05)*, volume 3679 of *LNCS*, pages 197–221. Springer, 2005.

[AT01]   Paul Anderson and Tim Teitelbaum. Software inspection using codesurfer. In *Proceedings of the first Workshop on Inspection in Software Engineering (WISE'01)*, pages 4–11, jul 2001.

[Ban79]   John P. Banning. An efficient way to find the side effects of procedure calls and the aliases of variables. In *POPL '79: Proceedings of the 6th ACM SIGACT-SIGPLAN symposium on Principles of programming languages*, pages 29–41, New York, NY, USA, 1979. ACM.

[BC85]   Jean-Francois Bergeretti and Bernard A. Carré. Information-flow and data-flow analysis of while-programs. *ACM Trans. Program. Lang. Syst.*, 7(1):37–61, 1985.

[BCM$^+$00] P. Bieber, J. Cazin, A. El Marouani, P. Girard, J.-L. Lanet, V. Wiels, and G. Zanon. The PACAP prototype: a tool for detecting Java Card illegal flow. In *Proc. 1st International Workshop, Java Card 2000*, volume 2041 of *LNCS*, pages 25–37, Cannes, France, September 2000. Springer.

[BDG⁺06] Dave Binkley, Sebastian Danicic, Tibor Gyimóthy, Mark Harman, Ákos Kiss, and Bogdan Korel. A formalisation of the relationship between forms of program slicing. *Science of Computer Programming*, 62(3):228–252, 2006.

[BDH⁺06] David W. Binkley, Sebastian Danicic, Mark Harman, John Howroyd, and Lahcen Ouarbya. A formal relationship between program slicing and partial evaluation. *Formal Aspects of Computing*, 18(2):103–119, 2006.

[BG96] David Binkley and Keith Brian Gallagher. Program slicing. *Advances in Computers*, 43:1–50, 1996.

[BGS97] Rastislav Bodík, Rajiv Gupta, and Mary Lou Soffa. Refining data flow information using infeasible paths. In *ESEC '97/FSE-5: Proceedings of the 6th European conference held jointly with the 5th ACM SIGSOFT international symposium on Foundations of software engineering*, pages 361–377, New York, NY, USA, 1997. Springer-Verlag New York, Inc.

[BH73] Per Brinch-Hansen. *Operating system principles*. Prentice-Hall, Inc., Upper Saddle River, NJ, USA, 1973.

[BH93] Thomas Ball and Susan Horwitz. Slicing programs with arbitrary control-flow. In *AADEBUG '93: Proceedings of the First International Workshop on Automated and Algorithmic Debugging*, volume 749, pages 206–222, London, UK, 1993. Springer-Verlag.

[BH04] D. Binkley and M. Harman. A survey of empirical results on program slicing. In Marvin Zelkowitz, editor, *Advances in Computers*, volume 62, pages 105–178. Academic Press, San Diego, CA, 2004.

[BHK07] David Binkley, Mark Harman, and Jens Krinke. Empirical study of optimization techniques for massive slicing. *ACM Trans. Program. Lang. Syst.*, 30(1):3, 2007.

[BHR89] David Binkley, Susan Horwitz, and Thomas Reps. The multi-procedure equivalence theorem. Technical Report 890, Computer Sciences Department, University of Wisconsin-Madison, November 1989.

[Bib77] K. J. Biba. Integrity considerations for secure computer systems. Technical Report MTR-3153, The Mitre Corporation, April 1977.

[BK01] Ulrik Brandes and Boris Köpf. Fast and simple horizontal coordinate assignment. In *Proc. 9th International Symposium on Graph Drawing*, volume 2265 of *LNCS*, pages 33–36. Springer, September 2001.

[BL73] D. Elliott Bell and Leonard J. LaPadula. Secure computer systems: Mathematical foundations. Technical Report 2547, Volume I, Mitre, March 1973.

[BL96]   D. Elliot Bell and Leonard J. LaPadula. Secure computer systems: A mathematical model, volume II. *Journal of Computer Security*, 4(2/3):229–263, 1996. based on MITRE Technical Report 2547, Volume II.

[BR05]   Gilles Barthe and Tamara Rezk. Non-interference for a JVM-like language. In *TLDI '05: Proceedings of the 2005 ACM SIGPLAN international workshop on Types in languages design and implementation*, pages 103–112, New York, NY, USA, 2005. ACM Press.

[BS96]   David F. Bacon and Peter F. Sweeney. Fast static analysis of C++ virtual function calls. In *OOPSLA '96: Proceedings of the 11th ACM SIGPLAN conference on Object-oriented programming, systems, languages, and applications*, pages 324–341, New York, NY, USA, 1996. ACM Press.

[CCHK90]   David Callahan, Alan Carle, Mary Wolcott Hall, and Ken Kennedy. Constructing the procedure call multigraph. *IEEE Trans. Softw. Eng.*, 16(4):483–487, 1990.

[CCL98]   Gerardo Canfora, Aniello Cimitile, and Andrea De Lucia. Conditioned program slicing. *Information and Software Technology*, 40(11–12):595–607, Dec 1998. Special issue on Program Slicing.

[CF89]   Robert Cartwright and Mattias Felleisen. The semantics of program dependence. In *PLDI '89: Proceedings of the ACM SIGPLAN 1989 Conference on Programming language design and implementation*, pages 13–27, New York, NY, USA, 1989. ACM.

[CF94]   Jong-Deok Choi and Jeanne Ferrante. Static slicing in the presence of goto statements. *ACM Trans. Program. Lang. Syst.*, 16(4):1097–1113, 1994.

[CFR+91]   Ron Cytron, Jeanne Ferrante, Barry K. Rosen, Mark N. Wegman, and F. Kenneth Zadeck. Efficiently computing static single assignment form and the control dependence graph. *ACM Trans. Program. Lang. Syst.*, 13(4):451–490, 1991.

[Che93a]   Jingde Cheng. Process dependence net of distributed programs and its applications in development of distributed systems. In *Proc. 17th Annual International Computer Software and Applications Conference (COMPSAC'93)*, pages 231–240. IEEE Computer Society, Nov 1993.

[Che93b]   Jingde Cheng. Slicing concurrent programs. In *Proc. of the First Int. Workshop on Automated and Algorithmic Debugging*, volume 749 of *LNCS*, pages 223–240. Springer, 1993.

[CM04]   Brian Chess and Gary McGraw. Static analysis for security. *IEEE Security and Privacy*, 2(6):76–79, 2004.

[Coh78]   Ellis S. Cohen. *Foundations of Secure Computation*, chapter Information Transmission in Sequential Programs, pages 297–335. Academic Press, Inc., Orlando, FL, USA, 1978. paper presented at a 3 day workshop held at Georgia Inst. of Technology, Atlanta, Oct. 1977.

[CPS⁺99]   Craig Chambers, Igor Pechtchanski, Vivek Sarkar, Mauricio J. Serrano, and Harini Srinivasan. Dependence analysis for Java. In *Proceedings of the 12th International Workshop on Languages and Compilers for Parallel Computing*, pages 35–52. Springer-Verlag, 1999.

[CX01a]   Zhenqiang Chen and Baowen Xu. Slicing concurrent Java programs. *SIGPLAN Not.*, 36(4):41–47, 2001.

[CX01b]   Zhenqiang Chen and Baowen Xu. Slicing object-oriented Java programs. *SIGPLAN Not.*, 36(4):33–40, 2001.

[CXY⁺00]   Zhenqiang Chen, Baowen Xu, Hongji Yang, Kecheng Liu, and Jianping Zhang. An approach to analyzing dependency of concurrent programs. In *Proc. First Asia-Pacific Conference on Quality Software*, pages 39–43. IEEE Computer Society, October 2000.

[DCH⁺99]   Matthew B. Dwyer, James C. Corbett, John Hatcliff, Stefan Sokolowski, and Hongjun Zheng. Slicing multi-threaded Java programs: A case study. Technical Report 99-7, Kansas State University, Computing and Information Sciences, 1999.

[DD77]   Dorothy E. Denning and Peter J. Denning. Certification of programs for secure information flow. *Commun. ACM*, 20(7):504–513, 1977.

[Den76]   Dorothy E. Denning. A lattice model of secure information flow. *Commun. ACM*, 19(5):236–243, 1976.

[DGC95]   Jeffrey Dean, David Grove, and Craig Chambers. Optimization of object-oriented programs using static class hierarchy analysis. In *ECOOP '95: Proceedings of the 9th European Conference on Object-Oriented Programming*, volume 952, pages 77–101, London, UK, 1995. Springer-Verlag.

[DHH⁺06]   Matthew Dwyer, John Hatcliff, Matthew Hoosier, Venkatesh Ranganath, Robby, and Todd Wallentine. Evaluating the effectiveness of slicing for model reduction of concurrent object-oriented programs. In *Proc. Tools and Algorithms for the Construction and Analysis of Systems (TACAS'06)*, volume 3920 of *LNCS*, pages 73–89. Springer, 2006.

[DHHO07]   Sebastian Danicic, Mark Harman, John Howroyd, and Lahcen Ouarbya. A non-standard semantics for program slicing and dependence analysis. *Journal of Logic and Algebraic Programming*, 72(2):191–206, 2007.

[dL01]   Andrea de Lucia. Program slicing: Methods and applications. In *IEEE International Workshop on Source Code Analysis and Manipulation (SCAM'01)*, pages 142–149, Los Alamitos, CA, USA, 2001. IEEE Computer Society.

[DRH07]   Xianghua Deng, Robby, and John Hatcliff. Towards a case-optimal symbolic execution algorithm for analyzing strong properties of object-oriented programs. In *SEFM '07: Proceedings of the Fifth IEEE International Conference on Software Engineering and Formal Methods (SEFM 2007)*, pages 273–282, Washington, DC, USA, 2007. IEEE Computer Society.

[Fen74]   J. S. Fenton. Memoryless subsystems. *The Computer Journal*, 17(2):143–147, 1974.

[FKS00]   Stephen J. Fink, Kathleen Knobe, and Vivek Sarkar. Unified analysis of array and object references in strongly typed languages. In *SAS '00: Proceedings of the 7th International Symposium on Static Analysis*, volume 1824 of *LNCS*, pages 155–174, London, UK, 2000. Springer-Verlag.

[FLL+02]   Cormac Flanagan, K. Rustan M. Leino, Mark Lillibridge, Greg Nelson, James B. Saxe, and Raymie Stata. Extended static checking for Java. In *PLDI '02: Proceedings of the ACM SIGPLAN 2002 Conference on Programming language design and implementation*, pages 234–245, New York, NY, USA, 2002. ACM.

[FOW87]   Jeanne Ferrante, Karl J. Ottenstein, and Joe D. Warren. The program dependence graph and its use in optimization. *ACM Trans. Program. Lang. Syst.*, 9(3):319–349, 1987.

[FRT95]   John Field, G. Ramalingam, and Frank Tip. Parametric program slicing. In *POPL '95: Proceedings of the 22nd ACM SIGPLAN-SIGACT symposium on Principles of programming languages*, pages 379–392, New York, NY, USA, 1995. ACM Press.

[GABF99]   Tibor Gyimóthy, Árpád Beszédes, and Istán Forgács. An efficient relevant slicing method for debugging. In *ESEC/FSE-7: Proceedings of the 7th European software engineering conference held jointly with the 7th ACM SIGSOFT international symposium on Foundations of software engineering*, pages 303–321, London, UK, 1999. Springer-Verlag.

[GDDC97]   David Grove, Greg DeFouw, Jeffrey Dean, and Craig Chambers. Call graph construction in object-oriented languages. In *OOPSLA '97: Proceedings of the 12th ACM SIGPLAN conference on Object-oriented programming, systems, languages, and applications*, pages 108–124, New York, NY, USA, 1997. ACM Press.

[GH96]   Rakesh Ghiya and Laurie J. Hendren. Is it a tree, a DAG, or a cyclic graph? a shape analysis for heap-directed pointers in C. In *POPL '96: Proceedings of the 23rd ACM SIGPLAN-SIGACT symposium on Principles of programming languages*, pages 1–15, New York, NY, USA, 1996. ACM.

[GH08]   Dennis Giffhorn and Christian Hammer. Precise analysis of Java programs using JOANA (tool demonstration). In *Proc. 8th IEEE International Working Conference on Source Code Analysis and Manipulation*, pages 267–268, September 2008.

[GH09]   Dennis Giffhorn and Christian Hammer. Precise slicing of concurrent programs – an evaluation of precise slicing algorithms for concurrent programs. *Journal of Automated Software Engineering*, 16(2):197–234, June 2009.

[GJSB05]   James Gosling, Bill Joy, Guy Steele, and Gilad Bracha. *The Java Language Specification*. Addison Wesley Professional, 3rd edition, 2005. http://java.sun.com/docs/books/jls/.

[GL]   Dennis Giffhorn and Andreas Lochbihler. Information flow control for concurrent programs via program slicing. Forthcoming.

[GM82]   Joseph A. Goguen and José Meseguer. Security policies and security models. In *Proc. Symposium on Security and Privacy*, pages 11–20. IEEE, 1982.

[GM84]   Joseph A. Goguen and José Meseguer. Interference control and unwinding. In *Proc. Symposium on Security and Privacy*, pages 75–86. IEEE, 1984.

[GM03]   Roberto Giacobazzi and Isabella Mastroeni. Non-standard semantics for program slicing. *Higher Order and Symbolic Computation*, 16(4):297–339, 2003.

[GMR94]   Deb Dutta Ganguly, Chilukuri K. Mohan, and Sanjay Ranka. A space-and-time-efficient coding algorithm for lattice computations. *IEEE Trans. on Knowl. and Data Eng.*, 6(5):819–829, 1994.

[GPB+06]   Brian Goetz, Tim Peierls, Joshua Bloch, Joseph Bowbeer, David Holmes, and Doug Lea. *Java Concurrency in Practice*. Addison Wesley Professional, May 2006.

[GS05]   Samir Genaim and Fausto Spoto. Information flow analysis for Java bytecode. In *6th International Conference on Verification, Model Checking, and Abstract Interpretation (VMCAI 2005)*, volume 3385 of *LNCS*, pages 346–362, Paris, France, January 2005. Springer.

[HBCC99]   Michael Hind, Michael Burke, Paul Carini, and Jong-Deok Choi. Interprocedural pointer alias analysis. *ACM Trans. Program. Lang. Syst.*, 21(4):848–894, 1999.

[HBD03]   Mark Harman, David Binkley, and Sebastian Danicic. Amorphous
           program slicing. *Journal of Systems and Software*, 68(1):45–64,
           Oktober 2003.

[HCD⁺99]   John Hatcliff, James C. Corbett, Matthew B. Dwyer, Stefan
           Sokolowski, and Hongjun Zheng. A formal study of slicing for
           multi-threaded programs with JVM concurrency primitives. In
           *SAS '99: Proceedings of the 6th International Symposium on Static
           Analysis*, volume 1694 of *LNCS*, pages 1–18, London, UK, 1999.
           Springer-Verlag.

[HD98]   Mark Harman and Sebastian Danicic. A new algorithm for slic-
           ing unstructured programs. *Journal of Software Maintenance*,
           10(6):415–441, 1998.

[HDZ00]   John Hatcliff, Matthew B. Dwyer, and Hongjun Zheng. Slicing
           software for model construction. *Higher-Order and Symbolic Com-
           putation*, 13(4):315–353, 2000.

[HGK06]   Christian Hammer, Martin Grimme, and Jens Krinke. Dynamic
           path conditions in dependence graphs. In *PEPM '06: Proceedings
           of the 2006 ACM SIGPLAN symposium on Partial evaluation and
           semantics-based program manipulation*, pages 58–67, New York,
           NY, USA, 2006. ACM Press.

[HH01]   Mark Harman and Robert Hierons. An overview of program slicing.
           Software Focus, 2(3):85–92, Januar 2001.

[Hin01]   Michael Hind. Pointer analysis: haven't we solved this problem
           yet? In *PASTE '01: Proceedings of the 2001 ACM SIGPLAN-
           SIGSOFT workshop on Program analysis for software tools and
           engineering*, pages 54–61, New York, NY, USA, 2001. ACM.

[HKN06]   Christian Hammer, Jens Krinke, and Frank Nodes. Intransitive
           noninterference in dependence graphs. In *Proc. Second Interna-
           tional Symposium on Leveraging Application of Formal Methods,
           Verification and Validation (ISoLA 2006)*, pages 119–128, Wash-
           ington, DC, USA, November 2006. IEEE Computer Society.

[HKS06]   Christian Hammer, Jens Krinke, and Gregor Snelting. Informa-
           tion flow control for Java based on path conditions in dependence
           graphs. In *Proc. IEEE International Symposium on Secure Soft-
           ware Engineering (ISSSE'06)*, pages 87–96, March 2006.

[HLB06]   Mark Harman, Arun Lakhotia, and David Binkley. Theory and al-
           gorithms for slicing unstructured programs. *Information and Soft-
           ware Technology*, 48(7):549–565, 2006.

[HLW⁺91]   John Hogg, Doug Lea, Alan Wills, Dennis deChampeaux, and
           Richard Holt. The geneva convention on the treatment of object
           aliasing, August 1991.

[Hoa74]   C. A. R. Hoare. Monitors: an operating system structuring concept. *Commun. ACM*, 17(10):549–557, 1974.

[How76]   John H. Howard. Signaling in monitors. In *ICSE '76: Proceedings of the 2nd international conference on Software engineering*, pages 47–52, Los Alamitos, CA, USA, 1976. IEEE Computer Society Press.

[HPR88]   S. Horwitz, J. Prins, and T. Reps. On the adequacy of program dependence graphs for representing programs. In *POPL '88: Proceedings of the 15th ACM SIGPLAN-SIGACT symposium on Principles of programming languages*, pages 146–157, New York, NY, USA, 1988. ACM.

[HPR89]   S. Horwitz, P. Pfeiffer, and T. Reps. Dependence analysis for pointer variables. In *PLDI '89: Proceedings of the ACM SIGPLAN 1989 Conference on Programming language design and implementation*, pages 28–40, New York, NY, USA, 1989. ACM.

[HRB90]   Susan Horwitz, Thomas Reps, and David Binkley. Interprocedural slicing using dependence graphs. *ACM Trans. Program. Lang. Syst.*, 12(1):26–60, 1990.

[HS04]   Christian Hammer and Gregor Snelting. An improved slicer for Java. In *PASTE '04: Proceedings of the 5th ACM SIGPLAN-SIGSOFT workshop on Program analysis for software tools and engineering*, pages 17–22, New York, NY, USA, 2004. ACM Press.

[HS06]   Sebastian Hunt and David Sands. On flow-sensitive security types. In *POPL '06: Conference record of the 33rd ACM SIGPLAN-SIGACT symposium on Principles of programming languages*, pages 79–90, New York, NY, USA, 2006. ACM Press.

[HS08]   Christian Hammer and Gregor Snelting. Flow-sensitive, context-sensitive, and object-sensitive information flow control based on program dependence graphs. Technical Report 2008-16, Fakultät für Informatik, Universität Karlsruhe (TH), Germany, November 2008. Supersedes ISSSE and ISoLA 2006.

[HSS08]   Christian Hammer, Rüdiger Schaade, and Gregor Snelting. Static path conditions for Java. In *PLAS '08: Proceedings of the third ACM SIGPLAN workshop on Programming languages and analysis for security*, pages 57–66, New York, NY, USA, 2008. ACM.

[Hub08]   Laurent Hubert. A non-null annotation inferencer for Java bytecode. In *PASTE '08: Proceedings of the 8th ACM SIGPLAN-SIGSOFT Workshop on Program Analysis for Software Tools and Engineering*, pages 36–42, New York, NY, USA, November 2008. ACM.

[JGS93]   N.D. Jones, C.K. Gomard, and P. Sestoft. *Partial Evaluation and Automatic Program Generation*. Prentice Hall, 1993.

[JM05]   Ranjit Jhala and Rupak Majumdar. Path slicing. In *PLDI '05: Proceedings of the 2005 ACM SIGPLAN conference on Programming language design and implementation*, pages 38–47, New York, NY, USA, 2005. ACM Press.

[JRH05]   Ganeshan Jayaraman, Venkatesh Prasad Ranganath, and John Hatcliff. Kaveri: Delivering the Indus Java program slicer to Eclipse. In *Proc. Fundamental Approaches to Software Engineering (FASE'05)*, volume 3442 of *LNCS*, pages 269–272. Springer, 2005.

[Kil73]   Gary A. Kildall. A unified approach to global program optimization. In *POPL '73: Proceedings of the 1st annual ACM SIGACT-SIGPLAN symposium on Principles of programming languages*, pages 194–206, New York, NY, USA, 1973. ACM Press.

[KL88]   B. Korel and J. Laski. Dynamic program slicing. *Inf. Process. Lett.*, 29(3):155–163, 1988. Reprinted in Berzins, 'Software Merging and Slicing'.

[KMG96]   Gyula Kovács, Ferenc Magyar, and Tibor Gyimóthy. Static slicing of Java programs. Technical Report TR-96-108, József Attila University, Hungary, 1996.

[Kri98]   Jens Krinke. Static slicing of threaded programs. In *PASTE '98: Proceedings of the 1998 ACM SIGPLAN-SIGSOFT workshop on Program analysis for software tools and engineering*, pages 35–42, New York, NY, USA, 1998. ACM.

[Kri02]   Jens Krinke. Evaluating context-sensitive slicing and chopping. In *Proceedings of the International Conference on Software Maintenance*, pages 22–31. IEEE, 2002.

[Kri03a]   Jens Krinke. *Advanced Slicing of Sequential and Concurrent Programs*. PhD thesis, Univ. of Passau, Germany, April 2003.

[Kri03b]   Jens Krinke. Context-sensitive slicing of concurrent programs. In *ESEC/FSE-11: Proceedings of the 9th European software engineering conference held jointly with 11th ACM SIGSOFT international symposium on Foundations of software engineering*, pages 178–187, New York, NY, USA, 2003. ACM.

[Kri05]   Jens Krinke. Program slicing. In *Handbook of Software Engineering and Knowledge Engineering*, volume 3: Recent Advances. World Scientific Publishing, 2005.

[KU77]   John B. Kam and Jeffrey D. Ullman. Monotone data flow analysis frameworks. *Acta Informatica*, 7(3):305–317, 1977.

[Lam73]   Butler W. Lampson. A note on the confinement problem. *Commun. ACM*, 16(10):613–615, 1973.

[LH96]   Loren Larsen and Mary Jean Harrold. Slicing object-oriented software. In *ICSE '96: Proceedings of the 18th international conference on Software engineering*, pages 495–505, Washington, DC, USA, 1996. IEEE Computer Society.

[LH98]   D. Liang and M.-J. Harrold. Slicing objects using system dependence graphs. In *Proc. International Conference on Software Maintenance*, pages 358–367, November 1998.

[LH03]   Ondřej Lhoták and Laurie Hendren. Scaling Java points-to using Spark. In *Proc. 12th International Conference on Compiler Construction,*, volume 2622 of *LNCS*, pages 153–169, 2003.

[LH08]   Ondřej Lhoták and Laurie Hendren. Evaluating the benefits of context-sensitive points-to analysis using a BDD-based implementation. *ACM Trans. Softw. Eng. Methodol.*, 18(1):1–53, 2008.

[LL03]   V. Benjamin Livshits and Monica S. Lam. Tracking pointers with path and context sensitivity for bug detection in C programs. In *ESEC/FSE-11: Proceedings of the 9th European software engineering conference held jointly with 11th ACM SIGSOFT international symposium on Foundations of software engineering*, pages 317–326, New York, NY, USA, 2003. ACM.

[LL05]   Benjamin Livshits and Monica S. Lam. Finding security vulnerabilities in Java applications with static analysis. In *Proceedings of the Usenix Security Symposium*, pages 271–286, Baltimore, Maryland, August 2005.

[LPM99]   Jaejin Lee, David A. Padua, and Samuel P. Midkiff. Basic compiler algorithms for parallel programs. In *PPoPP '99: Proceedings of the seventh ACM SIGPLAN symposium on Principles and practice of parallel programming*, pages 1–12, New York, NY, USA, 1999. ACM.

[LS09]   Andreas Lochbihler and Gregor Snelting. On temporal path conditions in dependence graphs. *Journal of Automated Software Engineering*, 16(2):263–290, June 2009.

[LT79]   Thomas Lengauer and Robert Endre Tarjan. A fast algorithm for finding dominators in a flowgraph. *ACM Trans. Program. Lang. Syst.*, 1(1):121–141, 1979.

[LWL05]   Benjamin Livshits, John Whaley, and Monica S. Lam. Reflection analysis for Java. In *Proceedings of the 3rd Asian Symposium (APLAS 2005)*, volume 3780 of *LNCS*, pages 139–160, Tsukuba, Japan, November 2005.

[LY99]   Tim Lindholm and Frank Yellin. *The Java(TM) Virtual Machine Specification*. Prentice Hall, 2nd edition, April 1999.

[Lyl84]   James Robert Lyle. *Evaluating variations on program slicing for debugging*. PhD thesis, University of Maryland, College Park, MD, USA, 1984.

[LZ05]   Peng Li and Steve Zdancewic. Downgrading policies and relaxed noninterference. In *POPL '05: Proceedings of the 32nd ACM SIGPLAN-SIGACT symposium on Principles of programming languages*, pages 158–170, New York, NY, USA, 2005. ACM Press.

[MCN⁺]   A. C. Myers, S. Chong, N. Nystrom, L. Zheng, and S. Zdancewic. Jif: Java information flow.

[ML00]   Andrew C. Myers and Barbara Liskov. Protecting privacy using the decentralized label model. *ACM Trans. Softw. Eng. Methodol.*, 9(4):410–442, 2000.

[MM07]   G. B. Mund and Rajib Mall. *The Compiler Design Handbook: Optimizations and Machine Code Generation*, chapter 14: Program Slicing. CRC Press, 2nd edition, Juli 2007.

[MMKM94]   Brian A. Malloy, John D. McGregor, Anand Krishnaswamy, and Murali Medikonda. An extensible program representation for object-oriented software. *SIGPLAN Not.*, 29(12):38–47, 1994.

[MOS01]   Markus Müller-Olm and Helmut Seidl. On optimal slicing of parallel programs. In *STOC '01: Proceedings of the thirty-third annual ACM symposium on Theory of computing*, pages 647–656, New York, NY, USA, 2001. ACM.

[MR07]   Heiko Mantel and Alexander Reinhard. Controlling the what and where of declassification in language-based security. In *ESOP '07: Proceedings of the European Symposium on Programming*, volume 4421 of *LNCS*, pages 141–156. Springer, 2007.

[MRR02]   Ana Milanova, Atanas Rountev, and Barbara G. Ryder. Parameterized object sensitivity for points-to and side-effect analyses for Java. In *ISSTA '02: Proceedings of the 2002 ACM SIGSOFT international symposium on Software testing and analysis*, pages 1–11, New York, NY, USA, 2002. ACM.

[MS04]   Heiko Mantel and David Sands. Controlled declassification based on intransitive noninterference. In *Proceedings of the 2nd Asian Symposium on Programming Languages and Systems, APLAS 2004*, volume 3302 of *LNCS*, pages 129–145, Taipei, Taiwan, November 2004. Springer.

[Muc97]   Steven S. Muchnick. *Advanced Compiler Design and Implementation*. Morgan Kaufmann, August 1997.

[NAC99] Gleb Naumovich, George S. Avrunin, and Lori A. Clarke. An efficient algorithm for computing MHP information for concurrent Java programs. In *ESEC/FSE-7: Proceedings of the 7th European software engineering conference held jointly with the 7th ACM SIGSOFT international symposium on Foundations of software engineering*, pages 338–354, London, UK, 1999. Springer-Verlag.

[Nan01] Mangala Gowri Nanda. *Slicing Concurrent Java Programs: Issues and Solutions*. PhD thesis, Indian Institute of Technology, Bombay, October 2001.

[NPW02] Tobias Nipkow, Lawrence C. Paulson, and Markus Wenzel. *Isabelle/HOL — A Proof Assistant for Higher-Order Logic*, volume 2283 of *LNCS*. Springer, 2002.

[NR00] Mangala Gowri Nanda and S. Ramesh. Slicing concurrent programs In *ISSTA '00: Proceedings of the 2000 ACM SIGSOFT international symposium on Software testing and analysis*, pages 180–190, New York, NY, USA, 2000. ACM.

[NR03] Mangala Gowri Nanda and S. Ramesh. Pointer analysis of multithreaded Java programs. In *SAC '03: Proceedings of the 2003 ACM symposium on Applied computing*, pages 1068–1075, New York, NY, USA, 2003. ACM.

[NR06] Mangala Gowri Nanda and S. Ramesh. Interprocedural slicing of multithreaded programs with applications to Java. *ACM Trans. Program. Lang. Syst.*, 28(6):1088–1144, 2006.

[NUS98] Diego Novillo, Ronald C. Unrau, and Jonathan Schaeffer. Concurrent SSA form in the presence of mutual exclusion. In *ICPP '98: Proceedings of the 1998 International Conference on Parallel Processing*, page 356, Washington, DC, USA, 1998. IEEE Computer Society.

[OO84] Karl J. Ottenstein and Linda M. Ottenstein. The program dependence graph in a software development environment. In *SDE 1: Proceedings of the first ACM SIGSOFT/SIGPLAN software engineering symposium on Practical software development environments*, pages 177–184, New York, NY, USA, 1984. ACM.

[ora85] *Trusted Computer System Evaluation Criteria (Orange Book)*. Number DoD 5200.28-STD. Department of Defense, December 1985.

[PBN07] Marco Pistoia, Anindya Banerjee, and David A. Naumann. Beyond stack inspection: A unified access-control and information-flow security model. In *SP '07: Proceedings of the 2007 IEEE Symposium on Security and Privacy*, pages 149–163, Washington, DC, USA, 2007. IEEE Computer Society.

211

[PC90]   A. Podgurski and L. A. Clarke. A formal model of program dependences and its implications for software testing, debugging, and maintenance. *IEEE Trans. Softw. Eng.*, 16(9):965–979, 1990.

[PCFY07]   M. Pistoia, S. Chandra, S. J. Fink, and E. Yahav. A survey of static analysis methods for identifying security vulnerabilities in software systems. *IBM Syst. J.*, 46(2):265–288, 2007.

[PFKS05]   Marco Pistoia, Robert J. Flynn, Larry Koved, and Vugranam C. Sreedhar. Interprocedural analysis for privileged code placement and tainted variable detection. In *Proceedings of the 9th European Conference on Object-Oriented Programming*, volume 3586 of *LNCS*, pages 362–386. Springer, 2005.

[PS91]   Phil Pfeiffer and Rebecca Parsons Selke. On the adequacy of dependence-based representations for programs with heaps. In *TACS '91: Proc. International Conference on Theoretical Aspects of Computer Software*, volume 526 of *LNCS*, pages 365–386. Springer, September 1991.

[PS03]   François Pottier and Vincent Simonet. Information flow inference for ML. *ACM Trans. Program. Lang. Syst.*, 25(1):117–158, 2003.

[qui]   Quis custodiet. http://pp.info.uni-karlsruhe.de/project.php/id=31 funded by DFG Sn11/10-1.

[RAB+07]   Venkatesh Prasad Ranganath, Torben Amtoft, Anindya Banerjee, John Hatcliff, and Matthew B. Dwyer. A new foundation for control dependence and slicing for modern program structures. *ACM Trans. Program. Lang. Syst.*, 29(5):27, 2007.

[Ram94]   G. Ramalingam. The undecidability of aliasing. *ACM Trans. Program. Lang. Syst.*, 16(5):1467–1471, 1994.

[Ram00]   G. Ramalingam. Context-sensitive synchronization-sensitive analysis is undecidable. *ACM Trans. Program. Lang. Syst.*, 22(2):416–430, 2000.

[RH04]   Venkatesh Prasad Ranganath and John Hatcliff. Pruning interference and ready dependence for slicing concurrent Java programs. In *Proceedings of 13th International Conference on Compiler Construction (CC'04)*, volume 2985 of *LNCS*, pages 39–56, March 2004.

[RHSR94]   Thomas Reps, Susan Horwitz, Mooly Sagiv, and Genevieve Rosay. Speeding up slicing. In *SIGSOFT '94: Proceedings of the 2nd ACM SIGSOFT symposium on Foundations of software engineering*, pages 11–20, New York, NY, USA, 1994. ACM.

[Ric53]   Henry Gordon Rice. Classes of recursively enumerable sets and their decision problems. *Trans. Amer. Math. Soc*, 74(2):358–366, 1953.

[RLS+01] Barbara G. Ryder, William A. Landi, Philip A. Stocks, Sean
          Zhang, and Rita Altucher. A schema for inter procedural mod-
          ification side-effect analysis with pointer aliasing. *ACM Trans.
          Program. Lang. Syst.*, 23(2):105–186, 2001.

[RMR01]   Atanas Rountev, Ana Milanova, and Barbara G. Ryder. Points-to
          analysis for Java using annotated constraints. In *OOPSLA '01:
          Proceedings of the 16th ACM SIGPLAN conference on Object ori-
          ented programming, systems, languages, and applications*, pages
          43–55, New York, NY, USA, 2001. ACM.

[Rob05]   Torsten Robschink. *Pfadbedingungen in Abhängigkeitsgraphen und
          ihre Anwendung in der Softwaresicherheitstechnik*. PhD thesis,
          Universität Passau, January 2005.

[RS02]   Torsten Robschink and Gregor Snelting. Efficient path conditions
          in dependence graphs. In *ICSE '02: Proceedings of the 24th Inter-
          national Conference on Software Engineering*, pages 478–488, New
          York, NY, USA, 2002. ACM Press.

[Ruf00]   Erik Ruf. Effective synchronization removal for Java. In *PLDI '00:
          Proceedings of the ACM SIGPLAN 2000 conference on Program-
          ming language design and implementation*, pages 208–218, New
          York, NY, USA, 2000. ACM.

[Rus92]   John Rushby. Noninterference, transitivity, and channel-control
          security policies. Technical Report CSL-92-02, SRI International,
          Computer Science Laboratory, December 1992.

[RWZ88]   B. K. Rosen, M. N. Wegman, and F. K. Zadeck. Global value
          numbers and redundant computations. In *POPL '88: Proceedings
          of the 15th ACM SIGPLAN-SIGACT symposium on Principles of
          programming languages*, pages 12–27, New York, NY, USA, 1988.
          ACM.

[RY88]   Thomas Reps and Wuu Yang. The semantics of program slicing.
          Technical Report 777, Computer Sciences Department, University
          of Wisconsin-Madison, 1988.

[Ryd79]   B. G. Ryder. Constructing the call graph of a program. *IEEE
          Trans. Softw. Eng.*, 5(3):216–226, 1979.

[Sch00]   Werner Schindler. A timing attack against RSA with the chinese
          remainder theorem. In *CHES '00: Proceedings of the Second In-
          ternational Workshop on Cryptographic Hardware and Embedded
          Systems*, volume 1965 of *LNCS*, pages 109–124, London, UK, 2000.
          Springer-Verlag.

[SFB07]   Manu Sridharan, Stephen J. Fink, and Rastislav Bodík. Thin slic-
          ing. In *PLDI '07: Proceedings of the 2007 ACM SIGPLAN confer-

ence on *Programming language design and implementation*, pages 112–122, New York, NY, USA, 2007. ACM Press.

[SH00]   Saurabh Sinha and Mary Jean Harrold. Analysis and testing of programs with exception handling constructs. *IEEE Trans. Softw. Eng.*, 26(9):849–871, 2000.

[SHR⁺00]   Vijay Sundaresan, Laurie Hendren, Chrislain Razafimahefa, Raja Vallée-Rai, Patrick Lam, Etienne Gagnon, and Charles Godin. Practical virtual method call resolution for Java. In *OOPSLA '00: Proceedings of the 15th ACM SIGPLAN conference on Object-oriented programming, systems, languages, and applications*, pages 264–280, New York, NY, USA, 2000. ACM Press.

[SHR01]   Saurabh Sinha, Mary Jean Harrold, and Gregg Rothermel. Interprocedural control dependence. *ACM Trans. Softw. Eng. Methodol.*, 10(2):209–254, 2001.

[SM03]   A. Sabelfeld and A. Myers. Language-based information-flow security. *IEEE Journal on Selected Areas in Communications*, 21(1):5–19, January 2003.

[Smi06]   Geoffrey Smith. Improved typings for probabilistic noninterference in a multi-threaded language. *J. Comput. Secur.*, 14(6):591–623, 2006.

[Sne96]   Gregor Snelting. Combining slicing and constraint solving for validation of measurement software. In *SAS '96: Proceedings of the Third International Symposium on Static Analysis*, pages 332–348, London, UK, 1996. Springer-Verlag.

[SRC84]   J. H. Saltzer, D. P. Reed, and D. D. Clark. End-to-end arguments in system design. *ACM Trans. Comput. Syst.*, 2(4):277–288, 1984.

[SRK06]   Gregor Snelting, Torsten Robschink, and Jens Krinke. Efficient path conditions in dependence graphs for software safety analysis. *ACM Trans. Softw. Eng. Methodol.*, 15(4):410–457, 2006.

[SS00a]   Andrei Sabelfeld and David Sands. Probabilistic noninterference for multi-threaded programs. In *CSFW '00: Proceedings of the 13th IEEE workshop on Computer Security Foundations*, page 200, Washington, DC, USA, 2000. IEEE Computer Society.

[SS00b]   Mirko Streckenbach and Gregor Snelting. Points-to for Java: A general framework and an empirical comparison. Technical report, Univerity of Passau, November 2000.

[SS01]   Andrei Sabelfeld and David Sands. A PER model of secure information flow in sequential programs. *Higher Order Symbol. Comput.*, 14(1):59–91, 2001.

[SS05]   Andrei Sabelfeld and David Sands. Dimensions and principles of declassification. In *CSFW '05: Proceedings of the 18th IEEE workshop on Computer Security Foundations*, pages 255–269, Washington, DC, USA, 2005. IEEE Computer Society.

[Ste96]   Bjarne Steensgaard. Points-to analysis in almost linear time. In *POPL '96: Proceedings of the 23rd ACM SIGPLAN-SIGACT symposium on Principles of programming languages*, pages 32–41, New York, NY, USA, 1996. ACM.

[Str03]   Martin Strecker. Formal analysis of an information flow type system for MicroJava (extended version). Technical report, Technische Universität München, July 2003.

[SV98]   Geoffrey Smith and Dennis Volpano. Secure information flow in a multi-threaded imperative language. In *POPL '98: Proceedings of the 25th ACM SIGPLAN-SIGACT symposium on Principles of programming languages*, pages 355–364. ACM, January 1998.

[SZC08]   Bernard Scholz, Chenyi Zhang, and Cristina Cifuentes. User-input dependence analysis via graph reachability. In *Proc. Eighth IEEE International Working Conference on Source Code Analysis and Manipulation*, pages 25–34, September 2008.

[TAFM97]   Paolo Tonella, Giuliano Antoniol, Roberto Fiutem, and Ettore Merlo. Flow insensitive C++ pointers and polymorphism analysis and its application to slicing. In *ICSE '97: Proceedings of the 19th international conference on Software engineering*, pages 433–443, New York, NY, USA, 1997. ACM.

[Tip95]   Frank Tip. A survey of program slicing techniques. *Journal of Programming Languages*, 3(3):121–189, September 1995.

[TP00]   Frank Tip and Jens Palsberg. Scalable propagation-based call graph construction algorithms. In *OOPSLA '00: Proceedings of the 15th ACM SIGPLAN conference on Object-oriented programming, systems, languages, and applications*, pages 281–293, New York, NY, USA, 2000. ACM Press.

[Ven95]   G. A. Venkatesh. Experimental results from dynamic slicing of C programs. *ACM Trans. Program. Lang. Syst.*, 17(2):197–216, 1995.

[VIS96]   Dennis Volpano, Cynthia Irvine, and Geoffrey Smith. A sound type system for secure flow analysis. *J. Comput. Secur.*, 4(2-3):167–187, 1996.

[VS97]   Dennis M. Volpano and Geoffrey Smith. A type-based approach to program security. In *TAPSOFT '97: Proceedings of the 7th International Joint Conference CAAP/FASE on Theory and Practice of Software Development*, volume 1214 of *LNCS*, pages 607–621, London, UK, 1997. Springer-Verlag.

[Wei79]   Mark David Weiser. *Program slices: formal, psychological, and practical investigations of an automatic program abstraction method.* PhD thesis, University of Michigan, Ann Arbor, MI, 1979.

[Wei81]   Mark Weiser. Program slicing. In *ICSE '81: Proceedings of the 5th international conference on Software engineering*, pages 439–449, Piscataway, NJ, USA, 1981. IEEE Press.

[Wei82]   Mark Weiser. Programmers use slices when debugging. *Commun. ACM*, 25(7):446–452, 1982.

[Wei84]   Mark Weiser. Program slicing. *IEEE Transactions on Software Engineering*, 10(4):352–357, July 1984.

[WL04]   John Whaley and Monica S. Lam. Cloning-based context-sensitive pointer alias analysis using binary decision diagrams. In *PLDI '04: Proceedings of the ACM SIGPLAN 2004 conference on Programming language design and implementation*, pages 131–144, New York, NY, USA, 2004. ACM Press.

[WR04]   Tao Wang and Abhik Roychoudhury. Using compressed bytecode traces for slicing Java programs. In *ICSE '04: Proceedings of the 26th International Conference on Software Engineering*, pages 512–521, Washington, DC, USA, 2004. IEEE Computer Society.

[WRW03]   Neil Walkinshaw, Marc Roper, and Murray Wood. The Java system dependence graph. In *Proc. Third IEEE International Workshop on Source Code Analysis and Manipulation*, page 55, Los Alamitos, CA, USA, 2003. IEEE Computer Society.

[YOT⁺02]   Reishi Yokomori, Fumiaki Ohata, Yoshiaki Takata, Hiroyuki Seki, and Katsuro Inoue. An information-leak analysis system based on program slicing. *Information and Software Technology*, 44(15):903–910, 2002.

[Zda04]   Steve Zdancewic. Challenges for information-flow security. In *Proceedings of the 1st International Workshop on the Programming Language Interference and Dependence*, 2004.

[ZG04]   Xiangyu Zhang and Rajiv Gupta. Cost effective dynamic program slicing. In *PLDI '04: Proceedings of the ACM SIGPLAN 2004 conference on Programming language design and implementation*, pages 94–106, New York, NY, USA, 2004. ACM.

[ZGZ03]   Xiangyu Zhang, Rajiv Gupta, and Youtao Zhang. Precise dynamic slicing algorithms. In *ICSE '03: Proceedings of the 25th International Conference on Software Engineering*, pages 319–329, Washington, DC, USA, 2003. IEEE Computer Society. Superseded by zhang05TOPLAS.

[ZGZ05]   Xiangyu Zhang, Rajiv Gupta, and Youtao Zhang. Cost and precision tradeoffs of dynamic data slicing algorithms. *ACM Trans. Program. Lang. Syst.*, 27(4):631–661, 2005.

[Zha99]   Jianjun Zhao. Slicing concurrent Java programs. In *IWPC '99: Proceedings of the 7th International Workshop on Program Comprehension*, pages 126–133, Washington, DC, USA, 1999. IEEE Computer Society.

[Zha00]   Jianjun Zhao. Dependence analysis of Java bytecode. In *COMPSAC '00: 24th International Computer Software and Applications Conference*, pages 486–491, Washington, DC, USA, 2000. IEEE Computer Society.

[ZL04]   Jianjun Zhao and Bixin Li. Dependence-based representation for concurrent Java programs and its application to slicing. In *Proc. 8th International Symposium on Future Software Technology*, Xian, China, 2004.

Index